The End of Silence

# The End of Silence

*Accounts of the 1965 Genocide in Indonesia*

*Soe Tjen Marching*

*With original photography by Angus Nicholls*

LONDON AND NEW YORK

First published in 2017 by Amsterdam University Press Ltd.

Published 2025 by Routledge
4 Park Square, Milton Park, Abingdon, Oxon OX14 4RN
605 Third Avenue, New York, NY 10158

*Routledge is an imprint of the Taylor & Francis Group, an informa business*

© Soe Tjen Marching / Taylor & Francis Group 2017

All rights reserved. No part of this book may be reprinted or reproduced or utilised in any form or by any electronic, mechanical, or other means, now known or hereafter invented, including photocopying and recording, or in any information storage or retrieval system, without permission in writing from the publishers.

*Trademark notice*: Product or corporate names may be trademarks or registered trademarks, and are used only for identification and explanation without intent to infringe.

ISBN: 9789462983908 (hbk)
ISBN: 9789463720847 (pbk)
ISBN: 9781003705994 (ebk)
NUR  692

Cover image: Ika Setiati (niece of Sriyono Wiwoho), holding photos of her lost parents (Asmoro Rahman Hadi and Rahayuni)
Photo: Angus Nicholls

Cover design: Coördesign, Leiden

DOI : 10.5117/9789462983908

Every effort has been made to obtain permission to use all copyrighted illustrations reproduced in this book. Nonetheless, whosoever believes to have rights to this material is advised to contact the publisher.

For Product Safety Concerns and Information please contact our EU representative:
GPSR@taylorandfrancis.com
Taylor & Francis Verlag GmbH, Kaufingerstraße 24, 80331 München, Germany

*This book is about the memories of the 1965-1966 genocide in Indonesia.
Because I am trying to prevent another genocide: the genocide of Memories.*

# Table of Contents

| | |
|---|---|
| Apology | 13 |
| Timeline: Indonesia, 1965-1967 | 15 |
| The Mutation of Fear | 17 |
| *The Legacy of the Long-Dead Dictator* | |
|     The Beginning | 17 |
|     The Creation of Fearful Memories | 18 |
|     The Genocide | 20 |
|     Gerwani | 25 |
|     Soeharto's Version of History | 26 |
|     Who Was the Mastermind? | 28 |
|     When the Victims Remain Evil | 30 |
|     The International People's Tribunal 1965 | 32 |
|     Real History and Memory: The 'Reality' of Oral History | 33 |

## Part 1    Accounts of the Victims: The Letter in the Sock

| | |
|---|---|
| The Letter in the Sock | 41 |
| Leo Mulyono | 42 |
| *Working for My Oppressor* | |
|     To Be Kept Safe | 43 |
|     Dating in Prison | 48 |
|     Being Transferred Again | 49 |
|     Back to Yogya | 51 |
|     Pramoedya Ananta Toer | 53 |
|     My Story | 53 |
| Oei Hiem Hwie | 55 |
| *The Amazing Library* | |
|     The Murder of the Generals | 55 |
|     Buru | 58 |
|     Pramoedya Ananta Toer | 59 |
|     The Beauty of Buru | 60 |
|     Building Houses | 61 |

Development ... 62
Staying or Leaving? ... 63
Going Home ... 64
Something Weird ... 66
The Birth of the Library ... 67

Antonius Pudji Rahardjo ... 68
*The Commander and His Mistress*
Moments before Gestok 1965 ... 68
Back to Surabaya ... 70
21 Musi Street – Surabaya ... 71
Kalisosok ... 71
Nusakambangan ... 73
Buru ... 73
The Giant Galiuk in Savanajaya ... 74
13 March 1972 ... 76
People from Overseas ... 77
General Soemitro's Visit ... 78
The Arrival of Families ... 79
Freedom ... 80
My Wife ... 80
After Buru ... 81

## Part 2   The Steel Women

Sri Muhayati ... 85
*Being Educated in Prison*
Educating Myself in Prison ... 89

Christina Sumarmiyati ... 94
*The Horrific Torture and Rape*
Our Children ... 102

## Part 3   The Accounts of the Siblings

| | |
|---|---|
| Sriyono Wiwoho | 107 |
| *The Lunch Box My Brother Never Received* | |
| My *Adik* and I at School | 110 |
| | |
| Adi Rukun | 113 |
| *Beyond the Look of Silence* | |
| My Brother and I | 115 |
| The Look of Silence | 117 |

## Part 4   The Accounts of the Children

| | |
|---|---|
| Usmantri Sukardi | 123 |
| *My Childhood with Strangers* | |
| Meeting *bapak* Again | 125 |
| | |
| Iwan Kamah | 128 |
| *Annus Horibilis* | |
| 1957-1965 | 129 |
| *Annus Horribilis* | 129 |
| Again: China | 131 |
| Antara | 132 |
| | |
| Irina Dayasih | 134 |
| *The Biggest Traitor in Indonesia?* | |
| My mama | 136 |
| The Secret of My father | 136 |
| After That ... | 138 |
| | |
| Wayan Windra | 142 |
| *Bapak was Slaughtered in Front of Me* | |
| | |
| Kristianto Budi | 148 |
| *My Family's Dark Secret* | |

Sari Marlina     152
- *The Flight of My father*
- Sumatra     155
- Sumatra: Again     156
- The Prison     159
- But Where Would Sabar Go?     161
- Sari Marlina     161
- Marriage     162

Rito Aji     163
- *The Son of Pudji Rahardjo*
- The Revenge against the Sasongko Family     166
- The Return of *bapak*     166
- The Sex Business     167
- Other Jobs     168
- Now …     169

Soe Tjen Marching     171
- *The Secret of My Name*
- I Became Chinese     172
- I Became Religious     172
- There Were Times …     174
- This is What She Told Me …     174
- The Unexpected Visitor     179
- The Story of When Your *Engkong* Was Imprisoned     179
- Her Suspicions     180
- I Was Born after His Release     181
- What is in a Name?     182
- Threats Were Always Near     183
- As He Got Older, His Temperament Got Worse …     183
- Years Later …     184
- One Last Secret     185

## Part 5  The Accounts of the Grandchildren

Kusuma Wijaya  189
   *The Day I Found Out about My Grandpa*

Haidir Svj  195
   *Born and Raised on Buru*
   The Time of Release  195
   Growing up on Buru  196
   The Argument  198
   Savanajaya  198

Diah Wahyuningsih Rahayu  200
   *My Grandfather's Earlobes*
   My *embah*  200
   The History Lesson  203

Kiky  205
   *The Eternal Fear*


Epilogue  211
   *The Corollary of Memory*

Bibliography  215

Index  217


## List of Photos

| | | |
|---|---|---|
| Photo A | Leo Mulyono in front of his home | 50 |
| Photo B | Oei Hiem Hwie in his library | 66 |
| Photo C | Pudji Rahardjo in his private library holding a book he wrote about Buru Island | 81 |
| Photo D | Sri Muhayati in front of the banner of Fopperham (Forum Pendidikan dan Perjuangan Hak Asasi Manusia, or the Human Rights Education and Advocacy Forum), a human rights organisation with which she has been involved | 92 |
| Photo E | Christina Sumarmiyati in her home | 94 |

| | | |
|---|---|---|
| Photo F | Rahayuni, Sriyono Wiwoho's sister-in-law, who was raped and murdered for her involvement in Gerwani | 108 |
| Photo G | Asmoro Rahman Hadi, the brother of Sriyono Wiwoho, who was murdered for his involvement in Lekra | 109 |
| Photo H | Sriyono Wiwoho | 111 |
| Photo I | Adi Rukun | 119 |
| Photo J | Iwan Kamah | 133 |
| Photo K | Irina Dayasih at her apartment block in Jakarta | 138 |
| Photo L | Wayan Windra, holding a photo of his father in front of the spot where he was butchered and murdered in 1965 | 144 |
| Photo M | Wayan Windra, Soe Tjen Marching, Adi Adnyana (an 85 year-old ex-Buru prisoner) and his wife at Adi Adnyana's residence in Bali | 146 |
| Photo N | Rito Aji at his home in Surabaya | 169 |
| Photo O | Kusuma Wijaya in Surabaya | 193 |
| Photo P | Haidir Svj in Yogya | 197 |

# Apology

I have to apologise to my mother for writing this book. She has made me promise many times not to reveal anything about our family's background, and nothing about 1965-1966 in Indonesia – and I broke this promise.

My mother's trauma of witnessing her husband being dragged from our home by Soeharto's troops, one day in 1966, makes her believe that silence is a virtue. I am almost the complete opposite. For her, I am just like a broken record: I cannot keep quiet. I believe that I have the responsibility to reveal these stories so that more and more people find out about what happened in Indonesia half a century ago: the horrific injustice which befell millions of people, the impact of which continues even now.

But my mother keeps calling my conviction reckless, thoughtless and dangerous for our family; and I considered her a coward. It was Joshua Oppenheimer's 2012 documentary film *The Act of Killing* which made me understand my mother's fear better. The pride of the thugs for having murdered the alleged communists and the immunity they still have in Indonesia are brought to 'reality' by this film. As I was watching these thugs expressing their hunger to attack ethnic Chinese, I sensed my mother's terror: 'That's what my mother has been so frightened of!' I knew why she prohibited me from writing or even thinking about these incidents. I understand. But at the same time, my desire to record witness accounts of this genocide grew stronger.

For a while, I was in a conflict between my desire to respect my mother's wishes and my need to speak up by revealing the life stories of the people victimised by this atrocity. Between being a good daughter and a good activist, I decided to choose the second.

Many people have been very helpful in this project, especially all of my respondents and their families. I thank Joshua Oppenheimer for his incredible support. Saskia Wieringa, Darriel Jeffree, Maria Bikos, Robert Gillett, Andrew Conroe and Ian Nicholls have provided useful suggestions. I am grateful to all of my friends in Indonesia whose names I cannot mention one by one. Special thanks goes to Nada Holland, and I am always grateful to Angus Nicholls for his love and support.

I have many people to thank, but I know I will hurt one person who I really love by writing this manuscript. For this reason, this book has no acknowledgement but only an apology.

# Timeline: Indonesia, 1965-1967

**1965**

1 October      Dawn: six top generals of the Indonesian Army and one aide are kidnapped from their homes and murdered.
7.15 am: The radio announces that the murders were a pre-emptive act to prevent a coup against President Sukarno and that the Revolutionary Council is in control of the country.
2 pm: The radio announces that Sukarno is no longer in power.
7 pm: Soeharto announces that he now controls the Army and claims that the Revolutionary Council had tried to seize power from Sukarno.

3 October      The bodies of the generals are discovered in a disused well at Lubang Buaya in Jakarta.

4 October      Autopsy of the generals, with Soeharto present.

5 October      Burial of the generals. Propaganda against the PKI (Partai Komunis Indonesia, or the Communist Party of Indonesia) and the left-wing women's organisation Gerwani (Gerakan Wanita Indonesia, or the Indonesian Women's Movement) begins to spread widely in the mass media. It is reported that the six generals and one aide have been mutilated and sexually abused by the women of Gerwani.

8 October      PKI offices in Jakarta and other cities are burnt down.

18 October      The mass murder of people associated with the PKI erupts across the country.

12 December      President Sukarno tries to correct manipulated news about the communists, but to no avail.

**1966**

11 March      Sukarno signs the presidential decree called Supersemar,[1] the original of which is lost. Soeharto's followers claim that this document contains an agreement to transfer power from Sukarno to Soeharto.

---

[1] Supersemar is a document signed by President Sukarno that allegedly gave authority to Soeharto to take whatever measures necessary to restore order during the 1965-1966 chaotic incident.

| | |
|---|---|
| 12 March | Using the Supersemar, Soeharto starts expelling Sukarno sympathisers from the parliament and the military, and accuses them of being communists. |

**1967**

| | |
|---|---|
| 12 March | Soeharto is appointed Acting President. He is then appointed President on 27 March 1968. He continues in power until 1998. |

# The Mutation of Fear

The Legacy of the Long-Dead Dictator

## The Beginning

Studying mammals' fear in relation to their defence mechanisms, Arne Öhman and Susan Minerka argue: 'Early and reliable recognition of the predator is a prerequisite for effective defense.'[2] Fear is part of mammalian evolution, and an important factor in survival. For this reason, the deployment of terror can be an effective means of dictating people's behaviour. When people are overwhelmed by fear, they tend either to be in paralysis, to fight, or to take flight. The response can be shaped by how people read the situation and, as such, this had been used by Soeharto to dictate the Indonesian public's reactions to his advantage.

The use of fear as a key strategy in politics is nothing new: the despotic methods of discipline and punishment supported by law are generally the key factors used by totalitarian regimes. However, as I was gathering the personal stories of the 1965 victims, it was not the law that most of my respondents were worried about; rather, personal reasons (such as pressure from families and relatives not to speak out) were of more concern. I will explain this in more detail below. Indonesia is one example of a nation in which the use of fear is so effective that it has become like a very dangerous virus that mutates, and in the end comes to be accepted as 'natural' by many people.

Almost like fear, viruses are unseen and most people are only aware of them because of public information. Soeharto and his allies implanted fear as widely as possible not only in the victims, but also in the perpetrators and at all levels of society. The murder of the generals at dawn on 1 October 1965 was used by Soeharto to start a rumour that the communists were responsible for this incident. Accounts about the brutality of the communists as well as about the sadistic promiscuity of the members of Gerwani (Gerakan Wanita Indonesia, or the Indonesian Women's Movement) were spread widely in order to arouse public fear. Gerwani was aligned with the PKI (Partai Komunis Indonesia, or the Communist Party of Indonesia). Through these means, Soeharto and his allies effectively portrayed the communists and their allies as 'monsters'. This in turn inspired an irrational fear so that

2   Öhman and Mineka, p. 486.

Soeharto's troops could easily gain not only public approval but also support in conducting their mission in exterminating people considered to be on the political left in Indonesia.

Their strategy was so effectively sustained that fear has become so powerful and is seen as ubiquitous, accepted and undetected. This is what I call the 'mutation of fear'. In this situation, many former victims have been transformed into agents that preserve the very ideology that has persecuted them. It is no surprise that long after Soeharto died, the most persistent resistance that many of my respondents had to face in revealing the truth about their family histories came from members of their own families who had themselves been victims of the 1965 atrocities.

### The Creation of Fearful Memories

The bloodbath of communists and left-wing sympathisers in Indonesia was triggered by the murders of seven high-ranking generals in 1965. What has come to be known as the 30 September Movement in fact happened early in the morning of 1 October. At around 3 am, the troops under the leadership of Lieutenant Col. Untung left their bases to kidnap seven high-ranking generals: General Ahmad Yani, Major General M.T. Haryono, Brigadier General D.I. Panjaitan, Major General Suprapto, Major General S. Parman and Brigadier General Sutoyo. General Nasution, who was the seventh target, managed to escape by jumping over the wall of his house into the garden of his neighbour, the Iraqi ambassador. He hid there and was safe. However, his young aide, Lieutenant Pierre Tendean, was shot by mistake. A total of six generals and one aide were shot, and Nasution's five-year-old daughter, Ade Irma Nasution, was also accidentally shot and died a few days later. The corpses of the generals were dumped in a well in Lubang Buaya, East Jakarta.

The radio that day broadcast confusing and even conflicting accounts, creating a muddle that would from then on come to mark Indonesian history. At around 7 am, the state radio network RRI (Radio Republik Indonesia) broadcast the news that Untung's troops had prevented a plot led by the 'Council of Generals' against Sukarno. The announcement confirmed a rumour that had, in various forms, been circulating since 1961: that Sukarno's army chiefs, led by Nasution, had established the Council of Generals, which, with CIA support, sought to topple the President. This rumour had been particularly strong in the months immediately before the murder of the generals. In response, the radio on 1 October claimed that Lieutenant-Colonel Untung had conducted a *pre-emptive action*, and it reported that a 'Revolutionary Council' had been formed that day to handle the situation. The Revolutionary Council demanded that the media and mass organisations be loyal, and the radio also stated that the murder of the generals was an internal army affair.

However, at 7 pm RRI announced that Soeharto was now in control of the army, and described the murder of the generals as an *anti-revolutionary* act. The Revolutionary Council, according to Soeharto, had not tried to protect the President, but to seize power from Sukarno and for this reason, the 30 September Movement, or G30S as it came to be known, had to be crushed. Because the strategic reserve commander General Ahmad Yani had been murdered, Soeharto was next in line in the hierarchy. He took command of the army, and by the evening of 1 October was evidently in control of the national radio. Soon after, those newspapers considered as left wing and/or pro-Sukarno were suppressed. All of the media were then brought under army control.

Soeharto ordered an autopsy of the generals, which was performed on 4 October. The bodies were buried the next day, 5 October, in the Hero Cemetery in South Jakarta. On that same day, the army newspapers started reporting the profoundly shocking news that the autopsy results showed that most of the generals had been severely tortured and mutilated before they died.[3]

So began an orchestrated campaign by Soeharto's army leadership to blame and vilify the PKI.[4] On 8 October, the army and outraged members of the public burned down the PKI offices in Jakarta and in other cities, and the leaders of the party were hunted down. However, witnesses including Leo Mulyono, whose memoir can be found in this book, informed me that in Yogya, the anti-PKI propaganda started as early as 3 October 1965.

The slander and framing of the women's movement Gerwani for the murders started soon after the autopsy of the generals, mainly through the newspapers and radio. That October, articles started appearing with 'confessions' of Gerwani members, describing how these women had been present at Lubang Buaya on the night of the murders. They 'admitted' to dancing naked around the generals and torturing them, slashing and slicing the bodies of the generals, including their genitals, with razors and knives. The articles described the women as having celebrated the suffering of their victims, while at the same time conducting orgies with young communist

3    Anderson, pp. 110-111.
4    Vickers, p. 157; Wieringa, pp. 306-307.

men. This slander was successful in portraying the women of Gerwani as witches. After this spreading of fear about communism and its evils, more propaganda was still needed in order to motivate the public actively to persecute both real and perceived leftists in Indonesia.

Thus, between October and December 1965, newspapers including *Angkatan Bersendjata, Berita Yudha, Kompas, Duta Masyarakat* and many others propagated these reports. Gerwani women, it was now broadly assumed, had sexually abused and even mutilated the generals while dancing seductively to 'celebrate' their own brutality. The newspaper *Berita Yudha* quoted eyewitnesses who claimed that Gerwani women had cut the generals' genitals.[5] The stories, as the historian Saskia Wieringa explains, 'struck chords with the Islamic fear of the uncontrolled sexual powers of women [...] and the male fear of castration'.[6] As such, the rumour was extremely effective in stigmatising women and the left, and suited Soeharto's aim of taming unruly women. During Soeharto's governance, known as the New Order, the image of the submissive, obedient and religious woman was aggressively promoted, with the politically active, non-religious, critical and sexually overt Gerwani witch as a horrid deterrent.

The gruesome story of the torture was used to stigmatise the communists as well as to generate anger amongst the people. The description of communists as brutal and inhumane was designed to create terror amongst the people in preparation for the next stage: mass murder.

## The Genocide[7]

At this stage, fear escalated to another stage: it was used to instigate action, to motivate the fight against the 'monstrous' PKI. Soeharto instructed the commander of the special forces, Sarwo Edhie, to lead the eradication of the PKI. Sarwo Edhie used the fear of the people to incite their anger and to encourage them to join the fight against those accused of being communists. Vilifying the victims was an important part of the perpetrators' strategy, so that they could construct their attack as a just war: a war to protect and defend. As can be read in the accounts of the victims and their families in

---

5   Drakeley, p. 13; Robinson, p. 293.
6   Wieringa, p. 295.
7   Although, according to the UN treaty, the term 'genocide' relates to national, racial, ethnic or religious groups, I want to add 'political affiliation' to this category. For this reason, I use this term to describe the massacre that occurred in 1965-1967 in Indonesia.

this book, the people who dragged these alleged communists from their homes and were implicated in their murder were not only members of the army or the police, but also civilians.

The combination of fear and authoritative approval for conducting violence incited many people in Indonesia to support and even take part in this bloodbath. In October 1965, an all-out hunt for communists and their sympathisers began. Sarwo Edhie was on the move with his special forces to murder left-wing sympathisers, and he encouraged the involvement of civilians in this bloodbath. Edhie explained: 'We gathered together the youth, the nationalist groups, the religious organisations. We gave them two or three days training, then sent them out to kill the communists.'[8]

Using religious groups, Soeharto's army found it easy to turn people against communists and left-wing sympathisers. In Java, the Islamic groups were actively involved in this mass murder, and in Bali, religious leaders organised the massacre. Ida Bagus Oka, a Balinese Hindu leader and Governor of Bali from 1988-1993 and instigator of the mass murder of the communists in Bali, states that there can be no doubt that 'the enemies of our revolution are also the cruellest enemies of religion, and must be eliminated and destroyed down to the roots'.[9] With this kind of statement, he initiated a campaign of slander against the communists in order to ignite communal rage.

Rumours were then spread that the left wing had been planning a systematic extermination of non-communists.[10] Fear can incite people to attack in panic, lest they be attacked themselves. Once fear had been aroused amongst certain groups of people in Indonesia, aggressiveness was easily stirred (indeed, aggressiveness is common in mammals that perceive themselves to be under threat), especially when there was a guarantee that acts that would normally be considered criminal were allowed and approved. The murder, lynching, raping and torturing of the communists was done in the name of self-defence, in anticipation of their enemies' attacks. The brutality against communists was no longer perceived as violence, but as a protective strategy, a vaccination. People were terrified, and this created a situation in which it was difficult for them to perceive other options. For people in fear will believe that they have been victimised and oppressed by the opponent, and the opportunity to attack the opponent is thus a form of release of emotion: it is seen to provide a freedom from fear

8   Hughes, p. 151.
9   Quoted in Robinson, pp. 299-302.
10  Farid.

and oppression, and ultimately a victory. Thus the story of Wayan Windra told in this volume depicts how, for the mob, attacking his 'red village' to slaughter the communists was in fact a celebration. For these attackers, their actions were a manifestation of their liberation, as well as a pretext for conducting atrocities without feeling guilty. The looting, ransacking and murdering by the attackers seemed to make them feel happy; for this violence was considered not as irrational aggression but as a reclaiming of their power and of their rights.

Witnesses I interviewed also said that if the propaganda failed to infuriate a mob the army had selected to attack the communists, threats were used instead: 'Your head or their head'. Fear had enabled the regime of Soeharto to eliminate its opponent, to create anger among significant parts of the populace, and to make them fight his enemy. The communists were so dangerous, the army claimed, that anyone who was not willing to get rid of them would endanger others and even their own families. Edhie himself boasted that about three million people were killed,[11] though the actual number of the people murdered in the massacre is unknown to this day. Fear had thus become part of social identity: it was fear of the communists that united the people to declare that 'we were not communists'. While the fear of communism led to the mass murder of both real and perceived leftists, the murders themselves in turn created a new and heightened sense of fear, so that most people were no longer able to think rationally about who were actually communists or what they had done to deserve such severe punishment. In this climate, individuals began to concentrate on how to please those in power so that they were considered 'good people' (meaning: non-communist people) in order to save themselves.

The CIA has called the 1965 genocide 'one of the worst mass murders of the twentieth century'.[12] However, the support of the CIA and of several Western governments for the massacre should not be underestimated. Sukarno, who was close to the PKI, was perceived as a thorn that had to be eradicated. As the Cold War reached its peak, one of the missions of the West was to remove him. By the mid-1950s, the American government started to worry about the growth of the Communist Party in Indonesia. By December 1954, the National Security Council of the United States decided that the

---

11   Permadi SH, at the seminar '50 Tahun Indonesia Merdeka dan Problem Tapol/Napol', 28 January 1995, cited in Wieringa, p. 344.
12   Central Intelligence Agency, p. 71n.

US government should make all efforts in order to prevent Indonesia from becoming a communist-oriented country.[13]

In fact, the support of the American government was crucial to the success of the genocide, as it was able not only to justify but also to legitimate the genocide via several channels. The American government did not only use journalists but also academics such as Guy J. Pauker (who taught at the University of California at Berkeley from 1956 to 1963 and became head of the university's Center for Southeast Asian Studies) to spread the news about the danger of communists. Pauker, who had close ties with the US military, urged his contacts in the Indonesian military to 'fulfill a mission' and 'to strike, sweep their house clean'.[14]

A more recent Berkeley scholar, Peter Dale Scott, has revealed the deception that the CIA and Pauker conducted in order to tarnish the left-wing sympathisers in Indonesia.[15] Yet at the same time, the American government tried to project an image of detachment from what happened then in Indonesia. After his efforts to slander the communists in Indonesia, Pauker still expressed worries that his concern might not be shared as powerfully by others, as he was afraid that groups backed by the United States 'would probably lack the ruthlessness that made it possible for the Nazis to suppress the Communist Party of Germany'.[16] However, the scale of the butchery from October 1965 until mid-1966 alone proved Pauker's apprehension to be unfounded, as hundreds of thousands had been murdered. At the end of October and in early November 1965, when the American embassy in Indonesia heard of the mass killing, their correspondence demonstrated that they expressed sympathy with what Soeharto's army was doing.[17] The killings were seen as part of the strategy of spreading alarm and fear so that the communists would not recover as a political force: it was a strategy to treat them as a dangerous virus and to deflect attention away from the real problem or 'virus'. Fear was the virus being spread, but it was camouflaged in such a way that being frightened should be seen as natural. By stigmatising and demonising the enemy, the American government and its allies manufactured people's fear as a necessity to survive (to protect themselves against the threat). As such this is an effective strategy to spread communal fear, as the society would treat it not as fear but as the "awareness" of a

---

13  Kolko, p. 173.
14  Pauker, pp. 222-224.
15  Scott, pp. 1-12.
16  Chomsky, p. 122.
17  Kolko, pp. 181-182.

threat. In other words, the people were to poison themselves with the virus of fear, so that they could become the tools of the people in power without being aware of it.

The British government also conducted similar propaganda efforts in support of the 1965 bloodbath. On 5 October 1965, the British political adviser to the commander-in-chief in Singapore sent a message to the Foreign Office in London:

> We should not miss the present opportunities to use the situation to our advantage [...] We should have no hesitation in doing what we can surreptitiously to blacken the PKI in the eyes of the army and the people of Indonesia.

The Foreign Office agreed with the recommendation.[18] On 8 October 1965, the British Foreign Office sent a message to Singapore that encouraged the anti-communist propaganda:

> Our objectives are to encourage anti-Communist Indonesians to more vigorous action in the hope of crushing Communism in Indonesia altogether, even if only temporarily, and, to this end and for its own sake, to spread alarm and despondency in Indonesia to prevent, or at any rate delay, re-emergence of Nasakom Government [government including the PKI] under Sukarno.[19]

The support for the brutal genocide in Indonesia was also expressed by the Australian Prime Minister, Harold Holt, who commented in the *New York Times*: 'With 500,000 to one million Communist sympathizers knocked off, I think it is safe to assume a reorientation [in Indonesia] has taken place.'[20] For these Western governments, the tragedy suffered by millions of innocent people in Indonesia meant the beginning of the Western victory over communism. The massacre of communists by Soeharto and his henchmen was thus actively supported by these powers and greeted by them with ill-disguised delight. These forces therefore also have an interest in ensuring that Soeharto's version of history is preserved.

The strategy of the red scare in the United States was imported to Indonesia. In the cultural sector, the chaos had a huge impact and Soeharto

---

18  Curtis, p. 394.
19  PRO DEFE 25/170.
20  Raymont.

used the arts to implement and spread his propaganda. Artists who were members of the progressive union Lekra (Lembaga Kebudayaan Rakyat, or the Institute for the People's Culture) were considered communist supporters. A 1959 Lekra document had proposed social realism for the arts and demanded that artists be political. Yet many members were not involved with the PKI and were not all political. Nevertheless, they were hunted down and murdered or imprisoned. Indonesia's foremost author, Pramoedya Ananta Toer (known as Pram), was tortured, held prisoner for fourteen years on Buru Island and banned from writing. He was allowed to write again in the years prior to his release, however, he was not provided with sufficient paper or ink. Surprisingly, in 1978, a year before Pram was released, his book written on Buru Island was published and distributed in small numbers. How did this happen? The account in this book of Oei Hiem Hwie, who helped Pram with his writing on Buru, will help to solve the puzzle.

## Gerwani

The slander against the Gerwani women also supported the instillation of fear. Gerwani was originally founded as Gerwis in June 1950. In 1954, Gerwis changed its name to Gerwani and established a close link to the PKI. The aim of Gerwani was to promote gender equality and to advocate for women's issues in Indonesia. Under Sukarno's Guided Democracy, Gerwani leaned increasingly towards the PKI and Sukarno's interests and its focus shifted more onto economic and political issues rather than feminism. Due to its affiliation with the PKI, Gerwani membership numbers increased significantly. By 1965, Gerwani claimed to have around three million members.[21]

The fabrication of what the Gerwani women did to the generals was effective in supporting the view that the communists and their sympathisers were anti-religious and malicious creatures, and thus the witch hunt against these women became a 'sacred' duty to protect the country. Tens of thousands of Gerwani members were murdered or disappeared, with many more being imprisoned. Saskia Wieringa's interviews with ex-Gerwani members show that many spent up to fourteen years in prison. They were also raped by the army and brutally tortured.[22] Many of them had their genitals torn by broken bottles.

---

21 Wieringa, p. 140.
22 Wieringa, pp. 196-246.

The Indonesia specialist Benedict Anderson, who managed to get hold of the forensic experts' reports of 5 October signed by Soeharto, confirmed that the generals were never tortured or mutilated,[23] and thus Gerwani was evidently not involved in the coup. His article 'How Did the Generals Die?' reveals the blatant lies spread by Soeharto and the Indonesian mass media concerning the 1965-1966 purge.

However, Anderson's writing did not make much impact in Indonesia. The public's memory had already been shaped and the propaganda of Soeharto had permeated too deeply to be affected. Too many people had been involved in this atrocity: the crime was communal, so that they would rather not listen to another version of history. Most Indonesians have been in a pact with Soeharto, and when people are frightened or under threat, they will tend to seek refuge in a stronger party or authority. After Soeharto was able to convince many Indonesians that communists were the threat, and involved many civilians in violent attacks against the communists, those involved would also need to flee from their crimes. They would need protection either from communists seeking revenge or from being held accountable for the atrocities they carried out against the communists, or from both. They would need assurance, not only that their rights remain protected but also that their efforts are rewarded. Meanwhile, others who were not involved in the violence were often overwhelmed by uncertainty about the future after a brutal bloodbath and confusing news. Ignorance, in this case, is an essential ingredient in maintaining public fear.

The more widespread fear is, the more it will be embraced by the people as something natural. In this situation, the authoritarian government could gain more support, as the people viewed themselves as being under threat from another power: it was easier for the elite to create the figure of a 'Leviathan' (a powerful ruler with absolute sovereignty). The process of inducing fear prepared the people to accept such a ruler. The ruler was no longer the one who spread fear but the one who protected and saved the people from it: the one with the antidote.

## Soeharto's Version of History

Thus, the Leviathan was born: Soeharto. The use of fear continued. Soeharto manipulated the people to despise the communists, and many joined in the mass attacks and even in the mass murder of the people accused of being

---

23  Anderson.

communists. By employing fear, Soeharto had been able to get rid of the previous President Sukarno and place his cronies in power. To maintain his power, he had to maintain the fear. For this reason, the government of Soeharto wrote its own version of history. Though the murders happened on 1 October, they chose a day earlier. The Indonesian for 30 September Movement is Gerakan Tiga Puluh September, which allowed them to come up with the acronym GESTAPU, probably so that people would associate it with the terror of the Nazi Gestapo.

To sustain the horrific memories of communism, monuments and museums were built to portray its evil. At Lubang Buaya, Soeharto built the large Sacred Pancasila[24] Monument, which depicts the brutality of the communists and the sexual immorality of the Gerwani women. The dead generals were immortalised in large statues. The PKI Treason Museum was built in 1990 and contains 34 dioramas about the cruelty of the communists. In Yogyakarta (central Java), the monument Yogya Kembali was also dedicated to eternalising Soeharto's version of history. The monument and museum are full of warnings about the purported chief threat to the nation: the latent danger of communism.

Although Soeharto's troops had murdered millions of communists, to maintain his power he had to persist in demonising his victims. This use of fear was part of a deliberate attempt to silence the victims and their families, while also leading the populace to believe that the Leviathan Soeharto was still very much needed by the country. This national identity, born out of fear, had to be maintained, and thus the crucial distinction between communist and non-communist was emphasised over and over again during the Soeharto period. Former political prisoners were treated like virus carriers who were liable to spread their 'infection' to their families and the next generation. Thus, anyone who intended to work as a civil servant had to undergo a screening process to prove that they were from a 'clean environment' (not related to any political prisoner). The victims' evil was thus perpetuated, and by stigmatising the members of their families, Soeharto tried to impede any rebellion or vengeance in relation to the atrocities of 1965.

Soeharto's campaign against the communists permeated almost every aspect of Indonesian life. Even school textbooks were full of descriptions of the communists' cruelty. The categories 'communist' and 'atheist' became synonymous, and both groups were seen as betraying Pancasila, Indonesia's founding principles. Many of the films produced during this period also describe the evil cunning and immorality of the communists, and school children were urged to watch them, with tickets being sold in schools. But none

---

24  The state ideology and philosophy.

of these films had the same brainwashing power as the 'documentary' film *Pengkhianatan G30S/PKI* (The treason of G30S/PKI), a 1984 film sponsored by Soeharto. The words G30S and PKI are connected in the title, to marry the communists to the murders of the generals. Running for about four hours, the film depicts scenes of communists killing Muslims in the midst of their prayers, murdering generals in front of their families and Gerwani women slicing the generals while dancing seductively. School children were required to watch this traumatising film, and it was broadcast every year on 30 September until the end of Soeharto's reign. Interestingly, although the film indoctrinated generations, it incited *others* to talk about what *really* happened. An example in this book is Kusuma Wijaya's account: it was this very film that made his father reveal the family's secret history in relation to the 1965 tragedy.

During the governance of Soeharto, the survivors' identity cards also had to be branded with ET (*Eks Tapol* or 'ex-political prisoner'). This stigma was carried by their husbands, or wives, their siblings, children and grandchildren, including those who were born long after the tragedy happened. Those branded as ET, as well as their family members, could not attend state schools and universities or work as civil servants, and generally private companies did not want to employ them for fear of repercussions for supporting these 'communist' people. They also had to fulfil many requirements, such as reporting to the army and/or to local officials, attending dogmatic seminars and trainings, etc. The ET brand was only removed during the governance of Abdurrahman Wahid in 2000. Wahid also made a public apology to the victims, but he was quickly overthrown in July 2001. The long-term negative effects of the tragedy live on. The mass murder is still believed by many to have been a healthy process of eradication that the nation had to undergo.

After such a long period of terror, many have moulded themselves into whatever the regime wanted them to be. The New Order government was so successful and powerful that the repression had become a 'prerequisite' to be considered human. Many had to collaborate with those in power by denying their own convictions, and some even had to be the carriers of the New Order ideology, for they had no choice. For their families to be safe, the only way for them was to obey.

## Who Was the Mastermind?

The head of the troops that murdered the generals, Untung, was executed on 7 March 1966, but there was no proof that Untung was the mastermind of the murder of the generals. So, who actually engineered the murder of the generals on 1 October 1965?

In *A Preliminary Analysis of the Coup Attempt of the October 1, 1965 Coup in Indonesia*, published in 1971, the American historians Benedict R. O'G. Anderson and Ruth T. McVey claim that the murder of the generals was an internal army affair. The aim was to remove members of the Indonesian army elite who had worked with the CIA. The PKI and Sukarno were presented as scapegoats for this incident. Anderson and McVey reason that the PKI had been enjoying close relations with Sukarno, so that it would have been more beneficial to maintain this bond than to rebel against him.[25] Harold Crouch in his book *The Army and Politics in Indonesia*, also considers the movement an internal military affair, but suspects that the PKI was deeply involved.[26]

The Marxist historian W.F. Wertheim, by contrast, concludes that Soeharto was behind the plot, as the murders enabled him to take control of the army and dismiss the PKI.[27] The historian Saskia Wieringa does not agree that Soeharto was the mastermind but writes: 'Soeharto was both ruthless and very ambitious, and was able to wait patiently for the right moment to strike.'[28]

In his *Pretext for Mass Murder*, John Roosa also argues that there is no proof that Soeharto was involved in the murder of the generals. Roosa concludes that a section of the PKI leadership was involved. This was, however, used by Soeharto as a pretext for the massacre of millions of people with the aim of suppressing Indonesian communism, toppling Sukarno and seizing power.[29]

President Sukarno tried to correct Soeharto's anti-PKI propaganda on 12 December 1965, by stating that the result of the autopsy of the generals' bodies showed no mutilation or sexual abuse. But it was too late: the mass murders had already begun. Only the mainstream newspaper *Sinar Harapan* published Sukarno's statement, but the same newspaper, a few days later, published accounts of the debauchery and immorality of the PKI, as if denying Sukarno's statement. By then it was clear that Soeharto's path to power lay open.

25 Anderson and McVey.
26 Crouch.
27 Wertheim.
28 Wieringa, p. 293.
29 Roosa, *Pretext*.

On 11 March 1966, it was reported that Sukarno, in signing the Supersemar document, gave full authority to Soeharto to take whatever action Soeharto deemed necessary to secure the safety of the nation. The original of this letter is, however, lost, and its contents are still debated. Sukarno withdrew from power on 12 March 1966 and was put under house arrest. This was the start of Soeharto's reign, which would last until May 1998.

People still wonder at how easy it was for Soeharto to get rid of Sukarno, without much of a challenge from the troops who were still loyal to Sukarno. Why did Sukarno's troops not fight Soeharto? The chapter about Kristianto Budi, whose father was one of those army officers loyal to Sukarno, addresses these questions.

## When the Victims Remain Evil

Many of the perpetrators of the 1965 genocide acquired high posts in the New Order government, and even now are still close to high officials, so that their activities and businesses are protected. They still boast about the murders they were involved with in 1965-1966, as can be viewed in Joshua Oppenheimer's recent film *The Act of Killing* (2012), which takes place mainly in Medan, North Sumatra. At some point, these mass murderers even seem to be involved in what looks like a bragging competition in describing their 'bravery' in one of the biggest episodes of mass murder in human history: they are sure (or want to be sure) that their victims were traitors who deserved to be eradicated. These mass murderers also admit that they drank the blood of their victims, as they believed that this would give them the strength to kill and prevent them from going insane. Oppenheimer's film demonstrates that the power of the New Order ideology still reigns and that the victims of the genocide remain demonised and stigmatised.

The mass murderers perpetuate their legacy by maintaining the organisations Pemuda Pancasila (Pancasila Youth) and FAKI (Front Anti Komunis Indonesia, or the Indonesian Anti-Communist Front), which continue their propaganda of defending the Indonesian philosophy Pancasila by asserting the need of their presence to tackle the threat of communism. Thus, the fear of communism is maintained so that these people can keep acting as heroes who saved the country, with an easy target – because the enemies have never been allowed to adequately defend themselves. The right of Pemuda Pancasila and FAKI to bully, intimidate and even to loot 'these communists' is still granted.

Many of these mass murderers are family men and appear to be ordinary people, as shown by Oppenheimer's film. This has led to several critics equating the criminals' behaviour with Hannah Arendt's theory of the 'banality of evil'.[30] In her book *Eichmann in Jerusalem* (1963), Arendt writes about one of Adolf Hitler's henchmen who was responsible for the murder of millions of Jews: 'The deeds were monstrous, but the doer ... was quite ordinary, commonplace, and neither demonic nor monstrous.'[31] Arendt argues that Eichmann was somehow not capable of thinking independently. It was thoughtlessness that drove him, as the evil was so effectively normalised that its perpetrator did not recognise the cruelty of his deeds. It was his unawareness of this evil that made him able to commit such a monstrosity. The evil was so banal, that Eichmann had no capacity for reflection on the evil he had perpetrated.

This seems to be what we find in *The Act of Killing*, as some of the assailants at first seemed very excited about Oppenheimer's project, claiming to know the 'truth' and that this history should be revealed, so that young people would not forget the past. The 'truth' for them is their sustained heroism and the sustained slander and defamation of the so-called communists, their families and even descendants. It is these mass murderers who often exclaim about the evil and menace of their victims, to justify what they have done and to perceive themselves as heroes who conquered evil. However, are all of these murderers driven merely by the banality of evil? After all, people do have choices, although some may not be as beneficial for them as others. It was also the choice of Kristianto Budi's father, the former vice-commandant of an Indonesian army battalion, to be loyal to Sukarno that sent him to prison.

Oppenheimer has admitted that he gained the trust of the perpetrators because he was American, and because the United States supported the anti-communist violence. As he states: 'They loved American movies and Americans ... When I arrived, they just assumed, "Oh, this guy must love us."' This leads me to wonder whether these people may have been at ease performing their unawareness (or denial) that they had committed crimes against humanity, precisely because they were being filmed by a perceived ally. Later in the film, the film's main protagonist, Anwar Congo, shows remorse as he becomes aware of Oppenheimer's true intentions. Was Anwar previously really unaware? Or has Anwar's awareness of Oppenheimer's political stance somehow led him to demonstrate his awareness and his

30  See Whitington; Bjerregaard.
31  Arendt, pp. 3-4.

remorse concerning the crimes that he had committed? After all, we represent ourselves differently to different people. It is a game of representation that everyone has to play, even with themselves.

The murderers can only live 'in peace' if they misrepresent themselves (even to themselves), thus they need to keep telling themselves that their deeds were heroic. Several times in the film, the mass murderers state that their intention to make the film is to be remembered as heroes by the next generations. Thus, for them, the construction of collective memories is important because they need assurance and reassurance of who they are.

Consequently, they have to maintain their conviction that their victims were not victims but defeated evildoers who would commit monstrous deeds again if given the chance. As such, it is important for the society and the country to agree with them, so as to portray these perpetrators' convictions as the 'truth'. In this way, the victims are not allowed to have their independent memories, for this would represent the possibility of questioning the murderers' version of history. To sustain the murderers' sense of righteousness, the victims must remain dehumanised – indeed, witnesses told me that the murderers used to refer to their victims as 'chickens'. Soeharto's strategy of hunting the families and descendants of the communists fits in with this dehumanisation: for this reinforces the conviction that the victims are of a different species.

It is no wonder that Joshua Oppenheimer's second film, *The Look of Silence* (2014), has been banned in Indonesia, because in it a victim, Adi Rukun, is given a platform, in order to tell of how his brother was butchered by anti-communist militias in Sumatra. The people involved in such mass murders are 'threatened' by their own shadows: they are not only frightened, but also paranoid, so that a simple thing such as a documentary film was able to trigger a huge reaction from them. To preserve their own self-image, these mass murderers also rely on the image of the victims, and to maintain a certain image it is necessary for the victims to remain losers: the genocide of the victims' memories is thus a must. Adi Rukun provides in this volume his own account of being the main protagonist depicted in Oppenheimer's film, as well as of the film's subsequent impact upon his life and that of his family.

### The International People's Tribunal 1965

A group of Indonesians broke the silence surrounding the events of 1965-1966 by holding an international people's tribunal against human rights violations in Indonesia in 1965 – the International People's Tribunal 1965 (IPT 1965). Although not legally binding, the IPT 1965 was like a formal court. It began as a community initiative brought about by people who felt that the government had created and sustained a culture of impunity surrounding the events of 1965-1966. The tribunal was supported by members of the Indonesian diaspora, who have more freedom to speak out about the issue. The organisers believed that it was too risky to hold the tribunal in Indonesia, so it took place in the Hague from 10 to 14 November 2015.

Most of the victims who agreed to become witnesses in the IPT 1965 had to give their testimonies from behind a curtain and to use pseudonyms. As the British coordinator of the IPT 1965, I attended these hearings and interviewed the victims. Those who decided not to reveal their identities in public often did this because of their families. One witness, Titin Rahayu (pseudonym), who was imprisoned, tortured and raped, for instance, said that originally she wanted to testify openly. However, after a talk with her family, she decided that it was better for her to testify behind the curtain. Similarly, Basuki (also a pseudonym), who was imprisoned on Buru Island, originally wanted to testify openly. However, his wife was too worried and persuaded him not to do this.

And it was not only those living in Indonesia who decided to use pseudonyms: two Indonesian exiles, one living in the Netherlands and the other in Bulgaria, also testified behind the curtain because they were worried about the impact that their testimonies might have on their families who live in Indonesia. Aminah (pseudonym), the woman who is now a Bulgarian citizen, also explained how several members of her extended family still cannot accept her even today. Despite the caution of these witnesses, their bravery in revealing what happened to them has alarmed several high officials in the Indonesian government as well as the New Order cronies.

Highly placed officials in the Indonesian government, such as Vice President Jusuf Kalla and Minister for Political, Legal and Security Affairs Luhut Panjaitan, openly condemned the IPT 1965. Luhut tried to intimidate the people involved in the tribunal by claiming that they were acting unlawfully and he stated that they would be detained. It is apparent that these officials were themselves frightened of what might happen if the survivors of 1965-1966 started speaking up and therefore issued the threats in order to silence them.

## Real History and Memory: The 'Reality' of Oral History

My effort in collecting these accounts is a way of preventing the wholesale destruction of the memories of 1965-1966, especially because the stigma and fear are still alive and strong in relation to the incidents of 1965-1966.

First, I started to open up about myself. When Joshua Oppenheimer suggested to me in 2013 that I join him and fellow director Werner Herzog for an interview on National Public Radio in the United States and also for the *Wall Street Journal*, I told them openly about my father. I knew that if I revealed my family's past in public, it would give confidence to other victims and their families that their past was not something to be hidden. And if I opened up, the victims would trust me more and they would be willing to open up to me, too. Then, I made an announcement of my intention on Facebook and Twitter. I also approached several of my friends who I believed had been affected by this tragedy (from what they said, thought and wrote I could draw this conclusion). And most of the time, I was right. Although we might have been friends for a long time, we had kept quiet about our pasts in relation to 1965. My revelation about my family led to their revelations. Some of them, however, were not ready to go into detail about what had happened to their families because of the trauma associated with it.

In fact, by stigmatising the family members and descendants of former political prisoners, Soeharto was able to induce families to spy on each other, trying to find who had been on 'the list' and to spread fear even deeper. Because of this, a complete breakdown of familial trust is common amongst the family members of the victims. Sometimes I can sense a dynamic of hatred within a family, because they feel that whoever has been imprisoned has put the whole family at risk. People often blame anyone who can easily be blamed, rather than the real culprit. Soeharto's strategy was efficient in making the families of the 1965-1966 victims end up fearing and hating each other. Such sentiments are still alive and thriving, even now.

The stigma against ethnic Chinese also remains powerful. It is also an irony that while the genocide of 1965-1966 could not be separated from the long history of anti-Chinese sentiment in Indonesia, not many ethnic Chinese were willing to open up to me and take part in my project. Many of them (including my friends) told me that the risk was still too high for them. One of my friends, whose father was also imprisoned in 1965, told me: 'I am sorry, Soe Tjen. I only told you about my father, because you are one of my best friends; but never ever reveal it to anyone else.' In this book, besides me, there are only two other ethnic Chinese represented. One of them is Oei Hiem Hwie, who was imprisoned on Buru Island and decided to open up about his identity when he opened a public library. Another is a granddaughter of a PKI member, but she asked me to use pseudonym. Fear is still dominant amongst the ethnic Chinese in Indonesia, and they are more worried about the stigma and repercussions of openly discussing the events around 1965-1966 compared with the people who are considered not to be ethnic Chinese. Fear produced by the state and its apparatuses (the military, the paid gangsters) seems serious and obviously threatening, and has been discussed widely under the heading 'the politics of fear' by several academics and journalists. Nonetheless, there is another form of fear that is often more sustaining and has a more powerful impact on individuals: fear internalised within the family.

When state fear is domesticated, it becomes silent and usually unnoticeable. Nevertheless, half a century after the incidents of 1965-1966 and decades after the end of the New Order in 1998, it is this domesticated fear that is able to turn many people into agents of Soeharto: they teach their children to be afraid and to subject themselves to the New Order ideology. Several of the memoirs I have gathered depict how the parents ban their children from getting involved in politics or challenging the government; some siblings also asked their brothers or sisters not to get involved in my project, and some grandparents warned the family never to speak up. Many of these people who forbid others to speak up have been victims of the atrocities of 1965-1966. Out of fear, the victims have become the hands of the New Order regime, helping to sustain its ideology. The state has not even forbidden these people from writing, but the censorship is already there: internalised, psychologically embedded and personalised. Accordingly, most of my respondents had to negotiate with their own families before they were able to reveal the truth about their family histories. Fear is a very effective and inexpensive confederate for maintaining the power of despotic rulers.

Many people in Indonesia have passed the inheritance of fearful memories onto subsequent generations. Fear has become a meme – it has been transmitted through several channels, it has replicated and even mutated. When cancer cells mutate, they become more virulent and can conceal themselves better. So it is with fear. After their mutation, these cells usually move to a different part of the body, just as fear moves from the government apparatuses to the mouths of the victims and their families. This kind of mutated fear will then be camouflaged by different forms: it can appear as love, care, attention. Parents forbid their children from writing, because of their love for their children and out of concern for their safety: 'We don't want you to say anything in relation to what happened in 1965-1966, because we love you, because we are concerned about you'. When I asked a victim and his family whether they were afraid of talking about it, they answered: 'No, we are not afraid. But we just don't talk about it. It's in the past and we do not want to dig up old wounds. What for?' Fear has moved from the mouth of the government, to the mouths of the family members and has thereby become ubiquitous. It is what you breathe: it becomes simply a matter of paying attention to your surroundings and of avoiding situations that put you at risk.

The people who make efforts to search and reveal the truth have become the ones who are seen to create trouble for wanting to talk about the 1965-1966 anti-communist purge. Several ethnic Chinese, for instance, said to me after finding out about my intention of writing this book: 'We are allowed to speak Mandarin now. We can celebrate Chinese festivals freely. You cannot expect the government to be perfect, but at least we do not have to worry too much now, so what more do you want?' Thus, it is not fear that makes them disagree with my writing this book, but they believe that I will disturb the 'peace' that they have been enjoying since Soeharto stepped down. However, behind this is actually the fear that what they experienced during Soeharto's period of rule may happen again, and I have become the potential source of their fear.

Soeharto died several years ago, but the terror continues in another form: anti-communism had become a way for the New Order cronies to sustain their power on a more general scale, and to intimidate the public so that the people will remain subservient. Meanwhile, the history textbooks in Indonesian schools are still full of manipulation about the 1965-1966 genocide. 'Official' accounts of what really happened in October 1965 do not exist. As such, written records have provided a limited space for the survivors and their families, as they have been stigmatised and many were hesitant to write, and those who are willing to publish their stories often find difficulties in finding publishers who are willing to publish their works.

In this discourse of repression and stigma against the victims, often anonymous oral history becomes an alternative for these survivors and their families to express themselves. While documents and written materials about this case are not only scarce but also subject to manipulation, oral history can provide information about 'ordinary' people in relation to the legacy of 1965-1966 in Indonesia. Vannessa Hearman, who conducted research on the use of oral narratives in researching the 1965-1966 massacres, states: '[P]risoner memoirs and oral testimonies dealing with the 1960s period in Indonesia can provide a counterpoint to the histories that have thus far been promoted by the New Order.'[32]

Yet oral history is not free from problems, as it can raise questions about the reliability of the sources as well as their memories. Todd Brewster states that oral history has indeed been subject to doubt because an oral

---

32  Hearman, p. 38.

source 'however persuasive, inherently involves a certain vagueness and imprecision, for it is inevitably based upon memory – which over the years acquires hindsight'.[33] With so much historical confusion and manipulation in Indonesia, especially during the New Order, historical distance may give the respondents more clarity, as these events could only be discussed openly after Soeharto stepped down. Indeed, many of my respondents told me that as years went by, the events became clearer for them. Thus, there is a paradox here: the further one moves away from a certain event, the higher the risk that memories of that event will dissipate. Nevertheless, the distance also gives time for my respondents to hear and see their own histories in a wider scope so that they can place their memories within a clearer context. As events often relate to other events, this distance has given most of my respondents more data and a better perspective of what happened about fifty years ago.

Partiality, bias and imperfect memories are factors that are unavoidable in oral history, but written history can also be subject to similar inaccuracies. Moreover, as Indonesian history has demonstrated: written records have been constructed, manipulated and even forged. Consequently, oral narratives should never be dismissed, especially in a situation where the government is still repressive and the opportunity for publishing these memories is remote for many of these people. Indeed, Paul Thompson, one of the pioneers of oral history as a research methodology in the social sciences, writes that 'the use of interviews as a source by professional historians is long-standing and perfectly compatible with scholarly standards'.[34] To denounce or degrade the space in which the survivors and their families have the opportunity to narrate their pasts will only stigmatise them further.

From the testimonies of the survivors and the families of victims, the reader can see different perceptions and interpretations of the past. Yet, inaccurate perceptions cannot be equated with manipulation, and the stories in this book are not intended to present objective facts; rather, they show how historical facts about Indonesia are perceived by and have had an impact upon these respondents. This collection of their testimonies is just a small part of the fight against the obvious manipulation that the Indonesian government had conducted concerning the events of 1965-1966. The personal stories of these survivors and their families underscore the fact that historical falsification is completely different from interpretation.

33 Brewster, p. 76.
34 Thompson, p. 3.

It is from the personal stories of these 'ordinary' people whom I met that a new version of reality, a new history of the country, is emerging. History is often concerned with the ambitions of the powerful and tends to forget the people whose lives have been ruined by those ambitions, whose families have been victimised and traumatised for generations, and whose names may never be mentioned anywhere.

The people who share their memories in this volume are writing the 'real' history of Indonesia for me, for us – today.

# Part 1

Accounts of the Victims:
The Letter in the Sock

# The Letter in the Sock

Several children put a letter in a sock at Christmas, hoping that Santa Claus would grant their wishes. A prisoner on Buru Island also put a letter in a sock, but it was not addressed to Santa, for Santa could certainly not be generous enough to come with his reindeer to make a miracle happen on Buru.

The letter in the sock was a cry for help from the prisoners to foreigners. The control of the New Order government was so powerful that the only hope these prisoners had was the foreigner. This has nothing to do with race or ethnicity. Foreigners often have more freedom to express their opinions about a country without being threatened by the government of that country. Of course, governments are aware of this and for this reason the appeal to nationalism is a weapon governments use to shield themselves from the criticism of 'outsiders'.

That was what the New Order government had done: it indoctrinated the people with the necessity to pledge loyalty to the nation and the government, while at the same time manipulating the foreign media about the treatment of Indonesian political prisoners. The government gave the impression that the prisoners were treated well and cleaned up the prison only when there were international delegates around. When these visitors left, the prison was returned to its horrible condition. However, one of the prisoners managed to reveal the poor conditions though a letter sneaked into a sock.

The memoirs of the three prisoners – Antonius Pudji Rahardjo, Leo Mulyono and Oei Hiem Hwie – are united by this letter. The three of them were imprisoned in the same unit and they had all been punished because this letter was discovered by one of the guards. No one knows who had written it. I heard about it for the first time from Leo Mulyono, who told me that Oei Hiem Hwie might have been the writer. Oei Hiem Hwie, who was in the same unit as Leo, did tell me that he remembered this letter, although his story is slightly different from Leo's. Then I tried to find out about other prisoners from the same unit, who must have known about this letter. This brought me in touch with Antonius Pudji Rahardjo.

Antonius Pudji Rahardjo, however, has a different recollection. I had not yet asked him about the letter in a sock or a shoe, but he told me another story related or somehow similar to this. I do not want to conclude anything from these three memoirs, in relation to this letter. It is not for me to decide who actually put the letter in the sock. I will leave it to the reader.

# Leo Mulyono

## Working for My Oppressor

*I was in my hotel room in Yogya at the end of August 2013. Suddenly, someone knocked on the door. When I opened it, two elderly men were standing before me. Leo Mulyono introduced himself and his friend, Suparto, who is also an ex-political prisoner. I was really happy that they were willing to travel to this hotel to meet me. We had a chat in my room for a while, but then he whispered: 'The anti-communist groups are still strong and aggressive in this city. That's why we must still be very careful. You should not stay here.' He said that he could ask his friend, another ex-political prisoner, whether I could stay at his friend's house: 'But his house is really basic. Do you mind?'*

*'I can sleep anywhere. I don't even mind sleeping on the floor,' I said. I used to do it when I was a child. Leo and Suparto left my hotel and about an hour later, they came back with Buce, another ex-political prisoner. They helped me pack my stuff, and all of us walked to Buce's house, which was only about ten-minute walk from the hotel. At Buce's house, we chatted over snacks and coffee. This is Leo's story.*

I was born on 21 August 1945 in Blora, Central Java. I went to the ISI [Institut Seni Indonesia, or the Indonesian Institute of Arts], which used to be called ASRI. I studied graphic illustration there.

When I was in my second year, I joined CGMI [Consentrasi Gerakan Mahasiswa Indonesia, or the Unified Movement of Indonesian Students]. I was also active in the art house Sanggar Bumi Tarung (established by people from Lekra). There, I met Djoko Pekik, a very talented painter who was also imprisoned by Soeharto. After Djoko Pekik got out of prison, he had to work as a tailor for a few years, just to survive, but recently he has been working as a painter again, and his paintings are well-known now.

On 1 October 1965, my friends asked me to take part in the demonstration to support the revolutionary council and to oppose the Council of Generals, as we considered the Council of Generals sided with the bureaucratic capitalists and the new rich. Two days later, on 3 October, Yogya was full of posters with slogans like 'Get Aidit Now!', 'Hang Aidit!', 'Gerwani Are Whores', 'Communists Are Dogs', 'Fuck PKI'. I didn't know where they came from, but sentiments against communists grew as quickly as lightning. In the North Square, on 20 October, there was a rally to demand the abolishment of the PKI.

That day, I went to the North Square, because I wanted to see the anti-communist rally and what would happened there. The people at the rally seemed aggressive and ready to devour the PKI. Then, I decided to go to Res Publica University. There were so many people there; some were my friends and the rest I didn't really know. They immediately dragged me in, then gave me *janur kuning* [yellow coconut leaf] to be tied around my wrist. I was really confused: 'What is this *janur kuning* for?' In Java, we usually used *janur kuning* for parties and celebrations. But this time? I did what they asked me to do and tied the leaf around my wrist. 'We must guard this university', they said. 'If they come here, we must fight them', the others said to me. I was even more confused. What did we have to fight them with? 'Anything', they answered. Coincidentally, the university was being renovated. So there were many bricks around. We could use them as weapons. Then, we filled balloons with gasoline, to be thrown and exploded. But we did not want to attack them first. We were here only to defend ourselves and this university.

My friends were right. A group of people was approaching. They came with various weapons – knives, spears, axes, krises – and started destroying the signboard of the university. Many of them were the ones in the rally against communists, previously. Res Publica University was considered pro-communist then.

That was when I realised that the *janur kuning* was given to me to differentiate friends from enemies. The other group was getting more aggressive. So we started throwing bricks and balloons. Several of us also used slingshots. The others threw whatever they could find in the university: bottles, cement, anything. We knew this building better, so we could defend ourselves despite their violence.

Several of them decided not to go further, and some even retreated to the nearest post office. If anyone dared to go a bit further into the university, we just threw anything at them. In the end, all of them slowly left the university. We had not injured anyone seriously – which was good. So we felt quite relieved when we could no longer see them.

But suddenly, we heard some shots. A Panzer tank was approaching, led by the commandant, Major Kartawi.

## To Be Kept Safe

We were very relieved when we saw them. The soldiers had come; they would keep us safe and protect us. Suddenly, there were other shots from inside. The sounds of the pistols of the police. So the police and the army were there, at the same time. We were really confused. Several friends were taken at gunpoint. They were ordered to surrender any 'weapon' they used to defend themselves.

Then they searched all of us and we were herded into a corner. After a few minutes, while still pointing their guns at us, they ordered us to get out of the building. We were loaded into a truck, taken to the police office and questioned there. One by one, all of us were interrogated. A friend said that one of the army personnel managed to get in from the backdoor, and said: 'If anyone gets in here, I will shoot him.' So maybe the army was on our side, but the police were not and they were successful in trapping us. But I don't know the answer even now. Everything was so confusing.

We were about 130 people altogether. The police asked our addresses. I answered honestly, as I thought they needed it to send us home. But several friends were very suspicious and gave fake addresses. But it made no difference: whether you were honest or not, everyone was detained. When we asked why, the police said that because Yogya was still in chaos, it was not safe for us to be around. So we had to stay in the Wirogunan prison temporarily.

Indeed, we were in Wirogunan for a short while. But only to be transferred to other more terrible prisons. It turned out that this 'temporary' would take a very, very long time. I knew that worse things were awaiting us, when all of us were squeezed into a small space. The capacity of this room was maybe only for 30 to 40 people, but there were 134 of us there, so we could only lie down on our side and our legs were often on top of other people's legs. But we didn't want to be separated anyway. We thought, if we had to die, then we might as well die together. We were never sent home by the police. Our families were never notified. They presumed that I was lost.

From 20 October until the end of November, more people were placed in this space. This made the room completely packed and we could hardly move or breathe. Eventually, I was moved to another block fenced-in with barbed wire. Every now and then the officer would call a name, then we would never see this person again. So we knew to just keep quiet when our names were called. The officers would look for this person being called, but they did not always find him, and he would be saved, at least for that day.

There were many ethnic Chinese here, and before Christmas, some troops from Jakarta came in and barked: 'Where are the Chinese?' With the tip of their bayonet, they lifted our chins one by one, identifying the ethnic Chinese. Raymond Sulung said: 'I am not Chinese, I am Manadonese.' Indeed, many people from Manado look Chinese. But he was still asked to go forward, then they picked another Chinese; and the two of them were ordered to fight and punch each other. The officers watched while laughing. If they did not fight properly or if the officers thought they were not hitting the opponent hard enough, they would be beaten up by the officers. Teng Han was one of them. He didn't really want to hit his friends, so he was punched and thrown against the spiky fence. His body was lacerated all over because of this. But he was really tough. He got up and then whispered to us: 'That was just practice, to make my body stronger.' Later, we met again in Unit 4 on Buru Island.

When Eid was approaching, I thought I was going to die because we hardly had any food for a few days. Maybe because the guards had to fast then (all of them were Muslims), we had to fast as well. Suddenly, on the day of Eid, we were allowed to have a communal shower. It was only for a few seconds and we couldn't use soap, and we were given some food. Well, it was their day of celebration, so they were slightly more humane to us.

In March 1966, we were gathered in a yard in front of the prison. We were ordered to put our hands behind our heads. From the other side of the yard, other prisoners could see what was happening. I thought we would be killed then. We were told to go into a train carriage. The train was surrounded by soldiers and after we were inside, all of the windows were closed and nailed shut. Before the door was closed, we were given a small parcel of rice with a little side dish – it was as tiny as a pair of dice. We peered out of the tiny window slat, but we could only look down at the passing road asphalt that changed to grassland, then changed to stones. It reminded me of Hitler's Holocaust train.

When the train stopped in the morning, they asked us to get out while squatting with our hands on our necks. I saw water around me: 'Is this Nusakambangan?' I knew that this island was the place for serious criminals like murderers. My tears fell. I was imprisoned in a metal jail. Food was really scarce. Many of my friends died there from starvation.

If someone died, the guards distributed coconuts to the prisoners. The guards would ask one of us to help bury the dead and to pray with the coconut. Then the prisoner had to cut the coconut and spread the juice around the grave. This was the custom here. The flesh of the coconut was distributed to the prisoners, so we were really happy when someone died. We were even waiting for someone to die, so that we could eat coconut. Our sense of solidarity had disappeared because of hunger.

One time, I had to carry huge stones with a friend, using a long pole and a basket. I carried the pole at the front, and he at the back. He kept pushing me from behind. I scolded him, but he didn't stop. Finally I asked him to swap positions: he moved to the front. But then he was dragging me. It was like he tried to load more of the burden on me. Eventually I lost my patience. I threw the stones on the ground, then challenged him to a duel. His name was Suroto. He said, 'Mas [Brother],[35] do we really have to fight because of stones? Aren't we about to die anytime, anyway? The government is trying to kill us. We can die together if you are like this.' I almost cried. I realised at that time, there was no point in us fighting each other. His body was weak because he hardly had any food. That was why he didn't have much energy to carry this heavy load.

Later on, I was imprisoned in a prison called Nirbaya, on Nusakambangan. This prison was so terrible it nearly broke me. Many of my friends died here. I really didn't have anything, but I managed to sneak in a T-shirt from a friend from Res Publica University. I didn't dare to wear it because there was a picture of the CGMI torch. When my friends saw it, they asked me to burn it. But that was everything I had. And I only used it as a pillow.

Maybe because the conditions in this prison were so bad, and I thought I was going to die anyway, I decided to wear that T-shirt one day. My friends got very worried and thought I was mad. They were right. The guard summoned me. I had to see an officer named Dalim. He was huge and carried a club everywhere. He was one of the mass murderer commanders and wore a red-and-white shawl, maybe to show off his sense of nationalism. I was really nervous in front of him and was preparing myself with any excuse, like I had just cleaned up the coconuts and didn't have any clothes, so I had to wear this. Or what else could I say?

Dalim: 'Where are you from?'
'Yogya.'
'Studied at?'
'ASRI.'
'Can you draw?'

He didn't say anything about my T-shirt. I was very relieved. Then he called Pak Repto, his assistant. 'Pak Repto, could you go to Cilacap and buy some pencils, drawing brushes, paper and other tools for drawing?' I was told to help around the office for a while, before all those drawing tools arrived. That was in late 1967.

After the drawing tools arrived, I was required to draw heroes like Diponegoro and Kartini. Other commanders really liked my drawings, too,

---

35   A form of address for Javanese men.

and asked me to draw for them as well. Because of this, the guards were nicer to me. I could get in and out of the prison without being checked, so I could bring cassava to be distributed in the prison.

One morning, the people aged 20-50 and the students were called. I was so happy: we definitely would be freed now. We were asked to go to the train station. I left Nirbaya prison in a cheerful mood, and could walk quite well because of the better treatment I received when I was drawing. The others could hardly stand, so many of them had to crawl. They were only skin and bones, and the elderly ones had to be helped to get on the train. This time, the windows were not nailed shut. But why should they be nailed if we could hardly stand and we were about to be set free anyway? At the train station, there were several banana sellers, and the guards bought us bananas. It was such a happy day.

When the train was approaching Yogya, I was very excited. I would see my home, my friends, and my family again soon. At the main station, Tugu, the train didn't stop. So it would stop at Lempuyangan, a smaller station. But the train still didn't stop. Where would we be taken? Finally, the train stopped in Semarang. Would we be released here? We were ordered to get on a truck. The army surrounded us with guns, although it was impossible for us to run away, as we were already very weak.

The truck took us to Ambarawa, a market town in Central Java. When we were in Ambarawa, our family was informed of our whereabouts. Only at that point did my parents know that I was still alive. The prisoners' families could also send stuff for us: clothes, food, etc. The fathers of several of our Chinese friends could come and meet them. Maybe they paid bribes because our families weren't allowed to see us. But I heard one of our Chinese friends, Kim Siang, say to his father: 'Do not pay bribes, Pa. That makes me feel like a cow. After all, if they want to kill me, they will just kill me.'

In Ambarawa, I met a soldier who had been arrested (maybe because he still had enough of a conscience not to take part in this brutality). Because he knew several guards, his wife was allowed to visit him and she helped me to send letters to my mother. My mother tried to send some stuff to me, but I said to her: 'Bu [mother],[36] if you cannot afford it, don't send anything.' I had many siblings and they all needed to be fed. I knew that my mother had to sell her hair to earn money.

A few weeks later, the families were allowed to visit the prisoners. But we had to be kept apart by a few metres. The prisoners would stand behind the bars, and the visitors could look at us from afar. It was just like at the

36 *Bu* is the abbreviated form of *ibu*, meaning mother. It is also used to address older women.

zoo, with the prisoners as the animals. We communicated via writing. We wrote on towels with big characters and capitals to tell them our news: 'HEALTHY'. The visitor often wrote: 'WHAT SHOULD WE SEND?' Then the prisoners replied: *'KARAK'* [dried rice] or *'GETUK'* [sweet cassava]. If someone wrote: 'IT'S BEEN DRY' – this meant they were asking for money. In Ambarawa we already could buy stuff like cigarettes or soap.

We often wrote in code. The commander may have been suspicious of the code, since he asked us not to write, but to speak. We had to scream. Often, everyone screamed at the same time, and it was just like a bird market. So crowded. Everyone had to scream to be heard by their visitors. Luckily, I had a high-pitched voice (like a woman), so it could be heard more clearly than the others. Because of this, several other prisoners, especially the elderly ones, often asked me to shout messages to their families.

### Dating in Prison

Here, the female and male prisoners were not very far away from each other, and we could see each other. Some of the prisoners began dating. They used code and finger-movements such as sign language to communicate and to express their feelings to each other. No paper or newspaper was allowed, so it was impossible to write any love letters. The only reading material we could have were the Bible, the Quran and several religious books that were selected by the authorities. Basically, they tried to brainwash us with religion.

In Ambarawa prison, there were two tailors who could come out often, as the commander assigned them to make clothes. One of them asked me to help them and said: 'I'll teach you to sew.' Although I couldn't sew at all, that was a chance for me to be able to get out every now and then. Because of that, I met an officer's daughter and started dating her. She was still young, still in high school. I knew she had a crush on me, because although I was a prisoner, she thought I was educated. And when I was young, I was rather handsome. She often sent me all kinds of things: food, clothes.

Her father, Pak Karto, was Javanese, from Banyuwangi [East Java] and once said to me: 'Leo, when they have set you free, don't be worried. Just come to Banyuwangi, I have a *madumongso*[37] company.' He wanted me to marry her. But actually, I did not love her, I just loved her deliveries.

---

37  Sweet made of fermented black glutinous rice, usually wrapped in colourful paper.

In 1968, several people aged 20 to 50 were released. I thought this time I would be freed, but my name was not called. We said to the people who were about to be released: 'Please visit us.' We wanted to know whether they were really freed or murdered instead. Some of them visited us later on, and we knew that they were really free.

## Being Transferred Again

In 1969, we were transported again by train. When I got out, I thought somehow this place was very familiar. Then, I realised, we were back in Nusakambangan! But I was tougher by then, and I did not cry at all. Kim Siang, who had asked his parents not to pay bribes, was with us in Nusakambangan. He said he wanted to stay with his friends no matter what.

Many of the old commanders were still on this island, and they asked me to paint the buildings. Because of this, I could smoke and eat better. I did it really slowly, so I never finished. I just kept painting the same thing over and over again. In my cellblock, there was a *dalang* [puppet master], and in the evening he performed for the prisoners. He did everything with his mouth. He did the Baratayuda story, a capella, from start to finish, including the gamelan, the music, the drumming. Everything.

Finally, the day for us to move to another prison arrived. They gave me a leopard pillow, with a number. Starting then, we had no names, we were just numbers. There was no Leo. This was just like Hitler's camp. On-board the boat called Tobelo, we went to Buru. They turned on *dangdut*[38] songs. Only a few songs, the favourites of the guards on the boat, were played over and over again. For a few days, we had to listen to the same few songs. But the guards' attitude to us changed on this boat. They became nicer. Maybe that was the rule of the boat. Many people got seasick here, but I didn't. So I could eat their food, but then I got sick as well, because I ate too much.

On Buru, they put me in unit 4 [Savanajaya]. I was really impressed by how diligent the Chinese people here were. Whereas we always tried to be in shade while working, these Chinese were out in the sun, although it was really hot. Later, I realised why they were like that: they wanted to look darker. Because the guards liked picking on the Chinese, these people wanted to look more like us. Unfortunately, many could not hide their slanted eyes.

Sometime in the mid-1970s, when there was a foreign visitor, someone wrote a letter to tell this guest about the bad things here which were

---

38   A genre of Indonesian music derived from Indian and Arabic music.

covered up by the authorities. He tucked the letter into the guest's sock. But when the guest was about to put on his sock, the guard found out about this letter. Of course, the guards were furious. But no one admitted to having written it. We were then all punished – by running in the rain for hours and hours. I was amazed by the bravery of this man. I was glad that no one confessed. And whoever wrote the letter, had done so for us too, anyway, so if we had to die, then we might as well die together. Was it Oei Him Hwie? You have met him, right? Could you ask whether it was he who did it? I think he speaks English quite well, so he could write to the foreigner. I really want to thank him for this, because after that incident, international visitors sometimes came unexpectedly and this improved our condition.

After years on Buru, we heard the news that a boat would soon take us to Timor Leste. 'Good', we thought. 'Since the natives here have been indoctrinated by Soeharto, they hate us; but we know that the natives in Timor Leste hate Soeharto. We can form a rebellion there by working together with the natives.' So we tried to stay healthy as much as possible. Coincidentally, I was ordered to join a volleyball team here because I was quite tall. I practiced hard because I wanted to get fit, so I would have plenty of stamina to fight after arriving in Timor Leste. But after all of that planning and preparation, the boat to Timor Leste never came.

**Photo A   Leo Mulyono in front of his home**

## Back to Yogya

Finally, I was released in 1979, and got married in 1980. My wife is a former Plantungan[39] prisoner. She had often danced *genjer-genjer*,[40] and that was why they took her. The people who were dating in Ambarawa prison, none of them got married. I met my wife at church. I love her dearly and we are still together now.

After getting married, we were required to stay in Yogya, although we didn't want to because this city was really strict in keeping an eye on ex-prisoners like us. But we had no other option. My wife and I had to attend Santiaji trainings. These were basically indoctrination sessions for the ex-political prisoners. At every Santiaji training, we had to read about Pancasila, led by the district head and the political staff from the city council. They also often insulted us as communists, etc. We were required to pledge allegiance to the government and had to condemn the PKI.

At first, we had to attend these indoctrination sessions every week for several months. Then, they changed it to every fortnight, and later, every month. After a few years, they changed it to every three months, on the 17th. When my wife had just given birth to our fourth child, I told them that we could not come to Santiaji, but the authorities got really angry and scolded me. So after delivering our baby, my wife had to go straight to the office of the district government, with all the children and me. The kids had to come because there was no one to look after them at home. They came inside the room, where we had the training. Because they were quite tired and bored, they started whining. So the officer let them wait outside. Every now and then the kids peeked in the window to see what we were doing.

I joined the group called Merdeka [Independent] artists, without telling them who I really was. They didn't really want to know my history, anyway. Coincidentally, we had an order from Jakarta, and I used this opportunity to meet Pramoedya Ananta Toer (Pram). I didn't ask for any travel permit from the authorities (although at that time, it was forbidden to travel without one). But I was able to do it secretly.

In Jakarta, we had to decorate the huge posters of Soeharto and the Vice President at the time, Tri Sutrisno. The official staff asked me to wear my ID card on my chest. But you know, my ID card had this ET [ex-political

---

39  Plantungan is a district in Central Java, and the hospital for lepers there was turned into a prison for female detainees around 1965.
40  *Genjer-genjer* is the name of a dance (as well as the title of a song) which was associated with the communists.

prisoner] stamp, so I told the leader of the project about this (he was an ethnic Chinese). He just gave me his ID card. 'But the photo?' He asked me to wear his ID card on my chest turned the other way around, so no one could see the photo. I did as he said, although I was really nervous: If they found out, what would happen? Indeed, they didn't check my ID card, so I could keep working. I had to decorate an open car with faces of movie stars. The car was moving around so our work became a kind of spectacle for the people (many of them were businessmen and high officials). The director of PAM [the Indonesian water utility] approached me and said: 'The car will soon pass the stage of honour, where Soeharto sits. Please remember to turn around, and pay respect to him.' I would have loved to show my arse to Soeharto but I couldn't do it. My family and I still had to eat, so I obeyed him. I just had to remember to keep my ID card turned the other way around so no one could see the photo.

For the sake of survival, I was willing to do almost anything. I also had a project in Batam, when Habibie [a virtual stepson of Soeharto, and then, the Minister of Research and Technology] and Tutut [a daughter of Soeharto] started the World Trade Centre there. They even appointed me as the group leader. So I brought several young artists to this island. At the border, a group of soldiers stopped us and asked: 'Where are you going?' I explained: 'We had orders from the central government.' The soldiers were immediately very helpful. Even when they asked for my ID card and I couldn't show it, they didn't mind. They let us all in immediately. I just had to be careful. If there was any project outside of Yogya, I could only do it when there was no Santiaji training, because I always left without a travel permit. If there was Santiaji, then I had to miss the opportunity (which meant, I lost the income as well).

Right after we had finished working in Batam, the staff told us that Habibie and Tutut were coming. We were packing our tools, and many of them had already been put into the boxes. But the official asked us to take them all out again, so that Tutut and Habibie could see us work. Accordingly, we had to take everything out again and pretend to work, although we were quite tired already. Sirens were screaming everywhere when their cars arrived. Many people, including the artists I was leading, got very excited. They asked me to come forward, as the group leader, to introduce them and to take pictures with these two public figures. I said I was too tired to do that. Of course, this was just an excuse. Actually, I hated these two people so much. I just needed their money. Some of the artists got really angry with me: 'Why don't you want to do this? It will be such a memorable experience to meet and have pictures taken with them.'

## Pramoedya Ananta Toer

I met Pram in the 1990s, when Soeharto was still in power. At that time, Pram lived in his house on Kehakiman Street. When he learned that an ex-prisoner from Buru Island had come to visit him, the gate of his dark house that was covered with vines and foliage was opened. He invited me in, and we had a long chat. He told me to remain cautious. When he took a walk in the morning, there were people who wanted to hit him with a motorbike or a car: 'Many people want to kill me here. Maybe they are Soeharto's henchmen. They do not like seeing me alive and healthy.'

I asked him about Soeharto, and he said: 'If Soeharto needs to see Pram, he has to come here.' His gestures were still defiant despite the long torment he had experienced: 'And who is this Soeharto, anyway? He was nothing compared to Aidit.'[41] Aidit was much more intelligent than him.' To maintain his safety, Pram decided to move to Depok [a small town not far from Jakarta]. In this town, Pram did some farming and continued to write. He told me that he was somewhat disappointed that his children did not want to write, because of their trauma in relation to what had happened to their father, whose writings became a sharp weapon and put him into so much misery.

Unfortunately after that, I never saw Pram again, until he left us all.

## My Story

I rarely told my kids about my past when they were young. It was only after they went to college that I started telling them my story, bit by bit. But they weren't surprised because they had met my friends when we had meetings or gatherings. So in a way they had already known before I told them. I think it's better this way, so they weren't shocked, and they didn't feel like I was dictating to them that they had to believe in a certain thing.

For a while, we have been promoting Bung Karno [Sukarno]. Although I think Bung Karno also made some mistakes, and glorifying him would also be a kind of worshipping of authority. I don't actually believe in the worshipping of any public figure, but this is a start. We must always make compromises and be aware that it takes time to achieve our goal. We have to move step by step, and be very patient because they are still very powerful. The museum in Yogya still lies about what happened in 1965. If you go

---

41   Aidit was the leader of the PKI from mid-1950s until his death in 1965. Under his leadership, the PKI became the third-largest Communist Party in the world (after that of Russia and China).

there, look at the Monumen Yogya Kembali [Monument to the Recapture of Yogyakarta]. It tells a fictional story about the brutality of the communists and left-wing people. Our journey is still winding and long. Every now and then, I feel desperate, but if I talk to the younger generation who are concerned about this 1965 issue, like you and my daughter, I feel alive again. That's just about my only consolation at the moment.

*When Leo finished his story, it was already around 4 pm. We tried to get some food at a stall nearby, but it was closed. Where should we go then? 'Are you desperately hungry?', he asked me. I shook my head. 'You know, we used to be starving in the prison, so if we don't eat, it's not a big deal. I can just eat at home later. But you should eat soon.'*

*Before he left, he told me that his daughter, Pipiet, would love to meet me, but her child was ill. I stayed with Buce, who works as a masseur. That day, Buce refused to take any customers so that he could stay and have a chat with me.*

*At the beginning of July 2015, when I came visited Leo again, Pipiet told me that her father used to tell her funny experiences on Buru Island when she was young. So she thought that being a prisoner was fun. He told her about the suffering and torture much later. We still keep in touch via email to encourage each other. I often miss these people.*

# Oei Hiem Hwie

## The Amazing Library

*I met Oei Hiem Hwie for the first time in 2007, because I had heard about his amazing library in Surabaya. It contains many ancient Dutch books, old Chinese and Indonesian newspapers, as well as old printing machines. Anyone could come and use the library for free. He is very friendly and cheerful. Many of the ex-political prisoners I have met do have an amazing sense of humour, despite the suffering they have experienced. After asking my name, Oei said: 'It's good you did not change your name.' Soeharto did require people with Chinese names to change them to Indonesian names (which meant, in practice, any name, Indonesian or foreign, that was not explicitly Chinese, such as Akbar, Gracia and Henry would do).*

I was born in Malang [East Java], to a father who was originally from Hokkien, and a mother who had mixed ancestors from Central Java. Papa was educated in a Chinese school, but mama was educated in a Javanese school. She wrote Javanese characters really well. That was why I was interested in many different cultures, although I went to a Chinese school in Malang called THHK [Tiong Hoa Hwee Kwan].

In high school, I studied journalism. At that time, journalists were highly respected (they were considered the kings of the world). I later worked as a trainee at the newspaper *Terompet Masyarakat* in Surabaya. This newspaper was actually neither left wing nor right wing. It was trying to be in the middle. The director of the newspaper was a Chinese Indonesian: Poo An Goei. This newspaper was the leading paper in Java at that time, with 75,000 copies distributed throughout East Java alone. From the rickshaw drivers to big businessmen and officials, everyone read it.

In 1963, I was assigned to interview Sukarno for *Terompet Masyarakat*. I stayed for three days in Jakarta and, of course, I was very proud. After the interview, Sukarno gave me a watch and I still look after it carefully.

## The Murder of the Generals

Two years later I was in Malang when Gestok [the 30 September Movement] happened. I heard it on the radio. Only a few weeks after that event, tens of men in black robes and masks, with only their eyes visible, turned up at my house. They all carried weapons: 'We have been ordered to search your house.' Besides me, mama and my sister were at home. Papa had died in 1960. Mama and my sister were really brave. They were not frightened at all. These men took all of my books and documents from my home at Klojen Kidul 26 in Malang, then put them all in a large Russian jeep. But they could not fit all of my books in. Finally they left some. Next, they chucked me into a truck as well. My sister gathered all of the books that had been left behind and hid them in the ceiling. Most of them were Dutch books. Unfortunately, many of those were destroyed, either by rain or by being eaten by moths. The books that could still be saved are now here in my library.

Afterwards, I was arrested. First, I was detained in Batu [a small town in East Java close to Malang]. There I was placed in a former can factory, called Gap Sin. The factory had been closed, but there were still tins remaining. Someone told me that this factory had been owned privately, but then was seized by the army. The prisoners were mixed, from various backgrounds and organisations, such as Baperki, PKI, BTI.[42] All were men. If there were any women, they were isolated in another room.

They had found my writing about Sukarno. So they called me 'Sukarno-centric'. I said: 'So I am not communist, right?', hoping that they would let me go. 'But if we release you, you will defend Sukarno', they said.

Despite the detention, I was lucky. I wasn't physically hurt, because they had not yet decided that I was a communist. But the others were beaten up and tortured. After being detained in this camp for two months, I was moved to Lowokwaru prison in Malang on 12 January 1967. The fence surrounding the prison was three layers thick, and was spiked and electrified. Mama, who had not heard about me for months, thought I was dead. She'd already held a *selametan* [wake], for me at the house.

Soon after, I was sent to Kalisosok prison in Surabaya. The prisoners were fed hard corn rice with coconut, in which the pieces of corn could be counted on one's fingers. They were not given any drink, although it was incredibly hot there. The food was wrapped in teak leaves, and guards threw it to the prisoners while yelling: 'Rotten shit!' Often, they gave us our meals by pushing the food with their feet. I was given drink, and was fed somewhat better, because my status was not clear: Could they consider me

---

42  Baperki (Badan Permusjawaratan Kewarganegaraan Indonesia, or Consultative Body for Indonesian Citizenship) was an organization founded in Indonesia in 1954 by Indonesians of Chinese descent; BTI (Barisan Tani Indonesia, or the Indonesian Peasants Front) is the Indonesian farmers movement. Both of these organisations were considered communist, although the members were not necessarily communist sympathisers.

a communist or not? Once they classified you as a communist, you were immediately treated ruthlessly.

If the prisoners were thirsty, they stretched out their clothes, or any fabric such as torn underwear, when it rained. They would squeeze out the fabric in order to extract water to drink. Many had shrunken intestines from lack of food and water.

At Kalisosok prison, one night, I saw Murahman, the former mayor of Surabaya. He was also a legal advisor to the Chinese community organisation Baperki, and to BTI, the peasant union. Murahman used to be my law professor at the university. He was a very good lecturer, but he was not PKI. He backed Sukarno and Baperki.[43] I saw him from far away. Now, no one has any idea where he was taken or what happened to him. His picture does not exist in the mayor's office even today: it has been destroyed, because he was considered a communist.

After Kalisosok, I was moved to the Koblen military prison in Surabaya. In this prison, the food was better. But I had been there for only three nights when, very early in the morning, they moved me again. The troops who guarded us were led by Captain Muhadji Widjaja. He was the one who built Wijaya Shopping Centre in Surabaya. Later, he became the mayor of Surabaya. He checked the prisoners and asked all of us to wear yellow shirts with numbers. On my shirt was number 64. We were required to stay in a certain lane. He said: 'If you guys move to another lane, you will be shot, OK?' He yelled and threatened us, but never hit us.

When he saw me, he asked: 'What are you doing here? How did you end up here?' I told him I had no idea either. He said: 'OK, now write a letter to your mother.' He promised that he would try to free me from prison. Some people were indeed freed then, because they gave bribes. But I wrote to my mother: 'Ma, do not use money, because this is a political affair. Just use your money to make cake, and send the cake to me.' Muhadji said to me: 'I'll take care of this'. I was so relieved. I was sure Muhadji Widjaja would set me free.

In a few days, they did call my name. I was not freed but taken to Nusakambangan Island. Apparently, the examination process had been completed and it had been decided that I was a communist. Muhadji could not do anything. On Nusakambangan Island, I was thrown in Karang Tengah jail. There were approximately eleven prisons there. Karang Tengah was for political prisoners. I was not tortured there, I just had to do morning

---

43 Baperki established several universities called Res Publica. This phrase, which is Latin and means 'for the benefit of the public', was taken from a speech by Sukarno. In Jakarta, Res Publica now has been turned into Trisakti; whereas in Surabaya, it was changed to UBAYA.

gymnastics. The food was not bad, not like at Kalisosok, but often the guards took away the best food. We were given bulgur and salty fish (the head or the tail only) or a tiny chunk of tempeh. The bulgur given to us was made of leftovers from beer making, so it had no nutrients at all. Because we were still hungry, we looked for cassava skins. We chopped them into small pieces and mixed them with salt. We could often find skins in the garbage bins because when the guards ate cassava, they threw away the skins.

Sometimes, when we were sent out to hoe the land, we could also get cassava. If the wardens were nice, we could boil it and eat it together. But if the wardens were nasty, they would take away our cassava. One time, there was this very nice warden who allowed us to go out of our cells for a while in the morning, to get some cassava, but this was really rare.

In the prison, the guards had given us a large white barrel to defecate in. In the morning, two of the prisoners would be ordered to dump the contents of the barrel into the ocean, then wash it thoroughly using seawater. One morning, when I was throwing the poo out of the barrel, a prisoner passed by. I think he was Kusni Kasdut, the most well-known fine art thief in Indonesia. He said, 'Hey, do you want boiled cassava?' I couldn't believe how much he gave us. But how to hide it so we wouldn't get caught? We decided to put it in the barrel, where our poo had been.

And we were right. The guards didn't check. So we had a boiled-cassava party in the prison that night.

I was on Nusakambangan for about three to four months; they moved me from one prison to another there as well. One day, there were many red-and-white flags flying at half-mast. I didn't know why. Only later did I learn that Sukarno had passed away.

In 1970, I was picked up by the ship Tobelo to be taken to Buru Island. The journey took much longer than it normally would have, because of the fear of getting caught by the international media, so the ship took a clandestine route through small islands, not via the usual route where big ships would go.

## Buru

We arrived in the evening, but we could only get off the ship the next morning. We were escorted by soldiers with guns. Most of them were Ambonese. These Ambonese usually treated people according to their religion. If the Christians guarded other Christian prisoners, they were treated better. But if the Christians guarded the Muslims, they would be nasty, and vice versa.

When we arrived on Buru, there were already thirteen units. I was in unit 4, also called Salenko. Later, this name was changed to Savanajaya. Why? Because unit 4 used to be a savannah. After the political prisoners worked on it and grew rice, this place was becoming more glorious [*jaya*]. So Savanajaya: the glorious savannah. This unit was the closest to the sea: approximately 3 km away. There, the land was rather flat, and also there were no big trees, so we could farm quite easily. Other units were higher up in the hills, uneven and full of large trees. The prisoners had to fell the trees before planting rice. Of course, they had to work much harder. Savanajaya was actually for special people, said some security guards. The leaders of the party were usually placed at the top, so they suffered more; whereas unit 4 was mainly for college students, journalists, lecturers and professors who were considered sympathisers only, not party members. There were about 1,500 of us there, and if any of these, after further investigation, were found out to have been active in the Communist Party, they would be moved up to one of the higher units.

## Pramoedya Ananta Toer

Pramoedya was placed at the top of the hill, in unit 3. Many of my prison mates looked up to Pram as a great writer. I was also a fan. Incidentally, behind Pram's unit was the field I had to work on. When I spotted Pram, I really wanted to meet him. So I waited for an opportunity. If the guard seemed lazy and sleepy, I would sometimes chat with Pram briefly, and he gave me so much inspiration he made me forget my horrible time in prison.

I tried to borrow a typewriter from the unit's office and asked for some paper. I didn't expect that they would agree, but they did, although the paper they gave was really thin and of very poor quality. During the day, when everyone had a nap, I gave the typewriter to Pram so he could write again, but not for long, because I had to take the typewriter away from him again, and return it to the office. That went on for some months.

Pram wrote his story, and I corrected the typos. Then, we dug a hole. We wrapped the script in banana leaves, and hid it in that hole. We also made a covering from cement that looked like the ones used to cover a latrine. So when anyone saw it, no one would dare opening it. Later on, I got more courage. I would send cassava to Pram. I hid it inside my underwear.

After huge international protests, Pram was finally permitted to write again. At that time, the head of Kopkamtib[44] was Sumitro. He came to Buru and said: 'Pram, this typewriter is for you.' The typewriter was broken but Pram could fix it. They also gave Pram one ribbon. When the ribbon ran out, they did not give him another one. I was looking for some leaves that could produce colour. Fortunately, I could find them on Buru. I boiled these leaves and they yielded indigo liquid. I wet the ribbon with this liquid, then dried it – but I was not sure whether this would work. When Pram started typing, it was a bit messy but at least it did work!

Later, Pram ran out of paper. Indeed, they gave him some paper, but the paper got torn easily. When the paper ran out, they didn't give him more. Around that time, my friends were often ordered to go to Namlea [a nearby town] to barter for daily needs. Pram was able to get eggs from the chickens in the fields in his unit. He didn't eat them, but gave the eggs to the prisoners who would go to Namlea, so that they could swap the eggs for paper.

I gathered all Pram's writings and glued the papers with boiled cassava. Then, I pressed them with a lid we made ourselves and hid them in the hole that we had dug for them.

Eventually, Pram was allowed to write by the government. Later, Pram's scripts also had to be submitted to the officers to be given to Soeharto. I don't know whether he ever read them or not.

### The Beauty of Buru

Buru Island is actually really beautiful, surrounded by mountains and a pristine river. The stones at the bottom of the river were visible, and there were plenty of fish. People were prohibited from defecating or urinating in the water, so we could drink it. It's called the Waibini River.

On Buru, the government only gave us food for three months. After that, we had to work for our own sustenance. If we could plant rice, then we ate rice. If we could harvest cassava, then we ate cassava. Anything. But the soil was not very good for crops. It was mostly sandy and not enough organic matter. So even though we'd worked hard before planting, the crops often failed. One time, Pramoedya was summoned by the Attorney General, when the Attorney General came to Buru. He asked Pram: 'What's

---

44  Kopkamtib (Komando Operasi Pemulihan Keamanan dan Ketertiban, or the Operational Command for the Restoration of Security and Order) was a secret police operation in Indonesia's New Order.

happened here? Why is the soil like this?' Pram answered: 'This island is so different from Java. Java has been cultivated for thousands of years so the land contains plenty of organic matter. This island must be left a forest first for a few years. If we have to make it an agricultural area right now, it will be impossible.'

Later, the government sent an agricultural organisation: they were composed of young people from Java. Most of them were students and were quite inexperienced. By then, most of us had found out what the problems were, but the guards looked down on us, so they never listened to us. We let these students examine the ground and do whatever they wanted there. And we were right, they could not change the land to be agricultural soil in seconds.

## Building Houses

The commander of each unit was usually a colonel or a captain. We had to make a house for all these commanders. The houses were made of wood and brick, and they had to be very good. We had to make the bricks ourselves. We also had to make the moulds to shape the bricks. We manufactured paint by mixing limestone with sago. There are many limestone mountains on Buru, with different colours. Our handmade paint was very durable.

The leader of the builders, who was also a prisoner, told the warden that we had to perform a *selametan* [an inaugural ritual with a communal feast], before starting the building, otherwise terrible things would happen to the houses. The warden believed in this kind of myth, so he agreed to organise it and have the foods and equipment for this ritual prepared. Actually, this was just our leader's trick, so we could have a bit of a rest and nice food. He actually didn't believe in this kind of rubbish.

After some time, maybe because the guards and the warden got bored as well, there was entertainment every now and then. Sometimes, there was a *wayang*[45] show. If there were wardens or officials from Surabaya, there would be *ludrukan*[46] and we all could watch. Because many of the officials here were from Java, the entertainment was mainly in Javanese. I felt sorry for the Ambonese, because they couldn't understand it.

---

45  *Wayang* is a shadow puppet performance, which is very popular in Java.
46  *Ludrukan* is a form of musical theatre, popular in Surabaya and East Java.

## Development

In unit 4 they established a hospital, built by the prisoners as well. Then the government sent young doctors who had just graduated from the university. They were usually very fierce, even rude to us, maybe because we were just political prisoners. One time, I'd got the flu. At that time there was a severe flu pandemic – the Hong Kong flu. I could not even stand up. I went to the doctor, whose name was Hadi. He had just graduated from the University of Indonesia in Jakarta. He was very serious and patient. He paid close attention to me, until I was fully recovered. But doctor Hadi kept his distance from me. He only wanted to talk about my illness and nothing else. It was obvious that he was very tense, maybe because he had been warned and even threatened not to talk about anything else with us.

We were then ordered to build a mosque, a temple, a church, an art gallery and a library. We continued to build and build. After these buildings were completed, the religious indoctrination began. They gave us religious education and the library was full of religious books. We were required to adhere to one of the religions – either Islam, Christianity, Buddhism or Hinduism. If we were Muslim, we had to go to the mosque on Fridays and pray five times a day. In the mosque, there would be staff who questioned the prisoners: 'Do you pray five times a day or not?' If we chose Christianity, we had to go to the church on Sundays. They sent a priest and an imam from Java to Buru to keep an eye on us. And they kept an attendance list for all of us.

So many of us thought carefully before choosing a religion. Which one was more convenient? If we were Muslim and had to pray five times and that was tiring. If we chose Christianity, it was not too bad, but Buddhism was better. They could not find any Buddhist Priest to be sent to Buru, so we could just get together and have a chat without being watched. Amongst these 'Buddhist' people, there was *one* real Buddhist. Every now and then, we asked him to pretend to pray when the guard was approaching.

Savanajaya had become a showcase for the government: if there were guests from abroad [such as from the parliaments of other countries], they came to Savanajaya. Indeed, because this place was low and flat, it was the most easily accessible. So that was the reason why we had to build and build: to fool the international community. Our unit had the best facilities in comparison with those of the other units. If the international visitors came, we were not guarded as strictly.

Yes, I do remember the incident that Leo talked about. But I remember a shoe, not a sock, and I have no idea who wrote that letter. If I am not mistaken, that guest was from the Netherlands. He came to Buru around 1972. One of the prisoners put a letter into the Dutchman's shoe, but the guard caught it when the man was about to step into it. We were all punished, but we were actually thankful to the guy who had written the letter, so we didn't even mind the hassle!

One time, the guards gave us imported sacks of fertiliser. They said that this fertiliser was extraordinarily good, and asked us to use it all up. We didn't want to do it, because we wanted to save some for later. But still, it was an order. And the plants indeed grew very nicely. Not long after, guests from Amnesty International in the Netherlands arrived. Other visitors from all over the world followed. At that time we realised that it had been intentional. Everything looked green and prosperous. The visitors would think that we were being looked after well here.

But when the time of harvest came, there were not enough people and too many crops. Indeed, some of us already said that the crops had to be grown in turn, so they didn't all come up at once. Finally, the leftover crops invited pests like grasshoppers. So we decided to burn some of them. After that, there was no more fertiliser for us. The soil was also damaged; it became very hard. We could not even hoe it. We just had to eat cassava and its leaves. The leaves became a vegetable for us; and because they were quite rich, they also became our only source of protein.

## Staying or Leaving?

In 1978, Soeharto ran out of money for his development plan, maybe because the money had been stolen by his cronies. The Indonesian Foreign Minister was sent to the United States to borrow some money to continue the government's project. The American President at that time was Jimmy Carter. Carter said that the United States could lend money provided that the political prisoners were released. Soeharto also borrowed some money from the IGGI [Intergovernmental Group on Indonesia]. Several countries then became donors, in a council chaired by the Dutch International Development Minister Jan Pieter Pronk. Pronk also demanded that the prisoners of Buru Island be released, especially Pram.

After that, the government announced that we would be released soon. The guards on Buru asked us: 'Do you want to go home or do you want to stay and we will send your families here?' Those who stayed on Buru would be given a plot of land to farm and other facilities. Several people said yes, especially if they had nothing much in Java and felt that they had formed a bond with the prison mates. Many of us said no – we wanted to go home. Those who decided to go home had to give whatever they had to the ones staying on Buru. I decided to return to Java.

But the government often didn't care about what we really wished. They wanted more people to stay on Buru, because Java was quite full. Soeharto had this transmigration programme as well – sending people to less populated islands to develop them. So in a way, it was more advantageous for his project if more people stayed on Buru. For this reason, they brought over the families of the political prisoners without their consent. This became very chaotic, as many prisoners were not ready to meet their families in such poor conditions, and with so little self-esteem. Many of them got depressed and committed suicide.

The last group of prisoners to be released were those in unit 3, where Pram was detained. In unit 3, there was also Oei Hay Djoen, who used to be a very prominent parliamentary member of the PKI, and a relative of mine. Indeed, there were many important people in the party there, so I guess that's why it took the government a long time to release them.

### Going Home

I was released in 1978, but Pram and Oei Hay Djoen still remained in prison. Soeharto was still unwilling to lose his authority over them. But a year later, Pram and Oei Hay Djoen were released. Oei Hay Djoen was not brought to East Java directly, but was sent to Semarang and other cities in central Java. Over half a month, he was just transported from one place to another without being landed anywhere. Because of international protests, eventually the government returned Oei Hay Djoen to Surabaya. If not, maybe he would have been disappeared – the government might have wanted to kill him.

Before I was transported to Java, Pram entrusted me with his original manuscript of *Bumi Manusia* [*This Earth of Mankind*]. I also took home the cement lids of Pram's manuscript from Buru. A ship that was usually for the Hajj pilgrimage took us to Java. It was a nice and comfortable ship. The food was good, too. On the ship, I was very worried, because many of us were being checked. They would definitely find Pram's manuscript and these heavy cement lids; and I could have been plunged into the sea with this stuff. Luckily, no one checked me.

We docked at Tanjung Perak harbour in Surabaya, and then I was dragged to a big building called Gelora Pancasila. There we were warned not to be involved in politics ever again. After receiving the release letter, they took me to Malang. I had really missed my family. In Malang, the ex-political prisoners were picked up by members of their families, but after thirteen years in prison, I didn't see any member of my family at all. I waited for a long time but I couldn't see the face of my mother or my younger sister. So I decided to make my way home alone, by *becak* [cycle rickshaw].

I felt like Tarzan, entering a city from the jungle. Suddenly, the streets were much bigger and there were cars and motorcycles everywhere. The buses were so big, and there was a TV inside the bus? It was unreal! I was also very frightened because I had not been in Malang for years. Would I still remember my way home? But I did. My sister was there. The same home. She accompanied me to the police office to report. My sister also had to become the guarantor that I would not be involved in any organisation or political activity. When we came back home, I asked my sister where mama was. My sister told me: 'Mama died 50 days ago'. I felt the world had come to an end then. Even when I was imprisoned, I had never felt that sad. I was 50 days late.

After that, the heads of the district (RT and RW[47]), kept an eye on me. When they walked past my house, they would often stop for a while and stick in their heads as if there was something suspicious happening inside. My friends did not dare to come and see me. A friend who heard that I had just been released came over with a can of biscuits but did not dare enter my house. He left the biscuits by the front door, and then quickly slipped away.

I had to report three times a week for about a month, then they changed it to twice a week, and later once a week. If I wanted to go out of town, I had to get a travel permit. I didn't have to pay for this permit, but they asked me all sorts of questions: Where are you going? What is the purpose of your trip? How long will you be away? How will you get there? Where will you stay? Who are you going with? And so on.

I looked for a job for a long time and could not find any, because of the ET stamp on my ID card. Out of the blue, I was approached by a man – he was one of the staff members of Hajj Masagung,[48] and he asked me to come to Surabaya. Haji Masagung asked me to work with him in Jakarta. From then on, I worked for him. Because Haji Masagung was quite well known, I got any permit straight away without any trouble.

---

47  The branches of government hierarchy in Indonesia reach down to the smallest level of social group, to make it easier to control and keep an eye on the citizens. RT stands for *rukun tetangga* (neighbourhood association) and RW for *rukun warga* (citizens' association). An RT usually consists of around 40 to 50 households. An RW is a step higher than RT, a sub-district consisting of 5 to 15 RTs.

48  A Chinese Indonesian Muslim who was the owner of a huge bookstore company.

## Something Weird

Something weird happened when I just got out of prison. Pram's work *Anak Semua Bangsa* [*Child of All Nations*] was suddenly circulated when Pram was still imprisoned. Pram was released in 1979, but his book appeared in 1978! I didn't publish it, although I had his manuscript. Indeed, I printed it using a stencil machine, but only 10 copies were printed and I gave them to the people I really trusted and asked them to keep this book a secret. So who did this?

Later, I found out that a priest had sneaked a copy of Pram's manuscript out from Buru. Religious leaders on Buru didn't get checked when they went in and out. It was also this priest who gave the work to a publisher, and finally Pram's novels were published by Hasta Mitra: *Bumi Manusia* [*This Earth of Mankind*] in 1980 and then *Anak Semua Bangsa* [*Child of All Nations*] in 1981. Unfortunately, the novels were banned soon afterwards. But in their very short lives, these books were a huge success. They were reprinted several times and translated into many languages as well.

After Pram was released, I intended to return the original manuscript to him; but he said: 'No, just give a copy to me.' Apparently, he was afraid that the manuscript would be confiscated by the authorities. So I have kept Pram's original manuscript and will never sell it to anyone.

**Photo B    Oei Hiem Hwie in his library**

## The Birth of the Library

In 1999, I stopped working for Haji Masagung and moved to Surabaya. I bought a house in this city, then I transferred all of my books from Malang to my new house. But my home was too small. With my books, there was hardly any room for humans. The books became a real burden for us, but I loved them. Fortunately, my wife was very patient.

That year, two Australians came to see me. One of them was Associate Professor Charles Coppel from Melbourne University. They wanted to buy my books, journals, newspapers and magazines; and offered me one billion Rupiah. That amount of money was really huge at that time. I could buy a luxury house with that. But I refused, because these books were all I had and they were priceless; and I really wanted the young Indonesian generations to learn from them; although I actually didn't really know what to do with all of them as well.

A friend of mine, the son of an ex-Baperki committee member, suggested that I establish a public library. Well, I had thought about this, but how about the money? How could I fund this project? Luckily, two big businessmen in Surabaya, Sindhunata Sambudi and Ongko Tikdoyo, heard about me. They bought me a house to be used as a library. And here we are at Medayu Selatan IV/42-44, Surabaya.

This library was finally established in 2001. Anyone can use the books for free, I just want my books to be useful for as many people as possible. I never regret what happened to me. I told my children about my past when they were at elementary school. I did it gradually, and my children are now really proud of me. I just consider my imprisonment as having been a time to contemplate and learn. I have been educated by Soeharto to be tougher!

*Every time I come home to Surabaya, I always pop by at Oei Hiem Hwie's library. When I come with friends, Oei will never get tired of telling his story. He repeats the same story to many people, still with the same passion as I heard it for the first time years ago. The last time I saw him was in June 2015. Although his health had deteriorated then, his spirit had not faded.*

# Antonius Pudji Rahardjo

The Commander and His Mistress

*In September 2013, I visited the house of Antonius Pudji Rahardjo in Surabaya with a friend, Djuir, who had known Pudji for several years. He took me on his motorbike there, because he said even if he gave me his address, it would be hard to find his house. He was right. We had to go via countless alleys before we arrived at a house with many plants outside. We had not told Antonius Pudji Rahardjo that we were coming. We just knocked on his door.*

*Pudji emerged from the house in his sarong and greeted us very warmly. I introduced myself, told him about my father, and my intention of writing his memoir. During our third meeting, he showed me his small library behind his house. The library was full of rare books, as well as his writings and newspaper clippings. A small yet very impressive library.*

I was actually born on 7 September 1929 but on my documents, the date is 7 September 1932. Before Gestok, I used to be a teacher at Pondok Takeran in Madiun [East Java]. The school belonged to Sarekat Islam.[49] Later, I found a job at BAT [British American Tobacco] in Surabaya. BAT was a huge corporation, which ran several cigarette and insurance companies and had plantations everywhere. First, I became an assistant accountant and, subsequently, I was appointed as head of accounting. After getting this post, I also became a trade union activist and, soon after, the nationalisation of foreign companies in Indonesia began. In 1964, I was given a mandate by Oei Tjoe Tat [a state minister under Sukarno] to nationalise BAT with the help of the military and labour representatives.

## Moments before Gestok 1965

On 27 September 1965, I left for Jakarta to attend a national meeting of union leaders, to discuss the problem of workers' social security. The meeting started on 28 September. On 30 September, I was still in Jakarta and at approximately 11:30 pm that day, I walked passed Menteng and saw many

---

49  Sarekat Islam (formerly Sarekat Dagang Islam, or the Union of Islamic Traders) was established in 1911, and its mission was to empower indigenous entrepreneurs and merchants.

armoured vehicles. At that time, I thought they were preparing for the celebration of the Armed Forces Day on 5 October.

Around midnight, a few friends and I arrived at our hotel and there was nothing unusual. But in the morning, at about 7 am, suddenly there was an announcement about the Revolutionary Council. This was what the radio said: the Revolutionary Council had saved Indonesia from an attempted coup by the Council of Generals. Sukarno's cabinet was declared dysfunctional, and governmental affairs were now to be administered by Lt. Col. Untung. All personnel of the armed forces above the rank of colonel would be lowered by two ranks; but all soldiers who had participated in thwarting the coup attempt by the Council of Generals would be promoted by two ranks. The radio emphasised that this was an internal army affair.

The next morning, we went around the town and walked past the office of the RRI [Radio Republik Indonesia]. It was surrounded by army personnel in green berets. Then at 3 pm, we walked past the RRI office again, and there were no green berets, but there were many army personnel in red berets [these were members of RPKAD (Resimen Pasukan Komando Angkatan Darat), or the Indonesian Special Forces].

The next day, on 2 October 1965, behind the Hotel Indonesia, we saw boys dressed in white with their thumbs tied together. They were all dragged into a truck, and according to those around, they were members of Pemuda Rakyat, the leftist youth club.[50] I headed straight away for the BAT office. There, I found Colonel Suwondo, who wore his camouflage uniform and a cowboy hat, and had guns hanging on his left and right. He looked so fierce that I did not dare ask any questions. But I knew that I had to leave Jakarta as soon as possible.

On 3 October 1965, my friend Kardono and I contacted another officer, Lt. Col. Mamesa, who was fortunately willing to meet us. I begged him to give us a consent letter to travel from Jakarta to our hometown [Surabaya], to guarantee our safety. After obtaining these letters, we immediately bought train tickets. Two days later, early in the morning, Kardono and I arrived at the train station. Throughout the trip, we saw the army with guns, as well as paramilitary personnel on the roadsides and in the rice fields, especially on the borders of every city. There was a rigorous examination of the vehicles. At Cirebon station, the train stopped a little longer, because there was a military operation in the carriage. Some people were ordered to get off the train by the army, including a woman who was sitting not far from me.

---

50   Pemuda Rakyat (People's Youth) was an organisation linked to the Indonesian Communist Party.

We were also being examined, but after showing the letters from Lt. Col. Mamesa, they immediately left us alone.

## Back to Surabaya

At 10 pm, we arrived at Pasar Turi station in Surabaya. When I got to my house, my wife and my four children had gone to bed. But my wife woke up and greeted me. I was happy that everything was fine.

In the morning, I went to work as usual. In the office, there had been a lot of changes. I was questioned and from then on, my activities were always monitored very closely by the corporate leaders. I had to report to them what I did, where I went, and when.

On 9 October in the evening, a friend told me that a journalist of the newspaper *Terompet Masyarakat*, Nyoo Ham Joe, had been imprisoned. After that, the activities of SOBSI,[51] the trade union federation, were halted. Two days later, when I was going to my office, a soldier stopped me on the way. He said: 'The army has surrounded your company. So it is better if you give in and follow me. Otherwise, you will be detained there.' So I followed him. I thought he just wanted to interrogate me.

I was taken to the local police station, and then to the military corps at Jalan Ngemplak in Surabaya. Four days later, I was sent to Koblen [a military prison] in Surabaya. At Koblen, our possessions were confiscated. I had just received my salary then, and they confiscated it as well together with my pens and papers. At that time, the total number of prisoners at Koblen was 76. On the first day, our food was OK. Sometimes, we got sweet food, like *kolak pisang*.[52] But every day, there were more people and we got fed less. We also could not sleep properly, because the room was getting crowded. We had to lie down like sardines, on the floor. The room that was supposed to be for 15 to 20 people was filled in with more than 60 people, so we could hardly breathe. Our rice was later mixed with sand, and the only vegetables we got were boiled *kangkong*[53] with the roots attached (which were really hard). Every time a new person arrived, there was new information about

---

51  SOBSI (Sentral Organisasi Buruh Seluruh Indonesia, or Central All-Indonesian Workers Organisation) was the largest trade union federation in Indonesia and was closely linked to the PKI.
52  *Kolak pisang* is a dessert made from banana, sweet potato, and cassava, boiled in water, sugar and coconut milk.
53  A type of spinach.

the sadistic torture and murder that the army was inflicting on people. This made us more aware of what happened and why we were here.

## 21 Musi Street – Surabaya

I was later sent to 21 Musi Street, which used to be the office of the labour union of the sugar factory in Surabaya. It had been transformed into a prison. At the top was the interrogation room. They asked me many things about the labour and trade unions and also about the nationalisation of BAT. Everything was just like a theatre. I am sure everything had been scripted. Before the interrogation, I had to sign a statement without being allowed to read the contents. The actual text was covered by a piece of paper.

Here, after we had been beaten up, we had to hear the screaming of others who were tortured, or the sound of heavy blunt objects hitting human bodies, at times accompanied by the sound of the radio. Then, the officers would call other prisoners who gathered at the back to carry their friends who had just been beaten up and could no longer stand up.

One day, in the morning, a guard summoned me. I was very nervous, but then I saw my wife there. She looked very pale, carrying our youngest child. When I was sent to jail, my wife was three months' pregnant. Now we could only talk for five minutes before I had to go back to my cell. Later, I was transferred to Kalisosok prison, then to another prison. I cannot remember which prison I was moved to then. Later, I was back in Kalisosok.

## Kalisosok

To reduce the number of prisoners at Koblen, some were sent to Kalisosok. Here we had to wash ourselves and get drinking water at 9 am. The bath was less than five minutes so if you were also washing underwear and clothes, there was no time to shower. If the whistle sounded, we had to finish. If not, you'd be punched. The ones who guarded us in the showers were criminal prisoners. Some of these criminal prisoners were really mean and loved hearing us scream. One of them used to count us by hitting us with a bat.

Eventually, my family could contact me through letters left with the prison guards, but we could not yet meet. The delivery of food from the family was only allowed once a week. But most of the deliveries were not passed on to us. Mainly those with money could get their deliveries in because they bribed the guards.

At some point, deliveries from families were no longer allowed, although prison food was very minimal and many people suffered from starvation. Many of them could hardly stand up, sit or even move. Eventually, they could hardly breathe. But as long as they could swallow water mixed with sugar, they were still OK. When they were no longer able to swallow anything, then we knew that death was waiting for them.

When families' deliveries were allowed again, sugar usually became the most wanted. We kept the sugar and would only consume it if really necessary. Only when we felt that our bodies had become very weak, then we would mix the sugar with water. Any unnecessary movements that took energy had to be eliminated. So we often tried to stay as still as possible, keep quiet and close our eyes, to save energy.

People who came from Koblen would sometimes only last for about a month before they died. We were required to report to the guard when anyone died. But often, we did not say anything, because we wanted to eat their food rations. Only if a corpse started smelling badly, then we reported it. Meanwhile, I kept a list, where I wrote down the names of the dead.

After being at Kalisosok for three months, I was moved back to Koblen. Before the move, we were searched. Knowing that, I put my list of the dead in my mouth and swallowed it, while pretending to cough. With that, the list of all the people who had died at Kalisosok disappeared.

At Koblen, I knew a painter named Masri. His wife was very beautiful. When she brought him some food, she was often invited into the office by the guards. After a while, one of them asked her to 'serve' him. However, she fought fiercely against him. But what was the officer's revenge? They tortured Masri severely, until he was mentally ill. Then he was taken away. No one knew or heard about him ever again.

When I returned to Kalisosok, a new man had arrived. I have forgotten his name now, but he was a former village head at Wringinanom in Gresik. I knew he had been imprisoned before and had been released. But why had he been jailed again now? He then told me that when he got out of prison, he found that the soldier who had arrested and beaten him up had married his wife. Obviously, he was upset and furious. So he decided to kill that man, and because of this, he was sent back to prison. But he said he did not regret it, he even felt relieved. 'At the very least, I have got rid of that bastard now', he said.

August 1969 saw the first stage of the prisoners' departure to Buru Island. We were told that the prisoners would have the freedom to manage the land and harvest the crops on the island. I was going to be sent on the second transport. One month prior to our departure to Buru, the prisoners were first sent to Nusakambangan Island. Our departure to Buru was scheduled for late June 1970. Two days before I was sent, I was allowed to meet my wife and five children. But they could not all meet me at the same time because of the limited space. During this meeting, my first child was crying incessantly, while the other kids just went quiet.

## Nusakambangan

Here, we heard that the students, scholars and intellectuals would be the last to be despatched to Buru. As we were categorised in this group, we had to wait. Every morning we had to exercise, then we were herded into the river to bathe. While bathing, we usually had an opportunity to find more food. When the officer who escorted us was a bit slack, we might take some cassava and eat it. One day, I managed to take quite a lot of cassava after having had a bath.

I hid the cassava in my underwear and also tucked some under the fold of my hat. When I entered the front of the prison and had to report to the guards, I forgot to take off my hat. The officer quickly snatched my hat off and threw it against my face. Because the hat was much heavier than normal, of course he was suspicious, and after he found the cassava in it, he beat and kicked me like crazy.

Even after this, he was still not satisfied. I was taken to a special cell. It was so narrow that I could hardly move and I was not fed. At night, it was pitch dark and the guard was at the checkpoint. I took that opportunity to take out the cassava from my underwear. I ate all of it quickly, so the guard would not find any!

Almost every day, we had to take turns working outside the prison, to clean the road. That was a good opportunity for us to get additional food. If we found lizards, mice or grasshoppers, we just swallowed them whole.

## Buru

After three and a half months on Nusakambangan Island, we were sent to Buru. Lots of friends got seasick, so the healthy ones had to clean up their vomit. As a 'reward', the healthy people could eat the food rations of the sick. So the healthy ones got healthier and the sick got sicker. On the seventh day, we arrived at the dock in Namlea, which is located at the tip of Buru Island.

When we got off the ship, we had to gather in a barracks, and the guards immediately searched us. If they liked any of our belongings, they would just snatch them. If we did not give them, they would punch us. Everything my wife gave me was taken away. From the barracks, we walked to unit 4 of Sanleko (later, we called this place Savanajaya). There had been four prisoner shipments to this island. The first had experienced the most hardship, because they had to open up the forest and make rice fields, roads, houses, and build many other things. I was in the second shipment. The last, which arrived around 1971, had it best, since by then there were roads and even shops.

Each unit was like a village. When I had just arrived, there were 29 units. The distance between unit 4 and unit 29 was approximately 44 km. We were prohibited from moving between units. Pramoedya Ananta Toer was tortured, just because he had wanted to meet his friend in another unit.

When we arrived in Sanleko, we were sorted into groups based on the division of work: agriculture, warehouse, marine, office and carpentry. We usually started working at 7 am, carrying our plates. They would give us bulgur rice with rotten salted fish. All work had to be done very quickly. If the work did not meet the target, we had to continue working into the evening, sometimes until midnight, using kerosene lamps.

One time, we had to work really hard to build a dam. The work was done by us with hardly any meals and barely any rest. If anyone was caught resting, the officers would punish him severely: often by making him do push-ups or similar exercises plus several punches as well. A friend of ours, Salim, suddenly fell over and vomited blood when he was carrying a heavy load of soil. His body was trembling and pale, and we decided to hide him in a safe and dark place to rest.

We also had to assemble boards to be sold by the unit commander. But some of us could smuggle and sell them directly to the purchasers. With that money, we could buy underwear. If the army needed women, we were told to make beds for them. The Japanese used to send some women to Buru during the Second World War, by telling these women that they would be educated, but then they were made sex slaves on the island. Well, some of those women were still there. Some of them had been awarded to the tribal chiefs.

## The Giant Galiuk in Savanajaya

The commander of Savanajaya was a lieutenant we called Galiuk, because he looked like the giant in puppet stories or comic books. Galiuk is short, has a large belly, and is a womaniser. I have forgotten this lieutenant's real name, so I will call him Galiuk.

First Lieutenant Galiuk had a 'courtier' called Willy S. He was one of our inmates, too, and his special duty was following Galiuk everywhere, finding and bringing him anything he wanted, including women. One time, Willy found a woman who was originally from Central Java. She was about 35 years old and lived with her husband, named Gondo, a retired armed forces officer with the rank of corporal. This couple had two children. The health of Gondo was very desperate because he suffered from chronic tuberculosis, while their financial situation was poor because of the low rank he had before he retired. He had to go for routine check-ups in Namlea, and, of course, this cost a fortune. Mrs. Gondo was quite beautiful; she had long hair, tanned skin and was curvy and sexy.

After Galiuk and Mrs. Gondo were introduced to each other, they made a deal. The requirements from Mrs. Gondo were: looking after the Gondo's family needs (including food, clothing and housing), as well as paying for the treatment of her husband. Galiuk agreed, and of course that meant extra work for us prisoners. First we had to renovate Mrs. Gondo's house. Then, we had to make furniture for her family, such as tables, chairs and beds. Almost every day (at least three or four times a week), Willy was summoned to Galiuk's office and we heard some dialogue like this:

Galiuk: Willy, come here quickly!
Willy: Yes, sir. Do you need anything?
Galiuk: You have to go to the queen consort's house, see whether she is home or not, and if she is, tell her that the commander will come.
Willy: Yes, Commander!

Willy had to report to the commander as soon as possible after performing this duty. If he returned a bit later than the time Galiuk had set, Galiuk would hit him. If Mrs. Gondo was home, Galiuk would depart from his office to Mrs. Gondo's with Willy following behind while carrying the commander's bag. On the way from our unit to Mrs. Gondo's was the Waibuni River. When there was no flood, the river reached above the knee. During dry season, the river was usually under the knee. But Galiuk did not want his pants or feet to get wet at all. So immediately he would order:

Galiuk: Come on, Semarang horse. Are you ready? [Willy originally came from Semarang.]
Willy: I'm ready, Commander, please get on.

Then Galiuk got on Willy's back to cross the river. When they arrived at Mrs. Gondo's, the commander would say:

> Galiuk: Willy, wait outside. Do not let any human get in here.
> Willy: Ready, Commander!

According to Willy, when the commander arrived, Mr. Gondo would go away with their two children. He would grab his stick, and lead out the children, ten and six years old, for a walk around the cassava farm. There, Mr. Gondo and his kids would sit and chat for a long time until Galiuk was finished with his wife.

## 13 March 1972

One day, I was cutting wood to make a dam. Not long after came Surento, a sergeant in unit 4.

> Surento: Make a double bed for me, please.
> Me: I am very sorry sir, I am really busy at the moment, because I have to finish this wood as soon as possible for the flood gate, which must be installed in that channel.
> Surento: I don't care [he hit me so hard that I fell off my stool].
> Me: OK, sir. I'll make one for you. But please give me a month.
> Surento: All right, but be careful if it is late. I'll give you clothes after you finish it.
> Me: Sorry sir, I have four friends here. So I'd rather have something else that can be used for four people.
> Surento: Well, then I'll give you sugar.

I finished Surento's bed in about three weeks. I hid it in a cassava plantation. Two days later, Surento asked about his order and I took him to the plantation and showed him the bed. He gave us a packet of sugar [approximately 5 kg]. Then, he ordered me to deliver the bed to the home of a tribal Butonese woman named Waambe.

I carried the bed with a friend, during our lunch break. On the way back, we passed Waibini River, not far from the home of Mrs. Gondo. I walked in front and my friend followed behind me. Unfortunately, when we were about to cross the river, Commander Galiuk appeared from the opposite direction. My friend had disappeared. Apparently he saw Galiuk first and had a chance to hide. I was beaten up and he ordered me to see him at his office.

At approximately 5.30 pm, I stood in front of his office. Immediately, punches started landing on my body as he fired questions:

Galiuk: Where were you this afternoon?
Me: I was fixing the bridge, because a board there was broken, sir.
Galiuk: Why did you have to go through the village?
Me: I did not go through the village, sir; I just had to cross over the edge of the river.

He asked me to go back to the hut and made me stand still, naked, for two hours, while mosquitoes feasted on my body. Of course, he would come and see me every now and then, to 'reward' me with hard punches. After he was satisfied with my punishment, he asked me to go to his office and thank him. As usual, while hitting prisoners, he asked another prisoner to watch and asked how his punches were. The prisoner had to give the desired answer: assuring him how badly he had hurt his victim.

In general, every inmate had to say 'thank you' after being beaten up. We sometimes laughed and called ourselves insane. Then one said, we said thank you because we felt fortunate that we were only beaten up, not trampled or strangled. Even if we were strangled but we did not die, we were still lucky in a way. So we said thank you because we could still speak, and dead people could no longer speak.

## People from Overseas

At the beginning of 1970s, visitors from abroad wanted to visit us, some of whom were from the Red Cross. Immediately, the government set up a clinic, but it was just cosmetic. There was no one even working there. Just before the visitors arrived, the government sent some people from Jakarta to the island. They filled up the library with books, the shops offered many things, and the clinic also had some nurses. They totally revamped our prison. But this was just a trick to make the visitors think that our conditions were good. When the visitors left, all of the stuff was transferred to the next place where the visitors were about to arrive.

We tried to outsmart them by speaking English with the guests. The military did not understand English. We did this when we were not being watched so carefully. But when these international delegates were around, the guards did not keep a very strict watch on us anyway. We asked these foreign guests not to go to the prison offices first, but directly visit other places, and we asked them to arrive there ahead of their scheduled visits, so they could see what it was really like here. Thus, a few of them indeed saw empty hospitals, empty health care centres and empty shops.

### General Soemitro's Visit

Before a certain General Soemitro[54] and his entourage came to visit Savanajaya, they called Prof. Dr. Suprapto SH, Pramoedya Ananta Toer and several other intellectuals to the office. I believe that the Buru Island officials just wanted to take advantage of the thoughts and ideas of our friends, in order to find out what they had to do next. Because despite their long and severe imprisonment, these intellectuals were still sharp and their minds were able to sail much further than this island.

The general gave a long speech concerning our imprisonment on Buru Island. He said that it was to direct and salvage us from the abyss of our previously misguided lives. He asked us to recognise our sins and repent. Only by doing this could we forget the past and obey the law and be good citizens. But how did he know our mistakes, if none of us had had any due process or trial in a court of law?

One of our friends, Edy Suparno SH, was questioned by General Sumitro.

> Sumitro: Do you know why all of you were brought here?
> Edy: I know, sir. I think we were just the victims of power struggles.
> Sumitro: What? Struggle for power? You are being really ridiculous. Come on, who had struggled for power?

Edy was speechless after that. He knew it was useless to express his opinion at all.

Some friends who happened to sit close to Edy urged him to remain silent. No matter what they said, we were only political prisoners, we no longer had any right to express our opinions, let alone to argue and disagree. In order to keep safe, the only way was to remain silent, especially after Sumitro had emphasised that our freedom depended on our attitude and behaviour, and asked us to obey the law.

---

54  Commander of the Indonesian secret police Kopkamtib (Komando Operasi Pemulihan Keamanan dan Ketertiban or Operational Command for the Restoration of Security and Order).

## The Arrival of Families

At the end of 1970s, the guards told us that some of our families would be summoned to the island. They asked us to build a small dock for their arrival. The prisoners whose wives were coming were gathered in unit 4 [Savanajaya], while many unit 4 inhabitants were transferred to other units. According to the information from the authorities, they were transferred to other units that still required the expansion of paddy fields. I was transferred to unit 13 [Giripura], the most distant and elevated unit, approximately 33 km from Savanajaya.

Not long before we were due to be released, two of our friends committed suicide. One of them was a vet. He was really sick and tired, but the guards accused him of being lazy and not wanting to work. He was taken to a special cell to be tortured, but he hung himself there. The other was a writer. The officers asked his wife to come to the island, but he was so ashamed of his life that he did not want to see her.

When the wives and children of the political prisoners arrived at Salenko, the men picked them up by carrying transport equipment such as carts or baskets on a yoke. Journalists also arrived to record that moment. But the foreign press were kept out, and local journalists had very limited access.

We helped the newcomers by making kitchen appliances and household items such as tables, chairs and beds. There was a building for a primary school, but there were no teachers yet. Fortunately, some of the wives were former teachers, so they took on those jobs. The junior or senior high school students had to go to Namlea. When the parents had no money to pay for their board, the kids had to go to Namlea and come home on a boat every day. When they were a bit established, the children could often rent a room in Namlea.

The wives and children of the political prisoners on Buru were considered political prisoners as well by the locals: they were not free, and the guards ordered them around and treated them badly. Often they became an entertaining spectacle for the officers and the indigenous people of Namlea. On holidays, the guards and Namlea people often gathered around to watch them, just like visiting a zoo. The guards would tease and jeer at these women, so the others could laugh at them. At times, they even touched or pinched the women, especially the young ones. Eventually, they sexually harassed them in front of the public. They treated the women as their possessions, and beat up the husbands in front of the public as well. Several of the women were raped.

## Freedom

On 30 August 1979, I was freed. After arriving in Java we were sent to the Gelora Pancasila building in Surabaya. The families who picked up the political prisoners had to wait outside. I looked for familiar faces from the window. There were so many people, that it was difficult to see. I had to search for a long time, and I heard a voice: '*Bapak* [father] ... *bapak* ...' The girl was crying hard: '*Bapak* ...' Then, I realised that she must have been my daughter, who had been separated from me for fourteen years. I didn't recognise her. I thought she was my fourth child. I called her name, but she corrected me. She was actually my eldest. She told me that her mother and sister were waiting outside.

The next day, accompanied by my brother, I went to the Secretary of the RT[55] to get my papers. The Secretary said that my name could not be found, so he could only record my name as a visitor. But, after my brother paid him Rp 500, everything was settled. Of course, I had the stamp 'ET' [ex-political prisoner]. I did make myself three years younger on paper. I had wasted my life in prison, so I did not want to retire early.

## My Wife

When I was arrested, my wife was also put under house arrest. Most of our possessions were seized by the army. Fortunately, we had hidden the title documents of our house at a friend's, so they could not confiscate my house. Later, my wife had to quit her job as a high school teacher. To find work again, my wife decided to get rid of all her certificates and start all over again. She went back to school and after she graduated, she became an elementary school teacher. She also replaced all of her papers, so she could claim her pension.

Several members of my wife's extended family had murdered members of the PKI. So when they heard that I was imprisoned, they tried to force my wife to divorce me and marry a more 'honourable' man. When she refused, her elder brothers started harassing her: they scolded her and even one of them beat her up to make her divorce me.

But my wife always stayed faithful to me, even though many soldiers courted her. One of them almost raped her. After my release, my wife and

---

55  The head of the RT usually knows everyone, and this was used as a means of keeping an eye on the citizens by the Dutch, which was continued by the New Order government. This system persists even now.

I decided to convert from Islam to Catholicism, because it was the only religion that welcomed us.

## After Buru

In 1999, some friends and I founded an organisation for the victims of 1965 called YPKP [Yayasan Penelitian Korban Peristiwa '65, or the Institute for Research on the Victims of 1965]. With the other ex-political prisoners, we demanded that the parliament rehabilitate our names. We demonstrated in front of the parliament building once a month, but we were always ignored. Therefore, I am very supportive of your project, so that our history is not forgotten. I still love to read, to do research, but my memory is really weak now. But I will never let go of our cause.

A final story for you. One of my son's brothers-in-law was a sea captain during the 1965 massacre. He said many were killed at sea, and the bodies were thrown overboard. On paper, they wrote that the prisoners 'ran into the forest'. The training for this mass murder, he claims, was done in Australia. Many of those deaths were never recorded or reported. They were forgotten just like that.

**Photo C    Pudji Rahardjo in his private library holding a book he wrote about Buru Island**

*Before I went home, Pudji showed me his small library, and said to me to tell anyone who wants to know about the history of 1965-1966 to come and read his collections any time.*

*At the beginning of June 2015, I visited Pudji again with my husband but he could no longer remember me this time. He had gone senile and had cut up his books and his own writings in his small library. According to his son, he sometimes did not even recognise his own children. However, he still remembered that he had been a prisoner on Buru Island. Though he had forgotten many things, the pain of having been a political prisoner had not been erased from his mind.*

# Part 2

## The Steel Women

# Sri Muhayati

Being Educated in Prison

*That afternoon on 4 July 2015, I was at Leo Mulyono's home. Pipiet (Leo's daughter) talked to me, while holding her mobile phone: 'There is a female ex-prisoner who would like to meet you. Her name is Muhayati.'*

*She then gave her phone to me, so that I could speak directly with Muhayati. 'Mbak, I was accused of being Gerwani and arrested, but was not tortured. Are you willing to interview me?'*

*We met at the home of another ex-political prisoner, Christina Sumarmiyati (Bu Mamiek), the next day.*

I was born on 6 December 1941, two days before the Japanese bombed Pearl Harbor. People said, perhaps because of that, I was so dark, unlike my fair mother and sisters. I am the first child and have six younger siblings: three boys and three girls.

After graduating from high school, I entered medical school at Universitas Gadjah Mada and joined the CGMI [Consentrasi Gerakan Mahasiswa Indonesia, or the Unified Movement of Indonesian Students], an organisation linked to the PKI. I loved this organisation because they were against cheating in examinations and rejected the practice of bullying in orientation programs. At that time, many senior students bullied new students during orientation programs. The bullying was so bad that it sometimes involved serious physical and psychological abuse.

Suddenly, at the end of October 1965, I was dismissed from the university for no reason. An announcement was posted on the bulletin board at my campus, stating that I was no longer a student there. My student number was 3616K. I still remember it, even now.

My father was a member of parliament for the PKI in Yogya at that time. On 17 November 1965, a bunch of soldiers came to our house and searched for weapons. After ransacking our house they did not find anything, but they took *bapak* [father], and told me that he would only be interviewed. But why did he not come home? Then, on 18 November, I went to the office of the local military, but they said that *bapak* had been taken to the Wirogunan prison. I immediately went to Wirogunan, but the clerk told me that I could not visit my father. So I just left underwear and toiletries for him with the clerk.

On my return home, there were already policemen waiting for me. They were looking for my father. I told them that he had been taken away. But the police still searched the house and ransacked everything. They also took our piggy bank, which was full of coins. Before leaving for the market every morning, my grandmother always put six Rp 50 coins into the piggy bank. The next day, the news came out in the Yogya local newspaper *Kedaulatan Rakyat:* 'A case of bullets has been found in the home of Muhadi, the PKI leader.' Apparently such slander was deliberately disseminated. They took a container of coins and told the public that they were bullets!

My lecture notes were also searched and seized. At that time, I was in the third semester. Incidentally, I wrote about PRPP (Punctum Prometrium Punctum Proximum) – this is a term in physics. However, they claimed that PR was the abbreviation for Pemuda Rakyat [the youth wing of the PKI], and that PP was the same as the PKI. They ordered me to get into their car. My mother was taken as well, but the car did not fit us all. So they returned me to our home, and asked: 'Can we trust you or not?' I replied: 'Well, it is up to you.'

I was summoned to the police station at Ngupasan in Yogya at 8 am the next day. I tidied up the house before I left, then I went to the police station, not carrying anything, because I did not know whether I would be arrested or not. I just brought my mother's medications, because, since 1959, my mother had been having kidney problems and hypertension.

I was accompanied by a friend, but I asked her to wait rather far away from the police station. I said to her: 'If in ten hours, I don't come back, could you please go home to pick up a pack of clothes that I have prepared this morning, just in case I am arrested.' At the police station, I met with my mother, who then in my presence was bombarded with millions of questions. She seemed really confused because she was never involved in my father's political activity: *ibu* was just a housewife.

Then it was my turn to be interrogated. They presented passport photos before me. The photographs were taken from the drawer of my father. Many of them were photos of high officials, such as mayor or the police chief. They asked: 'Were these people about to be murdered by your father?' The interrogator was the father of my good friend. I often came to their home. But now he seemed not to know me at all, and was really aggressive. I answered: 'This is nonsense. These photographs were for making the membership cards for the veterans. My father was the secretary of the organisation, so he was storing their photos. Could you please ask your commander to come here? His name is Darto. He was often present when there were veteran meetings at my house.' Indeed, my father used to be a freedom fighter but resigned in 1950.

When he asked me if I often attended underground meetings, I immediately flipped the question: 'Didn't you also attend meetings at the house of my father?' It made him rather nervous and he went silent immediately, because I knew so much information about him.

He did not question me again and asked me to leave instead. I was imprisoned immediately. *Ibu* was accused of being a member of Gerwani [Gerakan Wanita Indonesia, or the Indonesian Women's Movement] and was also detained with me. We were put in a dirty cell with a filthy floor, along with five other people. The size was about 2 x 3 metres. So seven of us slept in the narrow space, without any mat.

There, I had to cover my ears tightly, because the officers often harassed us about being 'Gerwani bitches' who had 'gouged out the eyes of the generals'. When night fell, we could not lie too close to the bars, because the officers would try to grab any parts of our bodies.

I often sang out the song 'Darah Rakyat' [Blood of the People] so that I did not hear the officers' abuse. I have forgotten the lyrics, but the song tells about the struggles and sacrifices of the poor. I sang it so loudly, that some male prisoners heard it and sang along as well. So we often sang that song together. Of course the guards were really angry, but I did not care. It was pitch dark, so they also had no idea that it was me who had started the singing.

After being imprisoned for one week, my mother and I were taken by a truck to the former American library named Jefferson, in Kranggan. Later, we were taken to the office of the military prison. The food was worse there.

Because I was the only one who knew about medicine, they asked me to work in the health department. I had to cure everyone who was ill: the prisoners, the guards and all the staff. Many of the guards and staff were nice to me, maybe because I insisted on being treated with respect. No one hit me. If any of the guards was about to hit me, other guards always stopped him.

Not long after, I was brought to Gondolayu prison, but my mother was left at Jefferson. There, I met many former Gerwani members and suddenly I realised that my mother was not present. I shouted hysterically: 'Where is my mother? Where is my mother?' They immediately picked up my mother, and I was united with *ibu* again.

Then I was moved to Fort Verdenburg, formerly used as a military barracks by the Dutch colonial government. The place was really dirty, fenced off and covered with barbed wire. People said that the back of this fort was haunted, because it had been used to massacre Japanese soldiers. Food rations came from the military prison and we only got about 20 ears of corn in the morning. Only at about noon would they give us rice with a small accompaniment. Here, a narrow space was filled with eight to ten people. I was imprisoned with my mother and met with the wife of Leo Mulyono.

On 27 April 1966 – I remember the date exactly, because it was also the National Prison Day or Correctional Day – my mother and I were brought by an open truck to Fort Pendem in Ambarawa. This fort was built during the civil war before the Giyanti Treaty, just before Yogyakarta and Surakarta split.[56]

When we arrived, I cringed because I felt that the fort was about to swallow us: the walls were at least 1.5 m thick. When I sat on the windowsill, I could lie my body down easily across it. The barbed wire fence was so high. In it, there were about 70 people from Central Java.

There we were given hard bulgur that was also used to feed horses. Some people were unable to swallow it. Many also had abdominal pains because they could not digest it properly. My tongue, throat and digestive system could barely stand this hard stuff: it went in OK, but the release was hard. The bulgur was so difficult to digest that I got haemorrhoids. Sometimes it came out of my anus like a green bean. I tried to treat this myself. Around the prison, there was a well made of hard concrete. When the sun was high, I sat on the well and pressed my bum against it. This slowly healed my haemorrhoids. The heat eventually restored the blood flow to my bottom.

The toilet in this prison was very long and disgusting. The compartments were only separated by low walls. No doors. We had to clean whatever we let out from above. The poo was often stuck and piled up at the bottom and stank so much, so that many prisoners did not want to use the toilet there if they did not really have to. Around the deposits of faeces, we planted *kangkung* [water spinach] and the plants became really fat.

That year, 1967, Eid fell on 13-14 January, a time that I can never forget. We got a ration of boiled cassava, but it turned out to be rotten: it smelled really bad. My mother and I did not eat it, but the hunger made others not care and eat the rotten food. Many suffered from food poisoning. Luckily, there were papaya trees nearby, and I told them to eat papaya leaves. Many survived, but some died. On 26 February, the guards said that they had to move some of us. We did not know who would be moved where or for what.

I asked one of the guards: 'Sir, could you please tell me who will be moved today?' He showed a list of 21 people: 20 men and a woman. I read the names of Pak De and *bapak*. Soon after a truck arrived. I saw my father and

---

56  The Giyanti Treaty was an agreement signed on 13 February 1755 between Prince Mangkubumi, the Dutch East India Company and Sunan Pakubuwono III. The treaty separates Mataram into two sultanates: Yogyakarta and Surakarta.

immediately I stretched open the barbed wire so that I could be seen by him. Surprisingly, the guards just let me do it. The other female prisoners stood behind me and watched from over my back. Once he saw me, *bapak* shouted: 'Are you OK?' I screamed back: 'YESSS!' He replied: 'Take care of your mother. I want your siblings to be successful.' That was the last time I saw him. Later I found out that these 21 people were executed in Wonosobo on 3 March in the Kaliwiro region.

In prison, we were required to participate in religious ceremonies. I did not mind it at all, because I did believe in God. My mother joined the Islamic group, but she was often harassed by the regular worshippers and called a whore. Many of my friends joined the Catholic group, so I decided to attend the Catholic mass as well. I was never cursed or harassed during the mass, and this caused me to keep participating in the Catholic mass even though I was Muslim.

In 1968, I was transported to the Bulu jail in Semarang, and was separated from my mother. My mother's health was getting worse, because the drugs that she had to take were not always available. She also developed cardiomegaly [an enlarged heart] in the prison. Perhaps because of this my mother was released a few months later. I was very worried. My *ibu* was beautiful, so she would be in danger outside, especially as I had heard that my sisters had been harassed by people from the military. Even after my father was imprisoned, the military and the police still often came to our home, looking for my father.

### Educating Myself in Prison

In Ambarawa prison, I met with many doctors, including Dr. Abimanyu. We worked together, and I learnt a lot from them. So my time in jail was also the time to educate myself. In 1969, in the Bulu prison, there was an outbreak of Hong Kong flu. It was so contagious that everyone was infected by it. Our medical team had to work day and night to treat them all. After almost all of them were better, they sent nurses to the prison. One of the nurses said that my face was really red. She measured my temperature: 40 degrees. But I kept on working as I did not feel ill. Later, I developed a bad cough. The nurse asked me to lie down, but my cough got worse and I started vomiting. So I got up and started working again. Apparently resting and lying down just made me sicker.

The health team gave me medication, but I kept vomiting. Finally, I was taken to the Dr. Karnadi Hospital, because I was vomiting continuously.

The doctor there asked me: 'Ma'am, when was your last menstruation?' I was really annoyed with this question: Did they think I was pregnant just because I had been vomiting? I asked the officers to take me back to the prison again.

Back in prison, I asked for spinach with chilli, but they refused to give it to me. So I asked one of the guards to get me some limes instead. In the prison, there were guards who we could order around, as long as we gave them enough money. As I had suspected, I was infected with the Hong Kong flu. My body ached and I could not see the light. After everyone else recovered, I collapsed with the flu.

In this prison there were all kinds of illnesses. For example, suddenly many suffered from itching and sores in the groin. The cause was unknown, perhaps it was because of mental stress in the prison. Of course, the facilities were very limited. So I tried to cure this by using *jarak* leaves.[57] I rubbed their scars with this leaf. Then I tried to clean the scars with hot water mixed with salt, or betel leaf. I got it, too, and I recovered because I rubbed *kencur* [*Kaempferia galanga*] on my scars.

Later on, there was a tuberculosis outbreak. The infected patients were required to sleep together in one room. Of course, this could be dangerous. For the first time, I had a look at the Koch bacillus[58] through a microscope. I was really careless then, because I did not wear a mask as I was working. My supervisor was quite angry with me. So I had to be injected with various vitamins to stay fit and strong. Luckily, I did not get infected with tuberculosis as well.

From Semarang, I was moved to Yogya and back to Wirogunan. There, I met my cousin, who was also arrested. Then I was released in 1970.

After my mother was sent home, she could not work so she never had any money. We were also subjected to all kinds of ridicule from the surrounding community, as a PKI family. My father had been very generous to these people, but they seemed to have forgotten about it. When *bapak* had the land, he allowed the land to be used by the public. Only a very few people remembered this.

From my brothers and sisters, I found out that when my *ibu* was still imprisoned, someone said to them: 'Your mother will definitely not return. If she comes home I'll drink my own urine.' Later, when I met the person who said this, I said to him: 'So, have you drunk you own urine now?'

---

57  *Jarak* or jatropha usually grows wild in tropical regions.
58  The causative agent of tuberculosis is *Mycobacterium tuberculosis*, which was discovered in 1882 by Robert Koch.

To make a living, I helped my grandmother sell batik in Beringharjo market in Yogya. On Sundays, when I sat in front of my shop in the market, I often saw my former college friends. I was really embarrassed, especially if the friends used to have much poorer academic achievements than mine. They had become doctors, and I? I was not permitted to practice medicine. So if I saw them, I quickly looked away or bowed my head, so that they did not see me.

Actually, I often helped other doctors after my release. Finally, father De Blot [a Dutch missionary] asked me to work at his clinic, which accommodated 1965 victims and their children. He also paid for my training, so I could learn how to work in a medical laboratory. Shortly after, I was assigned to the Indonesian Red Cross.

I told father De Blot that I did not want to convert to Catholicism, and he did not mind at all. My mother had asked me not to, because she was worried if I was baptised as a Catholic, I would not want to get married and would become a nun instead. Although I am not a Catholic, I have never married because I do not want to. This is my own decision.

One day, when I stopped by my old campus, the parking attendants and cleaning staff recognised me. They asked: 'Where have you been all this time? Which cities have you been working in?' Apparently, they did not know that I had been in jail. I just said that I had been working in the regions in which I had been imprisoned. I did work in the health department there, right?

Soon after *ibu* was released, many men proposed to her, but she declined them all. Every evening, mother sat in front of the house, by the door, waiting for *bapak*. She said: 'I have to, so when he comes home, he can see me.' I told her that *bapak* was dead, and of course my mother had seen that he had been taken away by the truck at the prison. But she still did not want to accept reality. After several years of this, I tried to convince her again that my father had actually died. My mother answered: 'If your father has passed away, I would no longer menstruate.' Not long after that, *ibu* suddenly stopped menstruating. This made her very distressed and she became very ill. Around the months of June and July 1972, mother had to be hospitalised at Pugeran in Gadjah Mada. So in the mornings I used to visit her, then go to the market, and in the late afternoon I would start working at the clinic.

One Monday afternoon in December 1972 my mother had to have a check-up with the doctors at a time when I had medical training at Realino Dormitory and had to stay there. At 3 am, father De Blot woke me up. My sister had turned up to tell me that my mother had passed away. I was so hysterical that I hit father De Blot.

**Photo D** Sri Muhayati in front of the banner of Fopperham (Forum Pendidikan dan Perjuangan Hak Asasi Manusia, or the Human Rights Education and Advocacy Forum), a human rights organisation with which she has been involved

Now I often help the research on the 1965 genocide. Many people have been brainwashed by the New Order, for example, with religious conservatism. I do not care about religion. The important thing for me is that I believe in God. Many were wondering what my religion actually is. Protestant, Catholic or Islam? I told them my religion is PKI *Protestan Katolik Islam*. All of them. I can do the Muslim prayer, *sholat*, but I can also sing Christmas carols, because in Ambarawa prison I joined the church choir.

In 1999-2000, I took part in disinterring the mass grave in Boyolali. I said to the team of diggers and forensic workers that there was a great possibility that my father had been buried there. I remember what one of the cellmates of my father in Wonosobo prison told me: 'Several people heard loud bangs from Situkup forest in Dempes village in Wonosobo, but the people were prohibited from approaching that place. They were also told that that place was used to kill monkeys. It is under a coconut tree.' I was determined to find it.

Indeed, we finally found several bones under a coconut tree: the skeletons of 21 people, but only 8 of them were identified. With the help of forensic doctors, I found the bones of *bapak*. My father's remains indicated that he had broken bones in one of his hands and one of his feet, and from the height and age, they determined that it was indeed my father.

We only wanted to have a more proper burial for the deceased, but even this modest request met with tremendous challenges from the surrounding community. In Temanggung in Central Java, someone claiming to be a representative of the Muslim and youth organisations said that all the locals opposed PKI skeletons being buried in their village. The reason was that if there were political prisoners buried there, then there would be a pilgrimage to the cemetery and this would likely revive the communist ideology. Several people were very aggressive towards us, and threatened us by brandishing knives. One of the men even tried to grab my face, but I had no fear, because that is my sole weapon: courage. I am determined to continue my struggle, no matter what.

*After the interview, we ate a meal together at the home of Christina Sumarmiyati (Bu Mamiek). Bu Mamiek provided a large variety of food. Incidentally, that day, 5 July 2015, was Bu Mamiek's 69th birthday. She invited four other female ex-prisoners besides Muhayati. We celebrated the day together talking about various sorrows in prison. However, we never forgot the funny stories, and tried to laugh at the sorrows, if possible.*

*Shortly thereafter, I watched the recording of the mass grave excavation conducted by Muhayati on YouTube: https://www.youtube.com/watch?v=svYdHm5073E.*

# Christina Sumarmiyati

The Horrific Torture and Rape

*Christina Sumarmiyati (Bu Mamiek is how she is called by many people) was born in Sleman, Yogyakarta, on 5 July 1946. My acquaintance with Bu Mamiek began with a remark by her son, Benny Putranto, on my Facebook page. On 11 March 2015 (the anniversary of the date when Sukarno signed the letter transferring his power to Soeharto in 1966), I wrote about the 1965 genocide. Benny commented on my page that his mother was an ex-political prisoner as well. Through Benny, I got in touch with his mother via Facebook.*

**Photo E   Christina Sumarmiyati in her home**

I still remember the applause when I talked about women's emancipation while dancing as crazy Srikandi, the female warrior figure. I also played in *ketoprak*,[59] and I usually acted as an elderly woman who could say whatever I wanted – this was great for me because I could speak my mind and utter any social criticism. I was indeed really active in the IPPI [Ikatan Pemuda

---

59   The traditional Javanese theatre.

Pelajar Indonesia, or the Indonesian Students Association].[60] This organisation was affiliated with the PKI. I became the coordinator in my town and I recruited many new members. We held arts events and took part in eradicating illiteracy. My father was the leader of the BTI [Barisan Tani Indonesia, or the Indonesian Peasants Front][61] in our town, so our home was always busy with visitors from our organisations.

In November 1965 my father was arrested. I knew I would be too so I moved and never came home. They kept looking for me but could not find me and they started threatening my family. They worked together with the head of our village, who called me and said that if I did not see him immediately, the soldiers would take away my mother and younger siblings.

I decided to come to the office of the village head, who asked me to report twice a day at 8 am and at 4 pm. But this was impossible because I went to university in Yogya, which is about 25 km from my town. So they asked me to come early in the morning, at 6 am. After reporting to the village head, I went to my campus and then I had to report again at 7 pm. After doing this for a few weeks, I was still arrested after the celebration of mother's Day on 22 December 1965. With two of the members of the family imprisoned, my mother, brothers and sisters had to bear the consequences as well. They were jeered at and scolded and our house was pelted with rocks almost every night because the people alleged that our home was also used as the Communist Party headquarters. My mother boldly confronted them and refuted their accusations. Indeed, my family had been mentally prepared because father and his friends had often discussed people who had to be 'detained, destroyed and disposed of' because of their idealism.

So when I was imprisoned, I was not afraid. I even thought that I could use this opportunity to see my father. Therefore I went to jail carrying a few of his clothes: trousers, a sarong and shirts. I also brought with me my mother's dress, so if I missed her I could just wear her clothes. I put *bapak*'s clothes right at the bottom under my underwear, so if the guard checked my bag, hopefully he would be put off by my old undies. Everything went as I had expected. When the officer opened my bag, he mumbled: 'What the hell are these?' My heart rejoiced as I had succeeded in bringing my father's clothes into the prison.

But now another task: finding my father. After the truck carrying us as prisoners arrived at the prison, I started looking around. The officers

---

60   The IPPI was a left-wing organisation whose members were mainly high school or university students.
61   The BTI, the Indonesian farmers movement, was a mass organisation linked to the PKI.

interrogated us one by one. They asked our names, addresses, etc. From the truck I could see the surroundings better ... and there he was! I saw my father. From behind the bars, I recognised his face even though he had been gone for a long time.

Immediately, I thought of a strategy to reach him. This place was actually familiar to me because I had done voluntary work here as a kitchen attendant during a Pemuda Rakyat training, which had ended on 30 September 1965. I had knowledge of the ins and outs of this place and I even knew some of the guards here. When there was excess food in the kitchen I always shared it with the soldiers' families, so I was able to sneak in my father's clothes along with some money.

In that place, there were about 500 men and women. Several of the women brought their children and babies as well, usually because their fathers had been imprisoned as well, so there was no one at home to look after them. Some of the soldiers here were quite nice to me and returned my favours to them from when I had worked in the kitchen by now giving me their leftover food. Of course, if the other soldiers found out, we could be in trouble, so they only communicated with me using sign language to let me know where they left the food and that I could pick it up after they went home. I usually shared the food with other inmates, especially with the children.

However, there were nasty soldiers there as well. They looked for a mark on us. I did not understand at first, but later on I realised that they were looking for a Gerwani mark on my body. They ordered me to strip naked and to turn around and around, but they could not find any Gerwani mark. So, they bombarded me with questions: 'Did you mutilate the generals? Were you at Lubang Buaya?' I asked them: 'Where is Lubang Buaya?' In the end, they asked me to sign a letter stating that I was only a member of the IPPI.

When a priest distributed communion in the prison, I did not waste the opportunity. I said to the priest that I was a member of PMKRI [Perhimpunan Mahasiswa Katholik Republik Indonesia, or the Union of Catholic University Students of the Republic of Indonesia]. I said: 'I've been a member of IPPI, but now I am a member PMKRI and I have not been expelled by my university. I still have the right to study at my campus.' I mentioned the name of my dean. Indeed, I did not tell them that I was a member of IPPI when I applied to the university.

Thanks to the help of that priest, I was released on 16 April 1966. Soon after my release, I looked for that priest and asked him to give me a recommendation so that I could go to college again. But that letter was not sufficient. I had to get letters from the police and the district military command as well as the head of the village, district, county and province stating that I was not involved in the G30S rebellion. Of course, this was not easy, but I was determined to get the letters from all of them in order to go to college again.

After I was able to go back to my university, I also applied to become an elementary school teacher to help my family by earning an income. I was accepted in the Wonosari area in Gunung Kidul. But getting from Gunung Kidul to my campus took at least six hours one way, so it was impossible for me to travel to both places every day!

I decided to meet the man in charge of placing the teachers. I begged him to move me to another place closer to my college. I told him how important this work was for me because I wanted to ease the burden on my mother. He asked: 'So where is your *bapak*? Why does your *ibu* have to be the breadwinner?' I replied: 'He has gone with someone else.' I was not lying, though. *Bapak* did go with someone else – with the soldier who took him away. If he found out that my father had been imprisoned, it would certainly have been a disaster. Fortunately, this school officer thought that my father had gone off with another woman. He felt sorry for me and agreed to move me to a school much closer to where I was studying.

I rented a simple room in Yogya and I had to juggle my teaching and studying. Sometimes I had to leave school early to get to a class on the campus, but I did not want my students to be disadvantaged by this. I left my notes and assignments for my students with fellow teachers so that they could look after my students when I went to the university. I was very grateful because my co-workers were very helpful and understanding. For two years I did both of these tasks with hardly any rest. I had to wake up very early in the morning and went to bed early, too. But I felt very happy because everything went according to my plan. I received a scholarship from the priest who had helped me in prison and my siblings also received money from the church.

One night when I was fast asleep, there was loud banging on the door. Still not fully conscious, I opened the door and saw six men pointing guns in my face. It was around 2 am. They grilled me with thousands of questions. They asked my full name and after I answered them truthfully, they were still not happy, maybe because they were actually looking for someone else. They accused me of lying and said that I had protected guerrilla fighters. My three housemates had woken because of the noise but they were all very frightened as well so they kept quiet and just watched.

The soldiers searched the house and found grenades and bullets.

'Whose are these?' they asked me.
'They belong to a guest who left the stuff here.'
'Where is that person now?'
'I don't know.'

Actually, the grenades and bullets belonged to me. They were given to me by a friend of mine who was in the army but who supported our struggle. He was also a former member of Pemuda Rakyat [People's Youth, the youth wing of the PKI], so of course I could not give them his name. Indeed, after I had heard that many of our friends had disappeared, I decided to participate in guerrilla politics. We had planned a people's armed struggle against the regime that had killed millions of innocent people because we did not want to remain silent and submissive forever. We created hideaway pockets in rural as well as urban areas. Friends who had lost family members were usually very helpful. They were willing to aid our comrades who needed food and give them a place to sleep and other help. We were studying martial arts and war strategies – we were prepared to fight with weapons. I never told any of this to the officer so I firmly stood by my answer: 'I don't know.' But because of this, my clothes were ripped off and I was ordered to climb the top of a round marble table in the house. Naked, I was bombarded with various questions, but I kept answering: 'I don't know.' In the end, they were blazing with anger and burnt the hair on my head as well as my pubic hair. I screamed the name of Jesus then lost consciousness.

After I awoke, they ordered me to get dressed and then handcuffed my hands and took me to the district military office. I was put in a cell with a man who was also handcuffed like me. In the afternoon, they took us to their office, without opening our handcuffs, to be interrogated about the guerrilla movement. I remained silent. And when they asked about my political activities, I replied that I did not have time for that because I was really busy studying at university as well as teaching. This answer drove them crazy and they gave me a choice: to confess or to be placed on top of the man. I answered: 'Neither, because there was no option for me to choose.' Instantly, they stripped both of us naked and lifted our bodies by force. We were placed on top of each other and at once I was in a complete darkness and could not remember anything else afterwards.

I found myself back in my cell, still with handcuffed arms. Soon after, I had a horrible fever for three days. The officers decided to send me to Wirogunan prison, which was also in Yogya but not far from the district prison. After the doctor in Wirogunan prison said that I was better, I was sent back to the district prison and was interrogated and tortured again. So they only cured me to enable them to torture me again. If there were new inmates, they often called me and questioned me in front of them, to see if my answers matched theirs. Once, just because a man said that I had come to his house, I was tortured severely.

They tried to force me to admit that I was a political activist but I kept saying no. Then eight men came and stripped me naked. They held my shoulders, competed for my body and forced me to kiss their penises one by one. Their hands greedily pushed my head on their crotches. After all that, they were still not satisfied. They dragged me to the middle of the room, then laid me down on the floor and trampled on me. I tried to get strength by remembering the martyrs, especially Saint Catherine and Saint Maximilian Kolbe. I also kept flashing back to the book I read when I was a student, entitled *The Letters from Vietnam*. At the beginning, I thought the book was a collection of letters but it actually narrated the story of a Vietnamese woman activist, Can Tin Nam, who was tortured by the American soldiers in a way similar to what I was experiencing. I mumbled her name several times as the men were mauling my body because I did not want them to possess my mind.

After that, my hair was shaved again. I was depressed, did not say anything and had no menstruation for about eight months. I was also not allowed to see my family for a year, but perhaps this was for the best because when my family finally came to meet me, my hair had grown back so I did not look too horrible.

Shortly thereafter, I was asked to work at the commander's home to care for his ailing mother who had asthma. She really liked me massaging her. One day, the commander's daughter lost her ring and I was accused of stealing it. Of course I denied this accusation and I pretended to be sick. I told them I felt dizzy and I made myself vomit. The ring was eventually found but I still pretended to be sick because I no longer wanted to work there.

I was finally returned to the prison because they considered me to be unhealthy. Of course this made me happier as I did not have to deal with further accusations from them. In prison, we sewed, embroidered and made fake buns from our hair, which was falling out, so that we would have something to sell. Sometimes we deliberately cut our own hair to create a bun in order to get additional food because the food ration was only 50 ears of corn. We carefully talked to an officer and negotiated this so that he could help us to sell our handicrafts. At night, we tried to console ourselves by performing drama, such as *ketoprak* or *wayang wong*.[62] I also often wrote and I hid my writings in my menstrual equipment. Back then, the menstrual equipment consisted of layers of cloths and a long thread. We made a pocket under the layers of cloth so that we could tie it around our waist. If it was already really wet, we washed it so we could use it again and again. Menstruating women were often called 'horse riding' and considered dirty. For this reason, the guards never checked my menstrual equipment.

In 1971, I was moved to Semarang where a good friend of mine died – a young activist named Girilyantini who was a former member of IPPI. She was still very young with a tremendous fighting spirit. She used to perform in our marching band, which was the pride of our organisation. I just tried my very best to survive because I did not want to give up to the savagery of Soeharto. I remained silent when interrogated, even though because of this I was more severely tortured. But later I found out how my friends who were more experienced than me were able to avoid severe torture. To avoid staying silent they gave the names of those who had died. After two weeks in Semarang, we were dispatched to Plantungan, the former hospital for leprosy patients in the Dutch colonial era. I saw the connection: we were regarded as political lepers.

There, the prisoners were all female, approximately 500 of us. We had to sleep with dangerous animals such as snakes and scorpions. Fortunately, there was a woman who was adept at hunting snakes so the scary animals became our meal. We ate everything we could find (dead or alive) and our favourite was snails – tasty and nutritious.

In Plantungan, there were several work divisions: agriculture, fishing, gardening, sewing, crafts, production and marketing. All the crafts could be sold and exchanged for whatever we needed. There was also a health unit led by Dr. Sumiyarsi, who was really proficient and could cure just about anything. Because of her, the stigma of Plantungan as a place for the dirty and amoral started subsiding as many people from outside of the prison came to seek treatment from Dr. Sumiyarsi, too. They often gave secret signs of gratitude, usually food. After some time, the demand from the public to be treated by Dr. Sumiyarsi increased so much she was allowed to go outside the prison to treat them.

In the prison, several of the women started dating the soldiers. Of course, this made many of us anxious, especially when the commander approached young girls and I knew what he wanted: to make these girls spies. Finally, I proposed to form a group with the name 'the Army of Durable Girls' whose

---

62   Javanese dance theatrical performance.

members were those who did not and would not go out with the guards. We strengthened and supported each other so as not to easily give in to the seductions of the officers. After we were freed, when we met with former prisoners, we still often asked each other: 'Still in the army?'

Many of us were determined to stand for what we believed in to the death. In every way, we also tried to prevent these young girls from being used by the guards, who lured them through dates to arts events and religious activities. Finally, we were also played off against each other, especially between the younger and older women. We were required to report on one another and to observe the movements of each other. These were the questions they frequently asked: 'What has your friend been doing? What has she said? Who has she visited? What did she talk about? Who has held meetings in prison? Who has tried to carry out ideological education?'

The cunning guards widened their network by recruiting the inexperienced young girls. They asked these girls to go out, gave them money, bought them gifts and even took them to visit their families. One of the girls used to get out at 3 pm and was back at 3 am. I knew what she was doing. In our Army of Durable Girls, we took turns in noting down what happened, which girls were out, with whom, and we communicated all of this information via relay messages. Eventually, these young girls discovered that we were 'spying' on them. They reported us and we were scolded as 'communist spies'. Not long after, babies were born: the outcome of the relationships between the girls and the guards, the commanders or even the pastors.

Meanwhile, about 45 of us were thrown into Bulu prison in Semarang because they said that women like us were nothing but communist old farts and we could no longer be fostered as loyal citizens who adhered to Pancasila. We were moved on 16 October 1976 during heavy rains. But we were more at ease in Semarang because all the officers were female. So we had no worries about being raped and after being moved to Semarang, an Amnesty International team arrived. Shortly thereafter, we were released on 27 September 1978.

For us, being released from the prison meant facing different problems. We were stigmatised as immoral, cheap, atheist women. I was certainly not young anymore after having spent a dozen years in prison. Even the women political prisoners who returned with severe disabilities due to torture had failed to touch people's hearts because the people had been brainwashed by Soeharto. Many women came out of prison only to see that their families and homes had been possessed by other people who did not want to have anything to do with the ex-political prisoners. Alone, without a job, insulted and condemned by everyone around them – this is what they had to cope with outside of the prison.

I was not as unfortunate as they were because my family accepted me back and my activist friends were willing to visit me. Shortly after my release, my parents talked about wedding plans. I was shocked and rejected them out of hand as I did not want to get married without having a job. Otherwise, how would I live? Depending on my parents financially forever?

But my future husband told me that he already had a garage. It turned out that he was also an ex-political prisoner. In fact, his entire family (father, mother and siblings) had been taken away by the soldiers. His father died on Buru Island. For this reason, he had been in touch with my family for some time. Finally, I understood my parents' choice for me and agreed to marry him.

I did not want a big party for my wedding, because I wanted the money to be used for my future. But my parents wanted to have a fairly large party. They told me: 'This is not just a wedding but our family celebration because you're alive.' I was finally able to enjoy the generous outpouring of love from my extended family. Unexpectedly, former political prisoners of Plantungan were also present. Many of these women even travelled from far away – from other cities and towns – to come to my simple home in a village. Everything was amazing for me although the party was prepared in an extremely short period. I got married on 25 November 1978, less than two months after I was released.

Not long after we got married, we decided to attend a court case of one of our friends who used to be a political prisoner as well. But we could not get inside because the room was rather full, so we just waited outside. After the court case was over and the audience started leaving the room, I saw a very familiar face unexpectedly. I immediately approached him: 'Sir, do you remember me?' He looked confused. 'Sir, my name is Christina Sumarmiyati.' He seemed shocked but did not answer at all. I will never forget his face or his name because he was one of my torturers. He left immediately and I also went home with my husband.

**Our Children**

On 6 May 1980, our first child was born: Diana Gabriella Asti; and on 5 May 1982, my second child was born: Benny Putranto. I decided to get sterilised after the second child. We have always been open to my children about our pasts so they knew who their father and mother are: former political prisoners who were persecuted by Soeharto. I did not want my kids to hear about us from other people.

I worked by selling anything I could – herbs, kerosene, whatever. I also raised my children to be independent. I asked them to deliver merchandise and gave them a salary to pay for their English courses. So I said: 'The course was paid by your own money' to motivate them to work harder.

One time, my children asked, 'Why don't you have cars? Why are you the poorest amongst our relatives?' I did not get angry with them and explained to them why it was hard for us to find proper jobs. They also watched the film *Pengkhianatan G30S/PKI*. That film was indeed disgusting but I used it as an opportunity to explain further about our pasts. First, I pinched Benny's penis lightly and he screamed. Then I said: 'If I only pinch your penis, you scream. Now imagine if the generals who had weapons were attacked by the Gerwani women who had nothing. Would these men keep quiet if the women cut their penises with razor blades? And how could these women leave the chopped penises anywhere so that they were discovered by other people – as has been reported by the media? Does this make sense?' The lengthy discussion continued and my children never blamed the PKI ever again nor were they willing to see that propaganda film again.

They grew to be so understanding of us and our situation. Both went to school at Kanisius, a Catholic school that offered us a discount but we did not take it because we felt that there were still many families of ex-political prisoners who were in a far worse situation than we were. One time I heard their conversation. Benny, my younger child, said that he did not want to go to Kanisius but to a public school as it was much cheaper, so that the money could be saved for his sister's study at college. However, the elder one, Dian, also said that she did not want to go to college and wanted to work so that Benny could study at university. I was really touched and felt so blessed with children like them.

When Dian was in high school, she heard that most of her friends were forbidden to date the children of ex-political prisoners. They also insulted ex-political prisoners, especially the female ones. This made Dian swear that she would work harder so that she could move to another country and change her citizenship, especially to a place more respectful towards women. Indeed, she finally married a Dutchman and now lives in the Netherlands with him, but she remains an Indonesian citizen and has no intention of giving it up.

Eventually my business was running well and I began to track down my old friends. I wanted us to work together and encourage each other. I am determined to continue seeking justice for the female ex-convicts of Soeharto for I am burning with anger for what happened to us. The downfall of Soeharto, of course, made me more confident to talk about the 1965 genocide. And it makes me really happy when I know there are young people like you, Soe Tjen, who are willing to continue our struggle. It feels like we have known each other for centuries! I really want to hug you now, my child.

*From 3 to 7 July 2015, I stayed with Christina Sumarmiyati. She is actively helping other female ex-political prisoners to get medical help and funds when they are in need. When I was there, she organised a meeting with me and five of the female ex-prisoners from Plantungan. In her small and fragile stature, I found a huge strength and her generosity is incredible.*

*On the weekend, I met her son, Benny, who told me that as a child, his parents promised to buy him new shoes. Suddenly, they said that he had to wait for a few months because they had just given the money for his shoes to one of their friends. Benny was really annoyed with them, but now he understands why his parents were doing it. Their sense of solidarity with other ex-political prisoners was so huge that they were willing to sacrifice their son's new shoes for it. Benny really appreciates and admires his parents' sense of humanity now.*

# Part 3

The Accounts of the Siblings

# Sriyono Wiwoho

## The Lunch Box My Brother Never Received

*I cannot remember how I got in touch with Sriyono Wiwoho, who lives in the small town of Sukoharjo in Central Java. He struck me as a very cheerful person. He makes a lot of jokes, but behind this cheerfulness is a severe tragedy, which he had kept hidden for years and years. Born in November 1952, Sriyono was only a child when the mass murder exploded and affected several members of his extended family.*

It has been about 50 years since I began to keep hidden the dark history of my family, this tragic event. I had been determined to bury it deeply, until the day I die. But with your project of gathering the life stories of the victims and families of the victims, my blood has begun bubbling again: I may be able to seek a bit of justice for the brutality that happened to my family.

*Bapak*, my father, was a Marxist: a Leninist adherent. And this is somewhat expressed by the birth of my brother who is two years younger than me, in 1954, by giving him the name Marsis. When his nephew in Solo gave birth to her second child, my father gave her the name Retno Leninsih. We lived in the cool and small town of Salatiga. Our parents opened a small restaurant there and *bapak* gave it the name Warung Sate Cinta Damai [Satay Café: Loving Peace].

We lived happily and peacefully. We were four brothers and sisters. The eldest was Asmoro Rahman Hadi. He was an artist, a journalist and a Lekra[63] activist. His wife, Rahayuni, sold vegetables and was a member of Gerwani [Gerakan Wanita Indonesia, or the Indonesian Women's Movement]. My second eldest sibling is a girl, Mbak [Elder Sister] Sardiyem. She married Sutaryo Sastrodihardjo, a furniture maker who was quite well known in our town. I call him Mas [Elder Brother] Taryo. Because they had a big house, Sardiyem and Sutaryo often let the IPPI [Ikatan Pemuda Pelajar Indonesia, or the Indonesian Students Association] have meetings there. Many of them also stayed the night, cooked and ate at my sister's home. Although Mas Taryo had many PKI friends, he was never active in politics.

---

63  Lekra (Lembaga Kebudayaan Rakyat, or the Institute for the People's Culture) was an art movement associated with the PKI.

In 1965, when I entered a junior high school, I also joined IPPI. I did not know what really happened on 30 September 1965 – I guess because I was too young then. All I knew was that my family got quite worried and tense. Everyone went very quiet. Even when speaking in our own home we had to whisper. Outside our home, in the streets, there were arrests by the police and the RPKAD [Resimen Pasukan Komando Angkatan Darat, or the Indonesian Special Forces]. My eldest sister's house was searched, the police confiscated four sacks of political books, along with pictures of world leaders and thinkers (some of which were those of Karl Marx). Then her husband, Mas Taryo, was arrested. Two of my uncles were also imprisoned.

A high official from the army then approached Mbak Rahayuni and asked her to leave her husband to marry him, so she could be safe. But Rahayuni stayed loyal to her huband. My eldest *mas*, Asmoro, and Rahayuni decided to leave home and run away. But they were separated during their escape. Because he did not want to betray his colleagues who had already been arrested, in January 1966 my eldest brother finally surrendered to Pekuper [the war implementing authority] in Salatiga. His wife? No one knows where or how she is. There was a rumour that she was captured before my brother surrendered, and other news said that she was raped by her captors before being murdered.

**Photo F    Rahayuni, Sriyono Wiwoho's sister-in-law, who was raped and murdered for her involvement in Gerwani**

Personal collection of Sriyono Wiwoho's family

**Photo G  Asmoro Rahman Hadi, the brother of Sriyono Wiwoho, who was murdered for his involvement in Lekra**

Personal collection of Sriyono Wiwoho's family

Mas Asmoro and Mas Taryo were imprisoned in different places. My *mas* was in the Armed Forces Centre. Mas Taryo was taken to Gedung Nasional Salatiga [the National Building of Salatiga], and then moved to the Balai Prajurit Makutoromo [the Warrior Hall Makutoromo] in the same town.

After the prisoners were allowed to receive deliveries, my younger brother and I brought food for our *mas* in a metal lunch box. My eldest brother always put messages on a cigarette paper folded up as small as possible and placed in the same container where his food had been (even though he was not a smoker – he in fact suffered from fairly acute asthma).

One day in March 1966, I already forget the date, I brought the last lunch box, the one he never received. For that afternoon, as soon as I arrived at the security post, the officer told me to go home. But I waited to see what was going on. Sometime after, there was a truck outside the yard and many policemen were coming out with their guns. This was followed by a group of men marching with their hands behind their backs, and their thumbs were tied to each other with shoelaces. I guess there were around 20 people there, and amongst them was my eldest *mas*. I remained standing near the security post, and my *mas* suddenly turned his head and saw me. Smiling slightly, he looked at me for a long time, and gave a sign of farewell. That day, I represented my extended family to say goodbye to him.

After my brother left, I ran home while carrying the lunch box and told my family what had happened. Everyone went quiet for a long time. 'He must be going to be killed in the Butak River', said my father. That river is in Boyolali (Central Java, about 30 km from Solo) and it was well known as a place to execute political prisoners.

At least Mas Taryo was still alive. Then, Mas Taryo was moved to a prison in Ambarawa, the place where the Dutch colonial government used to detain their prisoners (about 20 km from our town). Mbak Sardiyem and I were allowed to visit the prison only once a week, and even then we could not meet him. We had to leave the food for him with the guards and then stand in front of iron bars about 150 m away from him, so that we could not even see him properly. My eldest sister, Sardiyem, was six months pregnant then, and her first child was only two years old. She had to carry the toddler with her every time we went to Mas Taryo's prison. Some time in 1966, suddenly and without any reason, the guards returned our delivery and asked us never to come there again. It was useless asking them why. Mbak Sardiyem could not stop crying on our way back to Salatiga. *Bapak* concluded that my brother-in-law must have been killed. My parents remained incredibly strong. Mbak Sardiyem kept trying to find out what had happened to Mas Taryo for years and years afterwards, but in vain.

Maybe because we lived in the centre of the town, the people around us were not so nosy about what happened to us. Another possibility why they did not change their attitude much was that we lived peacefully with most of the ethnic Chinese around there. But the authorities were still not satisfied and wanted to inflict more suffering on our family. In 1967, my father was also imprisoned. He was already 63 years old then. At first he was placed in the Taman Harapan building in Salatiga. A year later he was moved to the Wirogunan prison in Yogya. In 1972, he was transferred to the Bantir prison in Ambarawa. Once a week our family visited him there.

Of course, we had all kinds of financial problems after my father was imprisoned. *Ibu* had to sell the café and tried to make a living by selling food in the street. I wonder how my mother could stay very strong despite everything. I have never seen her cry.

### My *Adik* and I at School

It was not enough for them that my brother, sister-in-law and brother-in-law were murdered, and that my father was imprisoned. My younger brother and I had to face all kinds of jeers at school, especially from my junior high school teachers and the principal. I was often called 'the PKI kid'. We were robbed of our holidays, and the time during which we could have expected to relax turned into a time of terror: every Sunday we had to go to school to be preached at with all kinds of indoctrination. We had to listen to the version of history made up by the New Order, and had to condemn communism and our own family. Finally, I just tried to toughen myself by saying, 'Let them do it, I don't care!'

My *adik* [younger brother] was very much affected by all of this, so that he could not finish junior high school. At my senior high school, fortunately, the teachers left me alone. I was able to complete high school in 1971 because I financed my study by running a bridal decoration business with my classmates. I was still lucky because many of my friends at high school seemed to accept me and did not mention anything about the PKI. I became more confident and enjoyed my life a lot more. My father was finally released in 1975. He never changed his principles about socialism and communism, and we tried our best to enjoy life. My *adik*, Marsis, is proud of my father and proud of the name *bapak* gave him.

Do you know, Mbak [Elder Sister][64] Soe Tjen, this is the first time I have opened up about my family's history. Even my wife and children have not found out about this, and I will never tell them. Let this be my secret to them. But, of course, until the day I die, I will never forget about this at all. Never. Our family is not vengeful, but we just want to be treated and respected like human beings. And I guess that is not too high a demand at all.

---

64  A form of address to Javanese women.

**Photo H   Sriyono Wiwoho**

*Not long after I finished interviewing Sriyono, a daughter of Sardiyem contacted me and sent a photo of Mas Taryo. This was followed by Nyom Mahaditya sending me a photo of his grandmother, Rahayuni. I uploaded the photos to Facebook with their permission. Seeing those photos, Sriyono said that he had been looking for them for a long time and told me how happy he was that the two younger members of his family found them.*

*At the beginning of July 2015, my husband and I visited Sriyono in his home in Sukoharjo. His extended family welcomed us warmly. His nieces, sister-in-law, wife, daughter, and grandchildren were there; some came from out of town. The daughter of Asmoro and Rahayuni was also present, and she told me about her bitter experience after both her parents were gone (her image is on the cover of this book).*

*After a long chat about 1965, I remembered how Sriyono had sworn that he would never reveal his family's history to his wife and children. But then, his wife and one of his children were present as we were chatting. So I asked him, 'When did your wife and daughter find out about your family's history?' He answered: 'Just now.'*

# Adi Rukun

Beyond the Look of Silence

*Adi seemed rather quiet when I first met him, but after a while, he became quite talkative, very sharp, and showed his good sense of humour, although he said that a motorcycle accident injury to his head a few years ago had made him rather 'slow'.*

*Adi was born in 1968 in Serdang Bedagai, North Sumatra, the youngest of eight children. He later moved to Medan and is the main character in Joshua Oppenheimer's 2014 documentary film* The Look of Silence. *From the confessions of the mass murderers in Oppenheimer's films and also from Amir Hasan's 1994 book* Embun Berdarah *(Bloody Dew), which narrates in detail how the author killed communists around 1965, Adi found out how his eldest brother was killed. Amir Hasan, one of the killers of Adi's brother, wrote the book as a historical record of his 'heroic acts' in murdering communists. In Oppenheimer's film, Amir claims the book is 'important for people who continue their higher education'. Amir also drew illustrations in the book and gave a copy of this book to Oppenheimer, who subsequently lent it to Adi.*

Our family lived in the village Serdang Bedagai, North Sumatra. I am the youngest of eight brothers and sisters. Most people in my hometown are not political and cannot be bothered much with politics. Most were illiterate, including my parents. Only their children went to school and even then only through to primary level.

My brothers told me that the head of the village always invited them to attend arts events. But then the head of the village had to list who were the communists amongst the people. At that time, my father worked as a labourer in a plantation owned by Socfindo [a large plantation company] and every now and then, he also worked as a fisherman. Neither of my parents liked getting involved in organisations. Maybe that was why my parents escaped being put on the village head's list – but not their three children. My elder brothers loved to get wrapped up in organisations, and my eldest *abang* [brother],[65] Ramli, was the leader of the Indonesian Peasants Front [BTI] in the village.

Ramli was only 23 years old when he was dragged into a truck at night by a group of mass murderers. In the truck, he saw my cousin. *But hadn't*

---

65 People in Sumatra call their elder brothers and other older men *abang*.

*he moved from this village, to go a university in Medan?* Then my cousin explained that he returned to his village to tell his family to be careful, but had gotten arrested himself instead.

Not long after my *abang* had been taken away, my father and mother heard the sound of gunfire, around 10 pm. Emak, my mother, said: 'Our son is finished now. That sound – that must have been them firing on communists.'

'Don't say that', my father said. 'That can't be true. Don't think about that.' Then, both went quiet for a long time.

But about an hour later, they heard someone calling weakly at the door: 'Mak, Emak, Ramli ...' Opening the door, my mother saw my eldest *abang* lying on the ground, leaning against the clothes pole. Immediately, my parents carried him into the house. My brother bled severely and his whole body was pale. His shoulder was almost broken and his intestines came out. There was a hole in his back from a spear. His body was covered with grass, sticking to his skin and clothes. His torn white shirt was stained by blood. Emak kissed him and asked who had done this to him, but my brother was so weak he could hardly speak. He was laid down in the living room, lit with an oil lamp. He just asked for a cup of coffee from my *emak*.

Apparently, in the middle of the road, my brother managed to fight and escape from the truck. His escape caused chaos, as all of the prisoners (about ten of them) joined the fight and tried to break free, even though their hands were tied behind their backs and they were surrounded by armed butchers. Five prisoners besides my brother managed to flee, but two of them were caught immediately and slaughtered in the palm plantation. Our cousin was also rearrested and massacred by clamping him to a cart and then dragging him until his tongue was sticking out. His body was then thrown into the Snake River.

As tension escalated, my father went to get help from my uncle (my mother's brother) who lived in a nearby village. He had to go through several rice fields and cross a river. But as he was approaching his brother-in-law's, he saw many people already crowded aggressively around the house. So my dad decided to turn around and return home. My third brother decided to pick up Ramli's wife, who was heavily pregnant. That night, everyone gathered around my brother, everyone was quiet, just tears flowed from our faces.

Around 4 am, the KOAKSI [Komando Aksi or The Commando Action] special forces picked up my brother. My family knew all of these people. KOAKSI said they had to take my brother for medical treatment. Of course, this was a lie. KOAKSI was the team formed by the government to execute the communists. KOAKSI was comprised of civilians and military people. Some of them were also the neighbours of my family and had been friends with my parents for a long time.

My father did not want to surrender my brother just like that, and was about to fight them with his machete. He'd already picked it up, but he was worried about his young kids. What would happen to them if he fought these people, some of whom had firearms? So he put his machete back in its place. What my mother regrets most even now, is that my brother's request for a cup of coffee was never granted. Even though Emak boiled the water, because of the fear and confusion, she forgot to make the coffee.

My *abang* was executed at the river near the village of Pekong Seirampah. When they believed he was dead, they just left his body there. Unexpectedly, at about 8 am, my brother moved up the riverbank and flailed around for help. But this became a kind of spectacle for the people there. They gathered around, as if watching an animal in a circus, and started laughing and ridiculing him. Some even threw stones at him. The men of KOAKSI eventually arrived and brought my brother to the palm oil plantation. There, he was executed and his genitals were cut off. Only then was my brother really dead.

The next day, *bapak* was searching for his son's body. Although he was butchered and covered in dirt, my father still recognised him and wrapped Ramli's head in grass-legume, and he was buried by my father and a few of his friends. Soon after his death, my other brothers, who were fifteen and eighteen then, were also detained and had to do forced labour. One of my sisters, who was only fourteen, was accused of being a Gerwani member although she knew nothing about politics and had not even finished elementary school. She was interrogated several times and her long beautiful hair was shaved. She was also required to do forced labour. Only after she got married and moved with her husband to his village did the forced labour stop, but she still had to come to our village to report. I never knew what happened to them in any detail. They never told me.

After the incident, my father became like an ATM machine for the head of the village called Juman. That bastard asked money of *bapak*, whenever he wanted it.

## My Brother and I

I was born about two years after my *abang* was murdered. Emak actually wanted a girl, but later she grew especially fond of me, because I looked so much like my dead brother. She believed that her prayer was answered by God, as He gave her 'a substitute' for my *abang*.

Ever since I was young, Emak talked a lot about Ramli, especially because all of the murderers of my *abang* lived close to us. She often cursed them and wished that their families would suffer for what they had done to us. That was all we could do, cursing them quietly, because they became more and more powerful. Amir Hasan even became the headmaster at our school, probably as a reward for having murdered communists. He used to be the art teacher, and when he asked the students to sing, the only song he taught them was 'Menanam Jagung' [Planting Corn] – maybe he thought of planting humans by burying them alive as he sang. Emak had no choice but to send me to this school, for there was no other school. I saw my brother's murderer every day, and every time I went to school, I had to walk past his house. The children in my village were scared of him, because many of their relatives were accused of having been PKI.

When I was in elementary school, my father asked me to come with him to Ramli's grave. We had to go secretly, because we were worried that someone might report us to the police or the army. Therefore, we could go to my brother's grave only once a year. The distance from our home to the grave was approximately ten miles. I always went on a bike with my dad: I was sitting at the front, on the iron bar. Travelling there was quite scary for me when I was young, because the grave was in the middle of a huge plantation, so there was hardly any housing or anything else there. We left our bike quite far from the grave, then looked around, just in case anyone followed us. If we thought there was no one else and it was safe, we continued our journey on foot. This fear continued until Soeharto stepped down in 1998. Emak hardly visited the grave because every time she came there, she would cry like crazy: 'Oh child, my child, why was your life so miserable? And you are buried in the middle of nowhere, alone. May God avenge your murderers with a worse fate than yours.'

However, later, the grave of my *abang* became a kind of a pilgrimage spot for many people. We found some frankincense and many flowers left there. Sometimes there were even bamboo mats [for praying], and we always took the mats home. We do not know who came there. I heard that they came to my brother's grave seeking good fortune. Maybe this was because they heard that my brother had some kind of supernatural power, which made him survive after the butchers had tried to kill him several times. Recently, some people built a tombstone and ceramic bench for anyone who wants to come to the grave.

My parents remain silent on this subject. We only talk amongst ourselves, but as we talk, their advice is always: 'Never mention it again. Forget about it. This is for our safety.' They both reminded us children never to associate with the children of the mass murderers. *Bapak* also forbade me to get involved in any organisation. He is worried that the tragedy will be repeated. But I cannot just keep quiet. I want to find out more and do something.

Once, I asked the chairman of KOAKSI in my village about it. He was one of the butchers in the 1965 tragedy. But his answer disgusted me. He did not feel guilty at all – he even thought of himself as a hero. He said that the PKI had to be slaughtered because they were atheists and had killed the generals in Jakarta. But my brother was not an atheist. In fact, all of us are Muslims and religious. For me, those mass murderers can be considered *kafir*. So I tried to explain to him that the murder of those generals had nothing to do with the PKI, especially not with my brother. I am persistent in revealing the truth, but of course what I do often puts me and my family in danger. This has caused rows between me and my family, too, because they do not understand why I keep doing this.

One time, I was involved in an argument with an ex-military man. He was so persistent that he was right about the 1965 tragedy. This made my blood boil. He was really furious, so I decided to get away from him as quickly as possible. I felt like hitting him and I was not afraid at all because he was already very old. I was sure he would soon turn into a corpse, without me beating him up. The problem is if he got injured by me, or he had a heart attack because of me, then it would have been my fault, right? I do not want to be the same as those murderers. I do not want to kill or hurt anyone, if possible.

When one of those mass murderers found out who my brother was, he even threatened me. Those butchers think that they are heroes. They even hope to get some awards and be respected. For what? But many people still believe that the communists are evil and must be eradicated. They are also frightened that the seed of communism will revive. The stigma is still strong. I often visited these people and said to them: 'The best ideology for poor people like you is communism, if you only knew better.'

## *The Look of Silence*

I often feel that I strive on my own, and feel lonely in this effort. Although my elder brothers and sister had also been victims of Soeharto's greed, they prefer to keep quiet. Even my wife does not really support me, because she is worried about the risks. When Joshua Oppenheimer was making the film from the victims' point of view, my friends and family discouraged me from taking part because they thought it would be useless. 'We are OK and safe now, why are you looking for trouble?' they said. They were worried that I would end up being like Ramli.

But I was persistent. Later, they tried to stop me again by saying that Josh might have been using me for his project. Well, talking about 'being used', I can say that I was actually using Josh, too. I wanted the story of my family to be known by as many people as possible, so I did want Josh to make this film. Only my mother was very supportive – I guess because she really wanted to be heard.

During the shooting of the film, people also thought that I did it because I got a lot of money from Josh, but I only got Rp 50,000 [about US$3.80] per day. Actually, my income suffered because of this film. I never complained and I did not tell Josh about this, because I wanted the truth about this murder to be revealed. Josh also gave me a camera and taught me how to shoot footage of my family.

During Eid 2009, when all members of my family gathered, I was then in the same room with my father, holding the camera given by Joshua. I was about to put the camera down when *bapak* started screaming. He suddenly thought he was lost in a stranger's house and someone was about to beat him up. He agitatedly crawled on the floor, asking for help. I did not know whether filming him in this situation was the right thing, but I turned the camera on. As I was recording, I was in a huge conflict with myself whether I had to continue or not. But helping him at this stage was rather in vain. My father had gone senile and did not recognise his own children. He could hardly be comforted by us, for he did not know us any longer.

In tears, I kept following him with the camera and, afterwards, gave the recording to Josh. I know several people who have seen the film think that that scene is an exploitation of my father. At first, some of them accused Josh of exploiting my father, and after Josh explained that I took the scene, I knew they would have thought that I exploited him, but they do not know the circumstances, they do not know what I really felt. My father had done that several times and we could not really help him. So, in the end I wanted the world to see my father in this situation. I wanted them to witness the endless misery the New Order has caused us, because too many people have been keeping quiet for too long. They do not want to talk about that tragedy and want to just forget about it, like the people in my *kampong* [community or village], although most of them have been accused of being communists. They think this is the best way, although the impact is still powerful, even now. Many of these people do not get to attend high school.

I am the only one who managed to finish high school. Many of them only completed elementary school. They think it is useless to study in school because even if they can get a degree, no one will want to employ anyone associated with communism.

Every day, they just go to the field, nothing else. But their economic situation is poor because they are sure that they will not be successful. So most of them do not even have their own fields – they only become labourers on other people's fields. Ignorance and poverty haunt them everywhere because of their past. When I went to school, the neighbours often commented: 'Why do you go to school? You will end up in a field, too. Don't dream of getting an office job if you are related to a communist.'

Well, indeed I do not work in an office at the moment. But I do not work in a field either, because I am unemployed now. It is indeed tragic if you get the label 'communist'. However, *The Look of Silence* has in some ways transformed me. I used to be quiet and reserved, but after making the film, I am more confident when speaking in front of people and more open. Another strange thing is also happening. Some people in my neighbourhood in Medan have started to respect and listen to me. Eventually, I was even elected to the committee of the mosque there. I am now the secretary of the mosque. I use this opportunity to talk more about 1965. I often talk to the students, as most of them do not know about this dark history.

**Photo I   Adi Rukun**

We still keep the white clothes my brother wore that night, the clothes with the stains of his blood. And if only, if only I could still speak to my brother, I would love to say: 'I have never met you, but will always remember you. I will strive to continue to live up to your aspiration.'

*I see myself in Adi. Both Adi and I are the youngest in the family. We were both born after the tragedy befell our families. We both did not witness it ourselves. We had been shielded from this tragedy by our families for fear of the repercussions and also the desire to protect us from this brutal episode in their lives. But because of this, we have developed an insatiable hunger for what they have been covering up. Our passion for revealing the history of 1965, for finding out what happened to our families, and for making this known to the world, are all a way for us to recover what has been hidden from us. The way Adi tried to get information in detail from other people and how he also made other people aware of the manipulated history reminds me of my own drive to straighten out what we consider wrong. We have received so much false history in our lives, even from those closest to us, that we have an unquenchable thirst for the truth: for presenting the public, even the planet, with real history.*

*After I met Adi in 2013, we kept in touch via Facebook. In mid-2014 when he was in Thailand with Joshua Oppenheimer for the preliminary viewing of* The Look of Silence, *he contacted me. He said that soon he would have to hide because the film was about to be released and his safety had to be protected from any powerful party in Indonesia who would be offended by this film.*

*Not long after, his face was in newspapers all over the world, as he was touring with Oppenheimer for their film.*

# Part 4

The Accounts of the Children

# Usmantri Sukardi

My Childhood with Strangers

*In writing this book, I often approached anyone who I suspected might be related to the 1965 tragedy via email or Facebook. One of them was Usmantri Sukardi. After I introduced myself and told him about my family background, he immediately revealed that several members of his extended family had been victimised by Soeharto's regime. Although at first he was hesitant to share his story, in the end he said how relieved and also proud he was for having been able to tell the truth. When I asked whether I should use pseudonyms for him and his family, he said no: 'We are proud of our names. Please write them down as they are and let people know what happened to us.'*

Sometimes I do not feel like talking about anything related to the mass murder in 1965 at all, because it is still very painful for me. But I also think that the reality should not be forgotten and the history of my family has to be told, as it has had a big influence on my political views. Because of what happened to my parents, I have become different from most of the people here: I am interested in reading about socialism and about left thinkers. When my parents were studying socio-political science at Gadjah Mada University in Yogyakarta, they were already activists. My mother was also very active as a member of Gerwani, an organisation of progressive women.

But because of this, *ibu* was jailed in Salemba from 1965 to 1974 and *bapak* was sent to Buru Island. All of their diplomas and certificates were burnt by Soeharto's troops. When they arrested my mother, my grandfather fled with my uncle (my mother's younger brother, who was only seventeen years old then), as both of them were quite active in communist organisations as well. But we never knew what happened to them. Even now, our family has not found out. They simply disappeared.

*Ibu* was born in 1938 and *bapak* in 1941. They were married in 1962. My *mother* was arrested in Yudonegaran Street in Yogyakarta, and my father was arrested in Sosrowijayan, which is now famous as a tourist destination and as a place to stay for those who visit Yogya. When my mother was arrested, she was three months' pregnant.

Marxi, my brother, was born in prison in 1966. Only the prison guards helped my mother at the time, because the family was forbidden to visit and also was not told to which prison she had been sent. In 1974, *ibu* was moved to Cijantung [the complex of Kopassus] in West Java, and was employed as a cleaner in an elementary school in Cijantung. Because of the immoral conduct of one of the army soldiers there, my youngest brother, Agus, was born. Marxi was taken to a friend of my mother's, Januar Suyono, in Jakarta, and stayed in this city [in Mampang]. Three years later, he was taken by my grandmother and brought to Yogya. Marxi thought that his father and mother were imprisoned in the same location, he does not know that our youngest sibling was born of another father. But after Agus was born, my mother was treated a bit better in jail. *Ibu* could write to us and afterward she could also send a bit of money to us. I never knew where that money was from.

Soon after my mother was imprisoned, Simbah[66] took me to Kidul Mountain. I do not remember my first days there, because I was only a year old then. The memory that still pierces my heart is when Simbah left to return to Yogya, and I was not taken: 'Why did she dump me in this awful place?' In the village called Kadisobo, I lived with a farmer, Pak Surawi, his wife, Bu Manis,[67] and their children who were still very young: Ngadiyo, Wagirah, and Sunardi. They were quite poor but I was treated very well, no differently to the other children, although I often felt very lonely. I still keep in touch with the family. Even now, our relationship remains strong. Pak Surawi and Bu Manis have died, but we still often visit the children. Only later, I found out why Simbah left me there: because Soeharto ordered a total extermination of the PKI children.

In that village, I helped them collect firewood for cooking, herd goats and make *tiwul*.[68] Our daily food was mainly cassava and *tiwul*. Not far from there, there was Jomblang cave, which became a mass grave for communist corpses. The distance from our village to the famous cave at Jomblang was only 25 km, so every now and then I heard rumours about what happened to the communists.

My life story sounds unbelievable to many of my friends. Just imagine, I lived on Kidul Mountain with people I did not know at all. Currently, Kidul Mountain is considered the most underdeveloped district in Yogyakarta. When I was young, it was worse. Life on Kidul Mountain was very, very hard then: the place was barren with limestone soil, water was scarce and illiteracy was nearly 100 per cent. The nearest school was in the village of Panggang, which was about eleven miles from Kadisobo. I had to walk there because there was no road for vehicles: it was a 22-mile round trip every day.

---

66 *Simbah* means grandmother in Javanese.
67 *Pak*: the abbreviated form of *bapak*, meaning father, also used to address older men.
68 *Tiwul*: traditional Javanese food made of cassava and grated coconut.

In 1978, Simbah took me to Yogya to meet my auntie. When I was playing marbles with my auntie, Simbah came with a shabby dark child, his clothes were old and had odd buttons (all with different shapes and colours). I did not know who he was, and then my auntie told me that he was Marxi. That was the first time I saw the face of my younger brother – when I was fourteen years old and he was twelve. The very first time we met! Simbah did mention a few years earlier that I had a brother, but it was like fiction for me. I did not even know whether I could miss him for we had never met. But he was now real. I felt more alive suddenly. There was another human like me, but this also made me sad, for he must have suffered so much as well. Simbah had been monitoring us from afar, and had been working hard so that both of us could be safe and could continue our studies.

During my elementary and junior high school years, I lived on Kidul Mountain. When I was about to start senior high school, *ibu* told Simbah to move me back to Yogya, because she was about to be released. *Ibu* was released in 1979 but the ET stamp on her ID card brought many problems. When I graduated from the college, I was hired by the TVRI [Televisi Republik Indonesia, the state-owned, public broadcasting television network]. In 1989, after they found out that I was a son of a PKI member, I was immediately dismissed. I knew it would be useless to complain, so I just applied for another job in a private company in Jakarta.

In 1996, on the eve of the burial of Oei Tjoe Tat,[69] I went to pay respect at the funeral home in Atmajaya. However, I was soon arrested by the security forces because they knew about my parents. I was accused of reviving communist ideology, although I came there only because of my empathy with Oei Tjoe Tat. He was one of the greatest men my mother knew, and had been severely victimised by Soeharto. I was interrogated for six days and they told my company to fire me. Fortunately, my boss defended me.

## Meeting *bapak* Again

My father was released a year after my mother, but he was mentally damaged. He was often angry and when he saw our youngest brother, Agus, he was furious and blamed my mother for the birth of this child. Then he walked out just like that, moved to Jakarta and no longer wanted to take

---

69   Oei Tjoe Tat was a state minister during Sukarno's era. He was arrested by Soeharto in 1965 and imprisoned without trial for over ten years.

care of us. I was very angry with him, but later I understood that he must have been severely traumatised by the inhumane torture on Buru.

In 1984, he got remarried – to a family member of a former prisoner. I rarely see him, although we live in the same city [Jakarta], we meet maybe only every two years. My brothers have never seen him again since *bapak* left home. The last time I saw *bapak* was in 2013. He was very unstable, his depression had gotten worse, his talk was disjointed and he was also very absent minded. Luckily, his new wife is really patient and understanding. She makes money by selling accessories in the Bethel church, while *bapak* tidies up the church before the service. His livelihood depends on the church people.

The memories of my parents and younger siblings are quite painful for me. Sometimes mother and I cry together, thinking about Agus, who does not know who his father is. *Ibu* never tells anyone. Agus never asks either, but from his eyes, I can see that he has so many questions. He must be wondering. He is really quiet and introverted, and it seems that he does not want to get married. After he graduated from university, he did not want to move out and find a job. He just stayed at home and helped *ibu* make paper boxes for food. He is almost 40 years old now, but still lives with my mother.

My mother is a tough person, and has been trying very hard to get over her trauma. She has never changed her mind about communism and socialism. She thinks these two systems are the best for the country. I am very proud of *ibu*. She still has a good memory, and likes to talk about socialism, Marhaenism[70] and Marxism with the students. I sometimes join them when I come home to Yogya. But I never talk about the 1965 tragedy with my brothers. It is like we have an agreement to keep silent about it, so we won't have further trouble in life.

My mother is the opposite: she never hesitates to speak up against the local officials. When they ask her to give a contribution she considers uncalled for, she will refuse to pay. If they pressure her to pay by threatening her, she will challenge them: 'Go on, imprison me if you dare!' Sometimes I am worried for her, but it also makes me smile seeing her like this: she has no fear whatsoever. When people mock her as PKI, ex-prisoner or atheist, she is not that bothered and never denies it. She and my younger brothers are active in a church in Yogyakarta. I am the only Muslim in the family. I became a Muslim when I was young, following the religion of the family who raised me in Kidul Mountain. However, many Muslims have called me *kafir* when they found out about my family background.

---

70   Marhaenism: popularised by Sukarno, is a socialist ideology in Indonesia.

Last night I called *ibu* and told her about you. When she heard about your activism, she got worried and said: 'This country is still murky. Please do not stir it too much. It is enough that I was victimised. You young people should be more careful and not sacrifice yourselves.'

*In September 2013, I met Usmantri Sukardi's mother in Yogya. She showed me her ID card: 'This is my name: Agnes Ramilah', as if stating that she did not want to hide her identity from me. Her stance seemed fierce, despite her suffering. She told me about her political activism with the workers when she was young, and also about her desire to keep making and selling paper boxes so she does not have to depend on her children. Before we parted, she hugged me tightly, very tightly. A few weeks after, I put on a photo with her and three other ex-political prisoners on my Facebook cover. According to Usmantri, this had made his mother really happy.*

*Then, on 21 July 2015, Usmantri contacted me: 'Good evening, Mbak Soe Tjen. On the 18th at around 12.15 am, my mother, Magdalena Agnes Ramilah, passed away, ten days after my father died. She had not been seriously ill, but she was just tired of the injustice in this country – that was also her last word before closing her eyes for good. She believed that you would continue her struggle to find justice in this country and looked at her photo with you for the last time, just before she died. Thank you for giving her attention and for making her proud.'*

# Iwan Kamah

Annus Horibilis

*Iwan and I have certain things in common. As the youngest child, Iwan is the one who knows the least about the history of his family during 1965. However, he is also the most keen to know. When I approached his siblings, they did not show as much interest in my project as Iwan did. They asked me to contact Iwan instead.*

*Maybe not knowing instilled in Iwan and me a desire to 'catch up' with the other members of the family, who know a lot more, and compelled us to keep searching. Maybe ...*

Why did the communist insurgency happen on the evening of 30 September 1965? Why not other dates? After or before? Does it have anything to do with the commemoration of the sixteen-year anniversary of the Chinese Revolution then? With the birth of the People's Republic of China on 1 October 1949? And why China? Because I believe that country played a major role in the 1965 event. China had been trying its hardest to get power in Indonesia. If any PKI rebellion had been successful, I believe the Indonesian Independence Day would not be on 17 August, but on 1 October. Well, I did not experience the dark events of 1965 myself. But I feel that those bloody events changed the lives and fates of our family. These events made me almost not recognise my father.

My family settled in Makassar in 1950, a year after my parents got married in their hometown, Gorontalo in North Sulawesi. A few years after, my parents moved to another house, right opposite of the South Sulawesi governor's office. That house was also used as an office for Antara, the news agency for the region of East Indonesia. My father was the head of this office, therefore, our house was always busy.

When night fell and *ayah* [father] happened to be at home, officers from Minahasa used to play bridge at our home, including people who took part in the Permesta rebellion[71] in 1957-1958. Permesta was a half-hearted rebellion against Jakarta. They believed that the centralised division of funding was unfair to the eastern part of Indonesia. My father was pro-Jakarta, but their friendship rose above political divisions. So they all still maintained their relationships despite their opposing political views. Ventje Sumual, who was

---

71  Permesta was a rebellion against the Indonesian government declared by civil and military leaders in East Indonesia in 1957.

then a colonel and the leader of the Permesta rebellion, continued to care for my father and our family. Later, he even gave my sister a job at his company.

## 1957-1965

During this period, many important events happened in Makassar. From the attempted murder and grenade attack against President Sukarno at the end of 1957, and the Darul Islam rebellion commanded by our neighbour, Kahar Muzakkar. Darul Islam is a fundamentalist Islamic group that demanded the establishment of an Islamic state in Indonesia and the application of sharia law. The radical group started in 1942 and led several rebellions in different parts of Indonesia during the 1940s and 1950s. Probably not many people knew that Kahar had a Caucasian wife. She wore a veil and both often came to our home. Kahar gave a draft of his book to my father. A few years later he was shot dead by the Indonesian army.

Because *ayah* had been involved in the biggest news station in Indonesia, we met many famous politicians and public figures, such as Adam Malik [the ex-Vice President of Indonesia], Djawoto [the last Indonesian ambassador to China before Soeharto came to power], and Arnold Monnutu [the first Indonesian ambassador to China in 1953]. Arnold Monnutu was also the person who changed the name Batavia to Jakarta, when he was the Minister of Information in 1949. 'When I came to Jakarta for the first time, I stayed with Djawoto', my mother recalled. Once my mother woke up in the middle of the night, and found Djawoto sleeping on a couch while a puppet show was playing on the radio. 'He woke up if the radio was turned off', mama said.

In 1962 my mother set foot for the first time on the island of Java and visited the headquarters of the Antara news station there. This was a shock for her, as our life in Makassar around this time was quite pleasant and organised. In the 1950s, many homes in Makassar already had gas for cooking, for instance. But Jakarta was so different. As soon as she looked out from the window of the Antara office, she nearly vomited. This was the scene she was watching: some people were defecating in the river, and not far from it, others were washing rice or brushing their teeth with the same river water.

## *Annus Horribilis*

When Djawoto became the ambassador to China in Beijing, *ayah* received an invitation to attend the Asian and African Journalists Congress, to represent Indonesia. In Beijing, my father met the Chinese Premier, Zhou Enlai. A few months later, it was my mother's turn to be invited to that country, as his wife. For three months she toured around China, a country considered as the Centre of the Earth.

I call the year 1965 the *Annus Horribilis* for Indonesia because of the incidents which led to tragedy for so many people and also for our family: the rebellion of 1965. After my mother had attended the commemoration of the Chinese Revolution of 1 October 1965 in Tiananmen Square in Beijing, she returned to Jakarta. But in Jakarta, *ibu* was immediately taken to a military office (next to St. Ursula school in Banten) and interrogated there by Umar Wirahadikusumah [later the Vice President of Indonesia from 1983 to 1988].

What about *ayah*? Things were even worse! It seems it was so easy to slander anyone then. People then would rather be accused of being a robber or a thief, than a member of the PKI. On the order of M. Jusuf [a general who was also the Minister of Industry], my father had to be 'secured'. In other words, he had to be put in prison. We did not really know why M. Jusuf did it – he was a very close family friend, so we trusted him. Would it have been terrible if my father had not been 'secured'? Or did M. Jusuf just follow orders in imprisoning *ayah*? Securing or imprisoning? We do not know the answer even now. We did not know anything about communism and my father hated this ideology. Perhaps it was because my father worked in an agency once led by Djawoto, who was then serving as ambassador in Beijing. Perhaps.

*Ayah* was arrested in mid-1966. *Ibu* told me that the car that picked him up was parked very far away from home, so as not to stand out and attract people's attention. He was jailed in Salemba [Central Jakarta] for a few months. There, he saw political prisoners go insane. Many of them had been important people and even famous public figures during Sukarno's government, but their lives had been turned around 180 degrees. One of them suddenly started watering plants during heavy rain; others displayed even weirder behaviour. My father was finally released by one of Soeharto's generals, Sutopo Juwono.

We were required to move to Jakarta in 1967. My mother had to feed eight children, some were teenagers and some were still babies. I am the seventh kid, and I had just been born at the time. Released from prison in 1968, *ayah* had to see another bleak reality: many of his close friends had crashed down from the top like jumpers without parachutes. Once they had enjoyed posts as high-ranking officials; now they were doing menial jobs such as driving taxis in order to survive.

*Ayah* tried to get any job, but in vain. Fortunately, there was Mr. B.M. Diah, a famous journalist and a good friend of *ayah*'s, who gave him a job as a columnist at his newspaper, *Merdeka*. Another friend of *ayah* who was an important figure and a donor to the Indonesian Democratic Party at that time, Gembel Soediono, asked my dad to work with him in the field of mass media. Because of this, our situation was not too bad.

I honestly do not know what happened to him in prison because I only knew *ayah* for a very short time. But I was very close to him. I still remember he breathed his last breath right in my eye. He passed away in 1972. Because we did not have much, Gembel Soediono financed the funeral. We did not spend a cent.

After *ayah* passed away, a friend of his helped us financially. But even this was often not sufficient. Almost every year, when we were supposed to pay the rent, we were very nervous: would we have enough money? In the end, my family was scattered. Only four of us lived with my mother; the other siblings lived with our relatives in Sulawesi.

In Jakarta, we only survived through the kindness of my parents' friends. We settled down temporarily in Dairi Street in Tanjung Priok. Not long after we had to move to Indramayu Street in Menteng, and then to another house, in Djatinegara. In Djatinegara, I discovered how many people had been detained without trial at the end of 1965. Their children were often ridiculed. In fact, people also taught me to mock one of my friends – 'Son of the PKI!' – because they did not know what had happened to my own *ayah*.

My mother had her own close brush with the law. At the end of the 1970s, a good friend of *ayah*, Joesoef Isak, dared to publish the works of Pramoedya Ananta Toer. Well, when my *ibu* came to his house in Duren Tiga in South Jakarta, he gave her a pile of Pramoedya's books. At that time the Attorney General, Ali Said, had just announced that it was strictly prohibited to own Pramoedya's books. Anyone who owned these books would go to jail. 'Mama could be arrested if the police found out!' we said. And it was only because of the books!

## Again: China

The tragedy of 1965 has turned many people's lives upside down, especially those of the ethnic Chinese. Indonesia broke off relations with China in 1967, and Chinese culture was immediately suppressed. Chinese script was forbidden in public from 1966. The Chinese flag was not allowed to be flown anywhere in this country, not even during an international event, such as sporting competitions. If China won in a certain competition, the flag raised was that of the organisation representing China. China often won the international badminton competitions, and the flag of the IBF [International Badminton Federation] was flown.

Magazines with any Chinese script were also censored. Many of them were covered with black ink, although the content might not have been political at all. Sinophobia had been going strong for about three decades in Indonesia. On the other hand, the radio in Beijing kept describing Indonesia unsympathetically, often using rude words, after 1965.

But this tension eased slightly in 1985, during the 30th anniversary of the Asian African Conference. The Chinese Foreign Minister, Wu Xueqian, and other Chinese high officials came to Jakarta, and that was the first time Soeharto shook hands with them, as long as he had been President. Then diplomatic relationships slowly resumed, and after the Prime Minister of China, Li Peng, visited Indonesia, the situation changed. The government allowed Chinese characters again, and Chinese culture was more accepted.

In 1989, Soeharto also visited Mikhail Gorbachev in Moscow for the first time. Following this visit, Soeharto announced on the national news: 'The people involved in 1965 can come back to Indonesia, as long as they are willing to be responsible for what they have done.' But what had they done? What did they have to be responsible for?

## Antara

*Ayah* never received his pension from his work at Antara, although he had given years to this company, from 1950 to 1966. He had sacrificed so much too for them: he refused an offer of a very prestigious and well-paid job by Manai Sophian [who was the ambassador to Russia at the time], because *ayah* had committed himself to his work at Antara. But what happened next?

A few years ago, during the era of President Gus Dur, I planned to bring my father's case to the then President of Antara, Mohamad Sobary. I did not want them to forget my father's dedication and hard work. My sisters disagreed with me. What for? Wouldn't it be like picking at old wounds? In the end, I did not do it.

Communism is extinct now anyway. It has become nothing but a dinosaur. The ideology, which has treated the people merely as numbers and has caused the suffering of millions, has collapsed. Well, with the openness of mass media nowadays, it is impossible for communism to grow. But maybe everyone has to carry his own cross. In my religion, Islam, we learn about submission: we just have to accept and surrender ourselves to faith. Submission – it is easier said than done. It has been very bitter for us. Very bitter.

**Photo J   Iwan Kamah**

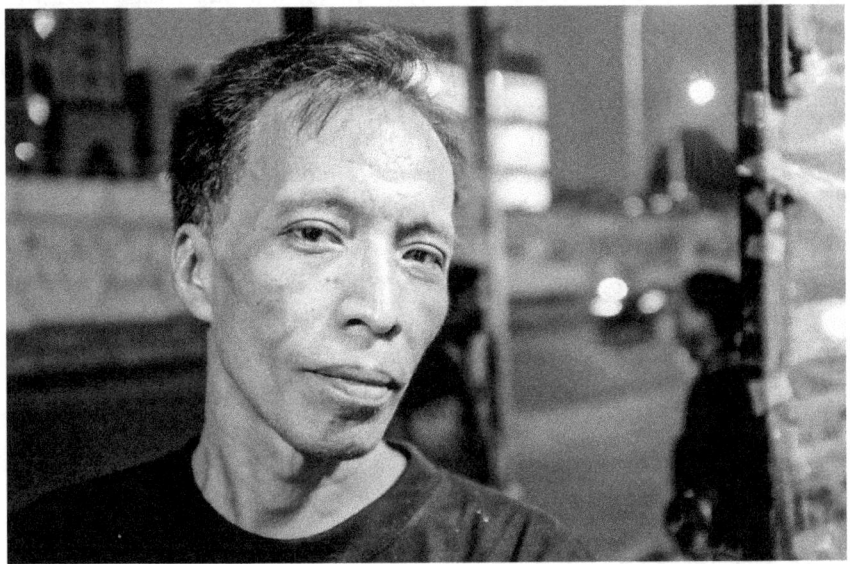

# Irina Dayasih

## The Biggest Traitor in Indonesia?

*Before I started writing her story, I had known about Irina for years, as I was one of the members of the advisory board of her organisation, Institut Ungu (The Purple Institute), which concentrates on women's theatre projects. We had never met, but we had kept in touch via email and Facebook. Little did I know that her father was a figure who was admired by my father. When I was a child, I knew the name Njoto from my schoolbooks as one of the biggest criminals and traitors in Indonesia. However, my father insisted otherwise: 'Njoto was a very intelligent man, much better than Soeharto!'*

*Of course, I thought my father was mad then ...*

*Now, in front of me, sits Njoto's daughter. A very simple woman, who tries to do anything she can for ex-political prisoners and their families. At a meeting with other ex-political prisoners and their families in Jakarta on 27 September 2013, those who had just found out that Irina is Njoto's daughter shook their heads in disbelief.*

*Njoto was a very important figure for many communist and left-wing sympathisers. He and Aidit were the top national leaders of the PKI, and he had been a state minister in Sukarno's cabinet. But Njoto was executed without trial, most probably at the end of 1965 or in early 1966. Even Irina does not know when and where her father was killed.*

For years, I never knew my family background, because I was separated from my parents and siblings since I was very young. I am the fifth child of seven brothers and sisters. My eldest sibling was born in 1956 and I was born in 1962. My mother was pregnant when Gestok happened. Just before that event, on 30 September 1965, we stayed at my auntie's home, because her son was about to have his first birthday the next day. Staying at our relatives when their children were about to have birthday parties was indeed our custom. But on his birthday, 1 October, mama received a phone call, telling us not to return to our home because of a critical situation that she did not really understand. After that, we lost our home. My family had to move from one place to another. We could only stay at one place for a maximum of two nights, otherwise it would have been too dangerous for the people accommodating us. Later, we lived in a student dormitory belonging to

CGMI,[72] and they were so kind to us. My mother was considered an aunt to the comrades there.

In 1966, my mother gave birth to my youngest sibling, a girl named Esti Dayati, but only two months after her birth, the soldiers found out about our whereabouts. They arrested my mother, who insisted that the children had to come with her. So we were taken with mama to the District Military Command in Budi Kemulyaan – Jakarta. I was there maybe for a few months, then my uncle took me to stay with him in central Java. I went to kindergarten there, also to an elementary school. Mama was only a housewife after she got married to papa. She was not involved in politics or any organisation at all, because in her ten-year marriage with papa, she had six children and was pregnant with the seventh when my father disappeared. The only reason for mama's imprisonment was being married to papa.

Mama was born in Solo in 1928, and grew up in the Mangkunegaran Palace [the home of the noble family of Solo]. She shares the same family lineage with Siti Hartinah Soeharto, known as Bu Tien [the wife of President Soeharto]. So my uncle tried to talk to Bu Tien about the release of my mother, but to no avail. Mama remained imprisoned. My eldest sibling, Svetlana, followed her into the prison, where the nine-year-old girl could hear the screaming of the tortured women in the prison. The next day, the officer usually asked Svetlana to clean the blood off the floor.

One of my uncles decided to pay a large amount of bail so mama could be released. She came back to us in January 1967 and I could meet her: 'My mama is back.' I finally had a mother again!

In June 1969, when I was in the first grade of elementary school, out of nowhere, a car stopped near our house. Several people entered our house with the mayor of Wonogiri [a town in Central Java]. My mother was taken away with my sister, Esti Dayati, who was only two years old then. I only had mama for a short while, then they took her away once more. I would not see her again until thirteen years later. Now that my mother was in jail for the second time, my siblings and I stayed with my auntie in Solo. But only two years later, my auntie's husband passed away. My auntie was stressed out because she did not work and did not have enough money. She had to sell her house and she could not cope: we had to be distributed to several relatives in different cities and islands. I was sent to South Sumatra, to an uncle whom I had never met before. Maybe because we were used to accepting

---

72   CGMI (Consentrasi Gerakan Mahasiswa Indonesia, or the Unified Movement of Indonesian Students) was one of the largest student organisations in Indonesia.

whatever condition we had to live in, no one complained. We never felt that we were being cast away. I just felt very lonely at times, because I had to face everything on my own. For years, I never met my siblings and we could only communicate by letter.

A child from Jakarta, who moved to a small town, especially outside of Java, was strange indeed. Usually what happened is the other way around: kids from small towns go to Jakarta to get a better education. But why did I do the opposite? I was quite confused myself. There were so many things that made me confused and wonder, but I never asked.

## My mama

After being moved from one prison to another, mama was released in 1978. I was still studying at a high school in a village in South Sumatra, so I could not see her. We also did not have much money to spend for this kind of thing. So I had to wait.

Mama was living at our relative's home. To earn a living, she did some sewing. After I completed my high school in 1982, I could go 'home' to Jakarta and meet my mother for the first time after we had been separated for thirteen years. My mother and three of my elder siblings rented a very simple house in Rawamangun in East Jakarta. For years and years to come, we stayed in the same *kampong* but we had to move to many different houses to get accommodation we could afford. My siblings and I eventually got a mortgage to buy a tiny house in Pamulang, Tangerang [about 25 km west of Jakarta]. That is where my mother lives now.

## The Secret of My father

Around the 1980s, when our family was still renting a house in Rawamangun, Oei Hay Djoen,[73] who used to be a close friend of papa, lived not far from us. He was active in Lekra and the PKI before being arrested and later sent to Buru. When we were chatting at his house one day, suddenly he asked me: 'Do you know who your father is?' I shook my head, because indeed no one had told me. Oei Hay Djoen continued: 'Do you know his name?' Again I shook my head. Not even my family had told me this information. Hay Djoen nodded his head several times then chuckled slightly. He asked

---

73   Oei Hay Djoen is also discussed in the memoir of Oei Hiem Hwie.

me to follow him, produced some slides and then showed them to me on a screen. I saw people at a serious political meeting. Hay Djoen pointed to one of the people there, and said that that was my father – the man was giving a speech in front of an abundant audience. *Is he an important person?* Then Hay Djoen said slowly: 'Your father's name is Njoto, one of the state ministers during the Sukarno's era, the Vice Chairman of the PKI.'

I was silent for a while. My heart pounded very loudly, I was confused about how to react. So this apparently had been the big secret of our family. We (including me!) turned out to be part of the political turmoil that was told in the history of this country. Imagine the horror! Yes, it turned out I was a child of one of the figureheads of the PKI! The name 'Njoto' had indeed decorated the school textbooks, as one of the greatest traitors and villains of the Republic of Indonesia.

Hay Djoen was very gentle and understanding: he was aware of my confusion and shock. He tried to console me by telling me how great my father was and also the great deeds that my father had done. Three of my eldest siblings had been aware that they were the children of Njoto. My elder siblings of course carried heavier burdens, as they were more aware of who their father was, and that the name Njoto was mentioned at their school and by their teachers as the bane of this country. They just had to stay calm and try not to get too angry about it.

And me? Although I had not known who my father was, every time the teachers told us about the evil of the PKI, I just kept quiet and thought to myself that that was not true. Somehow I knew that the disappearance of my father and the imprisonment of my mother had something to do with the PKI. I did not believe any of what the teachers said about the PKI, especially because mama was such a loving and kind person. I had never heard her complain or see her cry, despite what had happened to us.

After I found out who my father really was, other relatives told me that he had helped many people. He had paid for the studies of his friends' children when they did not have enough money. I think that is why no one minded helping us and also paying for our education after the 1965 tragedy befell us.

But amongst my family members, it is somehow still taboo for us to talk about the past, about what happened to our parents. About Njoto. So we hardly talk about it. We keep it silent. One of the reasons is maybe Njoto is such a big figure, and we cannot be compared to him. We are just very ordinary people – we are nothing compared to Njoto. Amongst us seven brothers and sisters, only the youngest has been able to go to the university. And that was because all of us had been working and could help her study. I am just glad that none of us has serious psychological problems.

**Photo K    Irina Dayasih at her apartment block in Jakarta**

## After That …

I was able to work as a teacher, because of a friend's help. However, later my employer at the school found out who I was and I got fired. Not long after, there was a friend who offered me a job at an NGO, because she knew I was unemployed. I was not actually an activist, but I worked for different NGOs for a few years. I mainly worked in administration. We were quite careful then, as there were many activists who were kidnapped.

In 2007, I quit working at NGOs because I got bored of working behind a desk. I wanted to do more fieldwork and interact with people. So I helped some friends who have moved out from Indonesia and live in Europe – most of them were the people who were banned from coming back to Indonesia by Soeharto because of their links to Sukarno or communism. After Soeharto stepped down, they were able to come back and did a lot for the country. Straight away, they helped the victims of the earthquake in Yogyakarta and the tsunami in Aceh. They donated some money, and we used the money to fund some small businesses run by the people in Klaten. Not all of these people in Klaten are the victims of 1965. We taught them how to make handicrafts, to grow certain crops or to raise chickens, etc. Then, we lent them some money to start their small businesses, such as selling handicrafts, raising chickens and selling the eggs or making sweets and cakes. They had to pay back the money we lent them, so we could use it for other people. This worked really well, and we could help many people to earn a living, as many victims of 1965 still lived below the poverty margin. Many villages that were known as the red ones did not get any funding from the government, so they became poorer and poorer. We tried to identify these villages and worked with them. Our activities worked very well and we managed to help about 130 people. However, it was a pity that one of the committee members embezzled the money, so our project was halted in 2008.

Our friends in Europe, however, did not despair. They kept raising donations by selling food, batik, books, etc. Finally, we could make another start. As more and more people heard about this project and wanted to apply for the funding, it was difficult for us to meet them one by one. In 2013, we decided to gather them at a building called Shanti Dharma in Yogyakarta, so they could explain to us about their plans and what we could do to help them. The meeting was scheduled for Sunday, 27 October 2013, at 11 am. About 15 to 20 people said that they would attend.

On the day, people arrived a few hours before the meeting started. At 8:30 am, several women from Pati were already waiting in front of the room. However, at around 9 am, suddenly there was a phone call, which told me that the head of the district [*camat*] and the head of the local police wanted to meet the committee members of this event. I am not sure how they found out about this meeting, but at about 9:30 am these officials turned up with some intelligence officers. Around ten of them altogether. I tried to explain that this was a meeting to discuss how to improve these people's economic conditions and we were not about to hold some political or ideological discussion. They insisted that this meeting had to be cancelled immediately, especially because we had not obtained any permission from the police to do it. This was such a strange excuse, indeed. Why did we suddenly need permission? I told them that they could attend the meeting as well, so they knew what it was all about, and that we were not about to cause any trouble at all. They agreed and we shook hands to confirm that we had reached an understanding.

However, about fifteen minutes later, the head of the police came back with a group of men. There were so many of them that I lost count but I think there were at least 50 people. Several of them wore uniforms with FAKI [Front Anti Komunis Indonesia, or the Indonesian Anti-Communist Front] written on it. They aggressively entered the room and some stood really close to me. The head of the police told me that these people wanted the meeting disbanded: 'It is our duty to guard the safety of the people, and for this reason, we must supervise all of you here.'

One of the men in uniform barked loudly: 'If they cannot be supervised, then...?' This was answered by a loud chorus: 'Then we must finish them!', followed by chanting: 'Yogya rejects communism! Communism is evil! Death for the communists! Killing the communists is halal!'

I tried to remain calm and told them that not all of the participants had arrived. I could not reach them as many of them came on their motorbikes and wouldn't answer the phone when they were driving. So I asked these people to be patient. The leader of FAKI, Burhanuddin, stood up and said: 'This is the congress of communist cadres, right?' I told him that that wasn't true: 'How could there be such a congress, if there were only a few people attending it and we would only talk for a few hours?' I asked him to attend the meeting and see for himself whether his 'accusation' was right. After a long discussion, finally we agreed to cancel the meeting as long as the police guaranteed our safety. The police agreed.

We shook hands again, but there was someone screaming outside. I asked the police to check what was happening. A man, still wearing a helmet, came into the front yard, covering his bleeding mouth: 'They hit me!' His lips were torn and his face swollen. The police came to him, but instead of helping him, they pushed him and demanded his identity card so that they could record who he was. He had come to accompany his father, he explained. Then he said softly: 'Please help my father. He is outside.' His father had also been beaten up quite badly and been knocked to the ground. Everything was very chaotic. I could not find that man's father. I panicked and rang my friends to get help. Finally, an ambulance came.

Five people had been injured quite badly during this incident. Later on, we found that man's father. Another attendant tried to help him by taking him away on his motorbike, but he ended up being beaten as well. As that man's father is 62 years old and was hit really hard on his temple, so his condition was rather critical. We talked to someone from Legal Aid, and they have been trying to help us. They have demanded the government take action. But nothing has been done even now. Nothing!

We just have to keep fighting, Soe Tjen. I wish I had met your father because he must have known quite a bit about Njoto. My father was born and grew up in Bondowoso [East Java]. My grandfather was an activist for Indonesian independence. He was detained by the Dutch and died in the death train which transported the prisoners from Bondowoso to Kalisosok prison in Surabaya. Without ventilation or water or food, 46 people died slowly on that train. As your father was active in the party and both our fathers were from East Java, there might have been members of our families who knew each other. I wish I could hear about my father from your father. I want to know what he thought of my father. But I am sure your father must be in peace now, and is proud of your work.

*I told Irina that I wanted to meet her mother some time, but Irina's mother, Soetarni, passed away on 6 September 2014, before I had the opportunity to meet her.*

*In mid-July 2015, I came to Irina's apartment in Jakarta, with several friends of the 1965 family. On my way to Irina's place, I texted Adi Rukun, who was also in Jakarta then. He made his way to her place straight away. Another small reunion of the 1965 survivors.*

# Wayan Windra

*Bapak* was Slaughtered in Front of Me

*Wayan Windra was born in Beringkit village in Bali in 1952. When I told him my intention about writing the stories of the victims' families, he was very enthusiastic and was willing to support me as much as he could. He stated that it was always his desire to have his story published, so that more people could find out the truth, but he also understands that many victims' families are still not willing to do this for fear of the repercussions.*

Dad often said to me: 'I really hope you can be a fighter pilot one day.' That was of course a mere dream. We were poor villagers, and father's only inheritance was a Dutch bike, which was quite a luxury in our village then. I have many beautiful memories of riding with father on this bike. He often took me to town to buy books, pens or dictionaries. We would often eat meatballs together. Sometimes, we watched a movie in town, or attended a carnival to welcome international visitors who came to Bali. In the 1960s, not many village children were like me, as many of them had never been to town. I had special experiences with my father, because he was active in the PKI. We often went to ceremonies held by the PKI or organisations linked to the PKI. Although they were often quite far away, father still biked there with me. We usually sat at the front, maybe because father was quite an important figure in the farmer's movement [BTI]. If we went to visit farmers from other villages, we usually brought some boiled cassavas or sweet potatoes and coffee for them. We often shared a simple meal with the members of mass organisations like the PKI, Partindo and Pemuda Rakyat,[74] and this spirit of togetherness I will never forget. This is what I always remember from my father: his enthusiasm of community spirit.

But because of this enthusiasm, father was slaughtered in our small village in Bali. I vividly recall that moment: Sunday, 5 December 1965, about 10:30 am. My mother had an asthma attack that morning, and I went by bike to buy an aspirin in the next village. But at the border of the village, I saw a line of men holding weapons, such as swords, batons, machetes, sickles and many other sharp things. Their faces were painted with charcoal, chalk, ink or other coverings that made them look more horrible and aggressive.

---

74  Partindo or Partai Indonesia (the Indonesian Party) is a nationalist party that strived for the independence of Indonesia; Pemuda Rakyat (People's Youth) was the youth wing of the PKI.

Maybe this was done to hide their true identities and also to frighten us more. I rushed back home to tell my family but father was no longer at home and everyone was already panicking.

Before this first massive attack, there had been other smaller attacks. A few men came and threatened us, and they also ransacked houses. However, that Sunday was not like before. Thousands of people and *tameng*[75] raided the village while cheering loudly, like they were about to have a party. Everyone in the village ran out of the house to find a hiding place. My grandfather ducked into a nearby kitchen fireplace, while my grandmother joined several other villagers who hid in a field on the edge of the river.

That massive group of people violently and passionately started destroying our village and were ready to devour us, as this was a feast for them. Indeed, our small village was known as a red settlement. There were only around a hundred households here, and we were surrounded by thousands of them. If the elders of the village had not submitted to this mob, our village would have been completely wrecked. But there would have been victims from the other side, because many people in our village were martial artists and many of them would have definitely gone over the edge if our warriors had fought them. There would have been a worse bloodbath.

My mother, her children and several other people sought refuge in the temple, but the mob ordered us out. The adult males were separated from the others. That was when I saw *bapak* amongst the crowd: he was dragged to the field next to the temple. According to several eyewitnesses, people in the mob took turns punching my father.

An ex-freedom fighter, father was also a member of Esti (a kung-fu group), so father did try to defend himself although he carried no weapon. He managed to deflect the swords and knives of his opponents. He could have kept fighting for longer, but they threatened if he did not give up, they would butcher his whole family. Because of this, he stopped fighting and let them beat him up.

That day, my father, my uncle, and two other people were killed. Their bodies, which were entirely battered by the ordeal, were lying on the road. When it was dark, we dragged their bodies away and held a funeral. Most of the adult males went to the grave, but I went along with my aunt. In our village, there was no electricity then, so we had to use flashlights. The rain made our trip to this dark, secluded area increasingly difficult. I felt really sad, afraid, anxious, angry, disgusted: everything was mixed.

---

75  A mass murderer in Bali is called a *tameng*.

The terror continued in our village. The crackdown to find communists in the village kept going. Cowards turned up everywhere. Many of the residents betrayed their own village: they blamed my father, uncle and my family for our leftist ideology, which led us all to be branded as PKI. In my small village, they ended up slaughtering at least fourteen people (including my father and uncle).

In the adjacent villages, two cousins of my father were slaughtered and my eldest cousin disappeared. A *tameng* from the neighbouring village proudly told my mother how he joined a troop of mass murderers to crush the PKI in Tegalbadeng village (which is rather far from our village). There, the stomach of a young mother who was pregnant was slashed until her baby came out, splattered in blood. Tegalbadeng village was wiped out. All the buildings were levelled to the ground because the village was 'red' and was accused of causing the death of a soldier.

**Photo L   Wayan Windra, holding a photo of his father in front of the spot where he was butchered and murdered in 1965**

We were increasingly ostracised by the villagers, because the people wanted to save themselves. Only a few months after my father and uncle died, my grandfather and grandmother also passed away, maybe because of the terrible sadness for having lost two children at the same time in such a brutal way.

Shortly after, another uncle of mine also passed away. The trauma from the tragedy as well as the endless fear made my mother suffer from palpitations.

I was still in the first year of junior high school then. I decided to quit school after one of my seniors, who was in the second year of junior high school, was picked up and murdered for no clear reason (many people said he was murdered at a graveyard). Most of our textbooks were also burnt at school. Moreover, because I was the eldest (with five younger sisters), I had to replace my father's position as the breadwinner and the head of the family. Every day, I hunted frogs, lizards, dragonflies, grasshoppers, moths, crickets, anything, to feed my younger siblings. I also had to work as a labourer to support them.

The year after, one of the committee members of a Catholic foundation requested me to go back to school. Fortunately, there were still Catholic foundations that were sympathetic to us, the children of the victims. I eventually went to the Catholic school; I had a uniform, but no books, pens or pencils. This situation made it hard for me to study, so I fell behind. I became a bad student, even though my family was full of intelligent people. My grandfather had his own views about life – he did not just follow what most people said or believed. He never prayed. Indeed, nominally, my family were all Hindus. But, in practice, each of us had the freedom to think and believe what we liked. My grandfather was an adherent of Samkya, an atheistic Hinduism, which is a forerunner of Buddhism. Its teachings were not far from Marxism. Father, uncle and I still prayed in the temple, but after praying they sometimes shouted 'Long live communism!' In the past, eccentric people like them were more accepted, but after 1965, the pressure to obey the ideology was crushing. Perhaps the appalling social and political conditions had abolished my desire to read and learn at school. I finished junior high school with much difficulty, while continuing to be a farm worker. Although I passed a senior high school entrance test, I could not afford to pay the fees. I was really disappointed that I finally had to leave school completely. I felt very helpless.

I decided to move to Jakarta to find a job to support my siblings and pay for their education. However, at that time, my mother's health was getting worse. In 1990, I had to go back to Bali to look after her. Indeed, after my return, mother's condition gradually improved, but her medication had severe side-effects, and her kidney was damaged. She passed away in 2006.

Even to this very day, many people still behave strangely towards us, because of the stigma of being the children of the PKI. The sad thing is that even though my village was known as the red village, the majority of the people there supported Soeharto and Golkar during the New Order period, because many of the people who had attacked and ostracised us were from PNI.[76] They were not politically aware, so they thought that the mass murder in our village was the fault of the PNI, of Sukarno's people. So, they became fans of Soeharto.

I just hope for a change. Perhaps this hope also gave me the courage to visit the home of a Buru Island ex-political prisoner, about 20 years ago. Because I did not know the exact address, I asked someone in a shop: 'Excuse me, do you know where Pak Adi Adnyana lives, sir?'

The person I asked stared at me for sometime, then asked, 'Who are you?' I replied by lying, 'I am also from Buru Island.' He seemed shocked and hugged me warmly, 'Oh brother, comrade, a true survivor ... I am glad we can meet!' What a great sense of solidarity and brotherhood he had!

**Photo M** Right to left: Wayan Windra, Soe Tjen Marching, Adi Adnyana (an 85 year-old ex-Buru prisoner) and his wife at Adi Adnyana's residence in Bali

*In mid July 2015, my husband and I visited Wayan Windra in his village. He welcomed us with his children and sister to the home where the tragic incident happened. They had no choice but to stay in the same place, as local custom prohibits them from selling the house. In the evening, Wayan drove us to visit*

---

76   Sukarno is one of the founders of the PNI (Partai Nasional Indonesia, or the Indonesian National Party). However, at the end of 1965, the party was split into left and right wings.

*Adi Adnyana, an eighty-year-old former Buru prisoner, who lived really simply with his wife. Adi told us that before the political prisoners were released, they were warned not to see each other and the authorities kept an eye on who they met. Although a few still saw other ex-political prisoners secretly, there was always the fear of discovery and that they would be imprisoned again. Now they can meet openly at last. Wayan visits this couple regularly and brings them food because the government does not take any notice of the victims, who have to look after one another.*

# Kristianto Budi

## My Family's Dark Secret

*I met Kristianto Budi (pseudonym) via a mutual friend of ours, Dede Oetomo, the most prominent gay activist in Indonesia. It turned out that we had been friends on Facebook for a few years, and he lives in my hometown, Surabaya. Because of his present post as a lecturer, he is still worried about revealing his real identity. We started chatting on Facebook, followed by meeting in Surabaya several times. He was one of the speakers when I held the public screening of* The Act of Killing *at the beginning of August 2014.*

When I had just begun my study at university, I was searching for my belongings in several cupboards and found my father's dismissal letter. A dismissal letter? What happened to my father, actually? No one had told me about this. No one had ever said that my father was sacked from the army.

*Bapak*'s dismissal is still a taboo in my family, especially for *ibu*. They have been hiding this from me even now, so that I can only sum up what happened to my father by remembering their past conversations or what others had said, by recalling several incidents when I was young and by looking at documents related to my father. There are many things I still do not understand, or cannot explain about my father.

*Bapak* was born in 1925 and was an Indonesian National Army officer. He had been sent to deal with several rebellions, such as Permesta in the eastern part of Indonesia and the Islamic rebellion (DI/TII), which aimed at establishing an Islamic state.[77] My father used to be the vice-commandant of Battalion 521 in Kediri [East Java], one of the battalions that were loyal to Sukarno. However, they did not fight against Soeharto's coup in 1965. Why?

Before the murder of the generals in Jakarta in 1965, my father already knew about the formation of the Council of Generals, that is, the group of subversive army generals which was plotting against Sukarno. Although he did not know exactly who the founders or the members were, my father heard that this council intended to get rid of Sukarno. After G30S happened, there was huge confusion amongst the officers. Many people were arrested

---

77 Although Indonesia is the nation with the largest Muslim population in the world, it is not an Islamic state. DI/TII stands for Darul Islam/Tentara Islam Indonesia (Darul Islam/Islamic Armed Forces of Indonesia), an Islamist group that aimed for the establishment of an Islamic state of Indonesia.

and murdered. Father and his troops were awaiting orders to move, but none came. Sukarno, as the supreme commander of the armed forces, did not give orders to them at all.

After the restructuring of the army [due to the events of 30 September], my father was reassigned as the deputy commandant of Battalion 530 in Madiun. Then, he saw a warrant of the commander to attend the Armed Forces Day Ceremony on 5 October. But the strange thing was that the battalion commander, Lt. Col. Bambang Sumpeno, received the order that the army had to carry weapons (command level I). This meant that they had to carry full combat ammunition. However, usually in such a ceremony, this was not allowed. Before *bapak* had the opportunity to enquire about this oddity, he had been arrested. Basically the officers who were loyal to Sukarno never got the chance to protect Sukarno.

There were also several officers in the suburban areas who did not agree with the massacre of the PKI members and sympathisers. Many of them were also arrested. Based on the story of *bapak*, the massacre of the PKI members happened only after the special forces, RPKAD,[78] arrived. One of the most terrible duties that my father still kept in his mind was arresting the followers of *mbah* Suro [the spiritual teacher in the border area of Blora-Ngawi-Bojonegoro]. *Mbah* Suro's training centre is right on the edge of the River Bengawan Solo. Indeed, most of *mbah* Suro's followers were PKI members or alleged communists. They came to the centre to seek refuge or to look for some peace of mind because of being terrorised by the army or the special forces. My father's army received no command involving murder or fire, so they were not armed. They just came to the training centre to arrest the people there. However, the RPKAD turned up later and shot them all. Their bodies fell to the ground near the river or into the river, and the Solo River was flooded with blood.

Many internal conflicts occurred, not only in the army but also within RPKAD. Because of this, one unit of the special force in Kandan Menjangan in Kartasura [Central Java] was sent to West Kalimantan, to guard the border with Malaysia. However, the news spread that this unit wanted to rebel and all of them were arrested. When I was young, I read the history of the communist rebellion in West Kalimantan involving the PGRS and Paraku.[79] I wonder whether this rebellion was related to the Kandan

---

78  RPKAD was a paramilitary force assigned to murder communists and their sympathisers. Under their commander, Sarwo Edhie (father-in-law of the ex-President of Indonesia, Susilo Bambang Yudhoyono), the force wiped out several 'red' villages. Sarwo Edhie also proudly boasted that his force had murdered three million people during this genocide.

79  The PGRS was the Pasukan Gerilya Rakyat Sarawak, or Sarawak Guerrilla Force, and Paraku was the Pasukan Rakyat Kalimantan Utara or the North Kalimantan People's Force.

Menjangan force. Most probably it was, also because their commander was Brigadier General Soepardjo [the senior officer who was accused as one of the leaders of the G30S rebellion]. This unit was wiped out.

Not long after that, the government house that was about to be given to my father became an issue. My family could no longer have the house. The last rank held by my father was major, and he could have been a lieutenant colonel if he had not been arrested and dismissed from the army.

The stigma on my father was further affirmed because my uncle, who happened to be a left-wing activist, sought refuge at my parents' house. This uncle of mine was later arrested at the home of my family. He was a teacher, living in the area of Yogyakarta. He was very intelligent and had been one of a delegation of Indonesian students in the KMAA [Konferensi Mahasiswa Asia-Afrika, or the Asian-African Students Conference] in 1950s-1960s. But due to the allegation that he was a communist, my uncle was thrown into prison until 1980, while my father was sent to the Rampal prison in Malang [East Java], and then to the Lowokwaru prison [also in Malang] from 1967.

When I was at elementary school, mother asked me to come with her to visit my father at the Rampal prison. On every visit, mother always lied and said to me that we were visiting *bapak*'s base camp. Because *ibu* said that my father was a soldier and we were in the military environment, I did not suspect that she lied. Maybe this was because my mother was really good at lobbying the officials, and also because my father still had friends or former subordinates in the prison, he was not strictly guarded.

Likewise, after my father had been moved to the Lowokwaru prison in the same city, I also often visited *bapak*. But I remember a strange conversation between my mother and my father. I heard them talking about a rice ration which was not edible. Then I asked: 'What's wrong? Is the food not good here?' But *ibu* quickly diverted the topic of conversation.

When *bapak* was released in 1977, I was about ten years old. My father told me when he came home that now he was retired from the military service, so he could stay together with my mother and me from then on. Basically, they were making every effort possible to hide the truth from me, so that I could remain proud of my father. They created the figure of my father as an army officer without blemish. Of course, my father's identity card was stamped ET [ex-political prisoner], but the creativity of my mother saved us. *Ibu* split the *Kartu Keluarga*,[80] so from then on, *bapak* had not been on

---

80 The *Kartu Keluarga*, or Family Card, records information about the members of a household. This card is usually needed when someone wants to apply for other documents such as a resident's card, passport, etc.

the same card as ours. He had a separate family card. My uncle did a similar thing, so that his daughter could get a proper education. He separated his daughter's Family Card, and joined her with my mother and me. So she became my eldest sister in the Family Card. Even with the ET stamp, *bapak* still tried to get any work he could, such as selling furniture or a bit of administrative work. My mother became the breadwinner of our family.

We were still lucky, because my mother did not get fired from her position as a judge. However, she could not get a promotion until her retirement in the 1990s: her rank stayed the same. Mother was a very smart lady, and she became well acquainted with various people in the bureaucracy, and also with high officials, which made our life easier. This was also all done to hide my father's identity. My friends, teachers, professors and others just knew that I was the son of a retired military officer.

Yet, I hit a stumbling block when I intended to become a lecturer at one of the state universities in Surabaya. At that time, I was the assistant lecturer for Dede Oetomo. He advised me to apply for a lectureship, and that was indeed my goal. Nonetheless, my application to become a lecturer was rejected. I suspected that this rejection was caused by the fact that I was the son of an ex-political prisoner. Most probably, the people at this state university checked my family background before making a decision. So I applied to a Catholic University in Surabaya in 2004. I was accepted there and had no problem at all. I am still a lecturer at the same university.

Around the year 1999, the era of President Wahid, my father with some friends tried to sue the military, because they had been fired, vilified and criminalised by the military without any valid reason. They had tried to do this for months, with countless meetings, but in vain. Even since my father died in 2001, the military still totally ignores all these demands. The story of my father has been kept within our family and close friends only, until recently, when I decided to reveal it to you so that people can know the truth about the massacre, about Soeharto's manipulation and about the pain that still burdens millions of people.

*The last time I met Kristianto Budi, he told me that he was required to teach citizenship at his university. This subject was created during the New Order era, to spread hatred against the communists. It was thus an irony that Kristianto was teaching it now. However, he saw it as an opportunity to influence his students.*

# Sari Marlina

The Flight of My father

*I had known Sari Marlina years before my project started, via the Facebook group Indonesian Atheist, in which we were both members. She replied to my announcement about my plan to gather personal stories of the families of the victims in 1965 Indonesia right away. A freelance photographer, Sari posts actively on her Facebook page, commenting on the social and political conditions in Indonesia.*

I was close to *bapak,* since I was young. We often watched the *BBC News* from London together until really late at night or even at dawn. Sometimes we sat outside, and while watching the moon, *bapak* told me a story about himself.

He was born in Klaten [Central Java], in 1945, the second child of six brothers and sisters. His parents gave him the name Sabar [meaning 'patient'], as they hoped that my father would be patient in facing difficulties in life, especially because they lived around gambling houses and other sites of petty crimes. But after members of the Communist Party got active in his village, gambling was gradually disappearing and the crime rate reduced. This attracted my father to the party.

When my father had not yet graduated from high school, his uncle Wardoyo, a party member in Jakarta, asked him to join. My father thought that he was too young, but Wardoyo assured *ayah* [father] that he was able to do it. One night, with three other men, young Sabar said his oath as a Communist Party member. Because Sabar was sharp, other political parties also wanted him to join them. To prevent Sabar from joining other parties, Wardoyo asked Sabar to come with him to Jakarta. Sabar got a job at the Directorate of People's Agriculture in the Pasar Minggu area and he lived together with Wardoyo.

In mid-1965, the gossip about the establishment of the Council of Generals from the army spread. This Council of Generals was believed by some to have planned a coup against Sukarno. Then, another rumour: the Cakrabirawa regiment [which had a duty to guard Sukarno] and the air force tried to counter the coup by kidnapping seven generals. But Sabar and his friends did not know for sure whether this was true or not. So every day they listened to the radio belonging to one of the party cadres.

On the morning of 1 October 1965, they heard that Colonel Untung with his Cakrabirawa troops[81] had occupied the state radio station [Radio

---

81  Cakrabirawa: the regiment with the duty of guarding President Sukarno.

Republik Indonesia, or RRI], and announced that they had established the Council of Revolution. They had arrested several generals to prevent the coup attempt. Later on, the announcement on the radio was completely different: Soeharto was in charge to save the country. Soeharto claimed the Council of Revolution had betrayed Sukarno.

Sabar and his friends knew then that there would be chaos – there would be a war between these two factions within the armed forces and they would be in danger. So they decided to stay together in that house, as this made them feel safer, while keeping their eyes open to see what would happen around them. One of the party cadres, a high school teacher, Kartinah, had to leave the house for a while because her husband was quite ill. Kartinah was also seven months' pregnant.

When Kartinah came back nearly at midnight on 1 October, they heard that there would be a search for PKI members and that the RPKAD had been spying on them. Straight away, the three of them (Kartinah, Wardoyo and Sabar) gathered all their party documents, as well as their ID cards and all their certificates. They tied all of these papers together and put them in the septic tank of the house. At dawn on 2 October, the three of them left the house by walking through the fields and bushes. They walked non-stop without eating for a day and a night – even Kartinah, who was heavily pregnant. Then they took the train to Bogor, and went straight to their friend's place. But it was impossible for them to stay there, so they had to continue their journey. They decided to go to Bandung. But Bandung was not much better: the troops were searching everywhere. They had to leave again, but where to? Finally, they headed further to the east, and arrived in Solo on 3 October. In Solo, they decided to split up. Kartinah and Wardoyo stayed in this city, while Sabar continued to Klaten and stayed there temporarily. The first two days were fine, but later on, Sabar heard that the RPKAD was entering small villages, including Klaten.

Arguments and conflicts spread amongst the people in the village, as they divided into 'left', 'right' and 'centre' groups. This made the PKI members more anxious, and several of them tried to hide in Pedan village. Thousands of them hid there, but the RPKAD surrounded this village as well. Luckily, they found a secret way to get out of the village, taking some food (usually rice with a little bit of some dish, wrapped in banana leaf) and some other essentials.

Then they were told that communists who had been caught had been brought to their homes and murdered sadistically in front of their families. What to do? Wait to be caught by RPKAD, or make another move? Sabar, his brother [Parlan], his cousin [Parno], and their friend Nardi decided to leave, for they did not want to be murdered in front of their families.

Towards dawn, they started their journey to the streets of a *kampung* there, as they knew that this was the time of day that the street pedlars started coming out. They were right – there were several vegetable pedlars passing by, and they asked them whether they could take their baskets and goods to disguise themselves. The vegetable pedlars seemed to understand their intention. Without saying much, they gave their baskets and vegetables to Sabar and his friends. With this disguise, Sabar and his friends got on a *dokar* [horse-drawn cart] to Ceper station. On the way, there were troops doing a search, and these four men covered their faces with the huge vegetable baskets.

At Ceper station, they got a train to Solo, and tried to stay with one of their relatives there. But their relative's house had been under the surveillance of RPKAD as well. They agreed to walk back to the station, barefoot, as they had no money left at all. Their clothes were dirty, their bodies smelled, and they carried a bag of clothes. This alerted the police, who asked them a few questions and ordered them to go back to Klaten. They promised to obey the police but it was a lie to help them escape. At the station, they went to Semarang instead, for Parlan knew this city quite well.

After they arrived in Semarang, they lived in a *kampong* of *becak* drivers for about three days, while making a plan to get out of Java to go to Sumatra. Parno and Nardi had stayed in Lampung before [South Sumatra], so they were familiar with the island. These *becak* drivers were very helpful, and they let the four men use the names of the *becak* drivers there. So Parlan became Samsuri; Parno became Parman, Nardi became Sunarjo and Sabar became Amijo. Several *becak* drivers got a travel permit (valid for three months), for these four new names. Before the four men left, the *becak* drivers also gave them clothes and sandals to make them look like real *becak* drivers. From Semarang, the four men went to Jakarta. The condition was very chaotic, as many people wanted to leave Java because of the uncertainty. At Gambir station in Jakarta, some travel agents helped them to reach Sumatra. These travel agents asked the four men together with other people who were going to Sumatra, to get in a car; then these agents took them to a two-storey building in a narrow alley. There, their money and belongings were snatched. That was the time when Sabar and his friends realised that these people must have been imposters. Because Sabar and his friends had almost nothing at all, the crooks got very angry and suspicious (actually the comrades had all hid their money inside their socks). One of the crooks was about to report them to the army but his friends intervened because they did not want to make things more complicated. So they let these four men go, while the others were still detained in that house.

Free from those sharks, Sabar and his friends looked for a bus to Tanjung Priok to find his relative, Siswo, who was an army officer. Siswo let them stay the night, and before they went to Sumatra, he also gave them money and some supplies for their journey. With Siswo's help, their trip to Sumatra went quite smoothly.

## Sumatra

Having arrived on this island, they walked to the village Raman Utara in Lampung. There, they decided to split so they did not attract too much attention. Sabar and Nardi went to a village called PC13, whereas Parlan and Parno went to Rejo Katon to stay with a friend. When Sabar and Nardi arrived in PC13, their friend told them that his family had been under surveillance as well, but this friend finally let them stay there. Sabar and Nardi tried to keep calm and tried to find a way out because they knew that their presence endangered this friend more.

The fate of Parlan and Parno was a bit better, because they stayed with a senior person in Rejo Katon village, and he was very well respected not only by the people but also by the head of the village. When the travel permits of Nardi and Sabar expired, they started getting very anxious. The head of the village also asked them to leave, or he would report them to the authority. The villagers had found out that they were fugitives from Java. Nardi and Sabar did not know where to go, so they went back to Java to renew their travel permit.

When they arrived in Semarang, they went to see their friends who got a huge shock. They told them it was a big mistake to come back to Java, as it was really dangerous for them: many of their friends had gone missing. So they decided to go to Jakarta. On the train to Jakarta, there was an incident in Cirebon, and all the passengers had to change trains. When they were waiting for the new train, they tried to get something to drink, but the sellers said that everything was sold out. Because they were so desperate and really thirsty, they kept pushing the seller to give them anything. Finally, he gave them water that had already been mixed with chilli – that was all he had. Sabar and Nardi drank it up straight away, although their mouths were burnt by the heat. They laugh about this, as that was very stupid indeed, and made them quite sick and weaker.

On the train, they had to hide in the toilet because they had no money to buy tickets. After arriving in Tanjung Priok, they went to meet Siswo, who was furious at them. Siswo said that their arrival in Java meant giving their lives to the army. Siswo told them how he had risked his career as an army officer to help them to get out of Java, but his efforts were in vain. Because of his anger, Siswo chased them away. Sabar and Nardi had to sleep with beggars and homeless people, but the army also kept an eye on them. Every night, the homeless people were asked to sleep under the light, and were inspected. Such a pressure made them very depressed, and they nearly lost their minds. Nardi wanted to kill himself, but Sabar tried very hard to prevent him.

He asked Nardi to get back to Siswo's house, and begged Siswo to help them again. He kept begging until Siswo was moved, and gave them money, but only enough to get on a one-way boat, back to Sumatra. At Merak harbour they had to undergo a security check. Many people were being interrogated. Without any valid travel permit, Sabar and Nardi would definitely be in trouble. The passengers were divided into two: male and female. The officers were taking a much longer time investigating the males. Sabar and Nardi made use of this, by sneaking in the female queue and pretending that they were too impatient to endure the long wait. Many women of course were very annoyed with them, and this chaos distracted the officers from checking the permits. They let the two men go. On the boat, they were trying to look for anyone who would be willing to lend them money to buy some food and to travel from the harbour to the nearest bus terminal. Coincidentally, an acquaintance was there, and they managed to borrow a bit of money from him to get them to Metro terminal, then they walked to Rejo Katon village. They were planning to live in the forest there.

## Sumatra: Again

Late that night they entered an empty hut in the village and stayed there. Several of the party sympathisers heard that these two men were back and tried to help them by sending food. They lived for about a month by being fed by various people. In the end, one of the sympathisers, Narto, asked them to live with him. Narto was a shaman in the *kampong* where Parlan and Parno had been staying, and he was well respected. So the four of them were reunited in the same *kampong*. They felt huge relief, as there was no one bothering them there. The *kampong* people seemed to protect them as well.

After about six months of living in this *kampong* without leaving it, they decided to visit one of their relatives outside it. In the house of that relative, they met another relative from Java, who had been looking for them. They panicked, thinking that the army must have found out where they were. They left the *kampong* immediately. Not long after they left, the army surrounded the *kampong*, but they had already gone. Their suspicion had been proven right!

Before they left, several of the sympathisers gave them an address to visit, and there they met other fugitives. These people had established an underground group, and tried to gather their followers. After that, they went from one house to another, from one room to another, from one stable to another, and one field to another. They made their trip via places which were hardly visited by other people, like old graveyards or 'haunted' alleys, and they always did it at night, or when it was raining heavily. This struggle to survive no matter what made them very tough. In that difficult situation, the party still tried hard to educate and hold discussions with the people, using the book of the former general secretary of the PKI [Sudisman], entitled *Kritik Autokritik*. They were trying to discuss the reformation of left-wing organisations and the management of the Communist Party.

The four men attended these meetings in a small village called Kali Gayor in South Lampung. This was a very secluded and barren village, and it was hardly touched by the government. This was the reason that the party chose it as a base. The tiny following of the party was slowly growing, but one time in 1968, a thief had entered the *kampung*. The police and security officers came to the *kampung* to look for the thief, and they were surprised to see so many non-locals there. Their intellectual appearance might have also aroused suspicion.

Using several inexperienced party cadres who lacked integrity and loyalty to their friends, the troops could capture other members of the party easily, from the top to bottom. Blood was flooding everywhere. In Seputih Raman and North Raman, the army killed every one, and not a single soul survived, except the few who managed to run away. Sabar, Parlan, Parno and Nardi were still together and loyal to each other. They managed to escape and hide in the bush around Seputih Raman.

But this time, the sympathisers had nearly all been murdered, and the residents' reaction to them was very different, because they now had to face a choice: either murdering the communist sympathisers or be murdered themselves. Many of the civilians took part in this mass murder because they had no choice. The four men lived among the high reeds, but as the dry season started, the farmers had to clear the land for planting rice. So the farmers and the army were cutting all the bushes and also the reeds. Parlan and Nardi ran as fast as possible, but it was in vain. They were caught straight away. Sabar and Parno managed to hide behind a thick bunch of high grass near an anthill. The troops passed through the area many times.

They searched but did not look behind the anthill. Then the troops left, taking only Parlan and Nardi.

In the late afternoon, the army and the people who had been brainwashed to help started the search again, but whenever they were near the anthill they just walked by it. One of the people suggested that they set the grass on fire, but fortunately none of them had a match. About the time of the Magrib prayer, they decided to stop searching and leave the place. After Sabar and Parno were sure that it was quite safe, they got out and decided to hide behind the banana trees behind the villagers' houses. They slept there, and covered themselves with dry banana leaves. The next day, the armed forces were more aggressive. They not only asked the local residents to look for these fugitives, but also brought helpers from Bali, who had spears and dogs. Then they set fire to the overgrown area. Sabar and Parno were watching everything from the far end of the field. After the army and the helpers saw everything burn (so if the two men were there, they would have been burnt to death), they left.

At night, Sabar and Parno came out of their hiding place and walked until they reached a dense field. They decided to live there. Every day, they survived by eating raw cassava. But this had made them weaker, because of a lack of nutrition. They were often dizzy as well, and assumed that this was because they did not consume enough iron. They decided to steal salt from a villager's kitchen. And they were right, for after consuming the salt they felt better. After about half a month living in that field, they left it and made a journey to see one of the communist sympathisers, Paijo. They were confident that Paijo would not betray them.

There was a full moon when they knocked at his house and Paijo got a shock when he saw two men who looked like Yetis. Their hair and beards were very long as they had not shaved for months and their clothes were very dirty and torn all over. He did not expect that Sabar and Parno were still alive. He gave them some scissors [to cut their hair and beards], but asked them to leave immediately for the threat for him was too high.

So Sabar and Parno were in the street again. They cut each other's hair and beards by the light of the moon. The next day at dawn, they were on a journey again, on foot, looking for anyone who was willing to help them. As they were walking, they realised that another loyal sympathiser lived not far away from where they were: Tarji. Around midday, they arrived at Tarji's house in Pringgodani Sukadana village, but he had already been taken away. His wife, however, was willing to help them under one condition: they could not stay in the house. So they were back in a field, not far from Tarji's. Every night, Tarji's wife would send food to them. In comparison to their suffering before, Sabar and Parno felt that they lived very comfortably in that field because they got proper food every day.

Meanwhile, the authorities were desperate as well as angry because they still had not succeeded in capturing the two fugitives. They told the political prisoners that in exchange for any information about Sabar and Parno, they would be released. Tarji's wife mentioned these two men to her husband. Tempted by the offer of the authorities, Tarji persuaded his wife to give them up, hoping that he could escape the brutality of the prison soon.

The day after, Tarji's wife sent food in the morning to the field where Sabar and Parno had been hiding. The two men were a bit surprised, as she did not usually come in the morning. Because they were hungry, they did not think too much about it and just opened the packet and ate the food. Soon after, they heard the sound of guns firing behind them. They ran away as quickly as possible, but Parno was immediately caught. Sabar ran across the road, but on the other side there were people waiting for him with various weapons in their hands, screaming: 'Kill him! Kill him! Kill him!' Sabar turned around and ran back to where the army was waiting. He was welcomed with a beating all over his body, until he was unconscious.

## The Prison

Both of them were taken to Puterpra [now, Koramil], the military district command there. There were tied, beaten and treated like animals. After three days at Puterpra, they were brought to another military station, and there they met the friends who had been manipulated to betray them. This was also to make sure that they got the right persons. The prisoners considered dangerous – about 60 of them – were separated. Sabar finally met his brother, Parlan, in the prison. Sabar, Parlan and Parno were amongst these 60 people, but Nardi was considered to be only a sympathiser, so he was moved to a district office and detained there. The authorities' promise to set free Tarji was never kept: he remained imprisoned.

Not long after Sabar arrived in that military command, he saw 23 men whose clothes were torn and who looked like beggars. These people told him that there used to be more than 2000 people detained in that place. Because conditions were so bad, many of the prisoners died and only these few people survived. The guards would put hundreds of people in a small cell, and these people often could not help stamping on each other, and killing their own friends that way. They also could not breathe properly, so by the morning many of them had collapsed or died. The dead ones would be tied on top of each other, piled onto a truck and thrown in a mass grave.

From these 23 people, three were ordered to join people who had just arrived. They were all placed in small cells without being allowed to get out at all. Each cell contained three to five people. Sabar, Parno and Parlan were in the same cell with another man from Lampung, named Slamet. The cell was about 2.5 x 2.5 metres with a toilet inside, without any lighting. The ventilation was a tiny window and there was a slot to put their meal in. They got one small bowl of unboiled water a day, for all the people in the cell. The first month, they only got rice and a small amount of vegetables. The second month, they were fed rice with *oyek* [dried cassava] without any vegetables. The third month, it got worse: only dried cassava without rice, and the cassava was dirty and rotten. The prisoners could hardly eat it because of the smell. Because they were really hungry, they washed the food using the water to flush the toilet, to get rid of the smell. Eventually, their health was getting worse because of malnourishment. One of the political prisoners, Supadi, who used to be a teacher, was paralysed because of this condition. To go to the toilet, he had to be lifted by his friends; and he had to be spoon-fed as well. For additional food, everyone had to be creative and tried to catch anything [edible] in the cell. If there was a mouse inside and they could catch it, that meant luck. If not, then they just had to put up with swallowing live lizards or dried cockroaches.

The criminal prisoners were treated much better than the political prisoners. They could have a shower and change their clothes every day, eat three times a day and do exercises in the morning. The political prisoners could see the much better life of the other prisoners from their cells.

Only after about five months were they allowed to get out of their cells to have a shower. They were asked to dry their bodies by baking themselves under the sun in the field. Most of them could not even stand up, so they had to crawl everywhere. Their bodies were merely skin and bone, but many of them tried to stay strong and entertained themselves by hunting for food around the cell, chatting or humming. During the day, they played communal chess with other prisoners, by sending estafette messages from one cell to another. At times, some of them would create communal stories, which were also transferred by an estafette. The thin plywood wall made it easier for them to communicate with each other in different cells.

In the second year, they were treated much better – just like the criminal prisoners. They got better food, they were given clothes and they could shower every day. Then, they were required to work as gardeners, builders or other workers needed by the military. Sabar became a typist in the office. After three years in prison, Sabar got the news that he would be released.

## But Where Would Sabar Go?

Not knowing where he should go after his release, Sabar decided to get married immediately to another political prisoner. She was a widow with three children, a former wife of a communist cadre who had been trapped by the authorities to betray his friends. Their wedding was organised by one of the staff at the military office, where Sabar used to work. After both of them were released, life was very tough as they had to face jeers and discrimination from the officials as well as the people around them.

## Sari Marlina

I was born in 1979, eight years after *bapak* was released. My second name was a combination of Marx and Lenin. Although *bapak* never intentionally discussed the PKI in detail, I heard about the PKI since I was young, because our family was ostracised and often called PKI. However, *bapak* taught us about the principles and ideas of the PKI, without naming them. Because of this, he had a big influence on me.

It is a shame that *ibu*, my mother, still adheres to Islamic law. She actually does not know much about politics. She was imprisoned just because of her first husband. When she was detained, she was three months' pregnant. She was allowed to give birth at home and soon afterwards she was imprisoned again, together with her baby. My mother still cannot forgive her first husband and somehow blames the PKI for what happened to her. She wanted us, her children, to have prestigious jobs and if possible, to earn a lot of money. Therefore, she asked me to be a midwife, because this profession is highly respected in my *kampong*.

On the other hand, *bapak* does not really care about what I wanted to be, as long as I was happy. His humanism has encouraged me to become an atheist and a socialist, and because of this, I joined the independent labour organisation in my city. I am now very interested in the history of Gestok, while my other siblings do not seem to show any interest in this. Even my elder sister used to idolise Soeharto, when she was young. She was indeed a very good student, and I think this was why she was also quite immersed in the dogma of the New Order education. *Bapak* never forced us to accept his opinion or to agree with him.

I guess because of our different ideological concepts, my elder sister and I have a very complicated relationship, especially after she found out that I had become an atheist. We have been estranged from each other, and we are not even friends on Facebook.

## Marriage

I got married for the first time in 2003. He was a Catholic. He had known the history of my family before we got married, but he did not mind it at all. In fact, he really respected *ayah*, because he was also an activist. My mother also did not mind him because he was willing to become a Muslim. This made her happy, as this meant I had converted someone to Islam. Little did she know that at that time, I had started becoming an atheist. But we got divorced in 2005.

In 2006, I got married for the second time, to a Muslim. He asked me to wear jilbab and I did it to make him and his family happy. But he was not satisfied with this, and asked me to keep obeying him, and if we had arguments, he would quote Islamic dogmas to say that women had to obey their husbands. Our first child was born in 2007, and he wanted her to become Muslim. On the other hand, I wanted my child to decide for herself when she was grown up, not to be made to follow certain convictions. The history of my parents was repeated in our marriage. The difference was that the conservative one was my husband, which made it even harder for me to challenge him, as he felt that he had more power and could force me to do what he wanted. He even reported me to his family if I upset him, and they asked me to divorce him. Because we loved each other, we kept trying.

Our second child was born in 2010, but in the same year, I decided to divorce him. He actually still loves me, and I have already forgiven him. After the divorce, he still asked me to go back to him. But I thought it was impossible for us to be together, so I told him honestly that I had become an atheist. Since then, he has stopped pursuing me.

After our divorce, I took off my jilbab, and this made my mother very upset. We had a long discussion, and I agreed to wear a jilbab when I meet a lot of people, but other than that, I will take off my jilbab. So here I am: an atheist with a jilbab.

*At the end of 2014, I heard that Sari Marlina had remarried. This time, to an atheist. In mid-2015, for the first time, I saw a family portrait of her (with her husband and two children), on Facebook.*

# Rito Aji

## The Son of Pudji Rahardjo

*I had known Rito Aji via Facebook for about three years, before he told me that his father had been imprisoned on Buru Island. Like many children of ex-prisoners who were born after their parents' arrest occurred, Rito has a huge desire to find out more, to get a clear sense of what happened and to uncover the truth about his family's history.*

When *bapak* was arrested in late 1965, I was still in my mother's womb, about two months along. I am the youngest of five siblings, the only boy. One of my uncles was also being hunted by the army at the time. He was a law student at Airlangga University, but could not finish his studies because he was on the run. Once, when he was hiding in our house, the police surrounded the place. My uncle managed to escape through the sewers. He has since changed his identity and become a Hajj (a religious devotee who has journeyed to Mecca).

*Bapak* had a good job at a big company, so without *bapak*, *ibu* had to struggle to feed the children. She used to be a teacher and lost her job, so she had to do whatever she could to make money, like selling food at the market. It was really hard for *ibu*, because on my father's side, there were many victims, but on my mother's side, there were many mass murderers. I was in my mother's belly for almost eleven months and weighed less than 2 kg when I was born. The soles of my feet were cracked, a sign of malnutrition.

My family did not need to tell me about *bapak*. From when I was young, I knew that my family was implicated in the PKI, because the neighbours liked calling me names. We lived in a *kampong* in Surabaya, predominantly Javanese, with some Arabic, Indian and Chinese mixed in.

Little kids there often said that I was a son of PKI who had no religion and was like an animal. Because *bapak* was jailed, our family's finances were falling apart. So we could not afford to buy a TV. The *kampong* children who did not have TV usually went to the house of a neighbour, who was a teacher. But I was not allowed in by him. If I tried to see the TV from the outside he would chase me away.

My neighbours also used to tell me how members of the PKI were beaten to death, dragged by cars or run over by steam trains. One of them, Sukemi, liked calling me over just to talk at length about this, so almost every night I had nightmares.

In this *kampong* lived a family of Indian descent. One of the sons, Ron, was four years older than me. He often knocked my head with his knuckles. One day, for no apparent reason, he pushed me really hard, until I plunged into a pond. Fortunately, Ron's own brother helped me out.

I was often home alone, so no one protected me. *Ibu* had to work all day. My mother was actually really beautiful, but she had blemishes all over her face, maybe due to being out too much in the heat. At home, *ibu* often complained to me. I was a toddler then, so I did not really understand what she was saying. I just knew she was exhausted. So I massaged her legs and back by stepping on them, to ease her fatigue.

I never told her how the neighbours treated me. The worst of my neighbours was the Sasongko family, who lived in front of our home. The son who was my age (at the time we were both five years old) often harassed me. He said: 'Your father was PKI, he was killed and chopped up.' Because he said this so many times, I lost it once and beat him really badly, until he was black and blue. His family got angry and they looked for me all day, while carrying a knife and a rope. Maybe they wanted to tie me up. I hid and did not dare come home.

Therefore, I preferred to hang around with street kids in other areas, and I could make money, too. Since the age of four, I often did not come home. I walked to Tunjungan, then hung out with the homeless children there. Some were mean and some were good to me. But at least they did not discriminate against me. Anyway, with them I found happiness. We looked for old bottles together while playing. Besides bottles, I also collected used light bulbs – I broke them and took out the copper. They were more valuable than bottles. Usually, there was a teenager about seventeen or eighteen years old who came every day with a cart and a scale. We sold the bottles and copper to him.

When I was in the fourth grade in elementary school I finally found out where those bottles were sold, and I went there on my own. At a flea market, I sold the bottles to the Makassarese and Madurese.[82] I earned quite a lot of money from this. My neighbours at that time could only buy regular rollerblades, but I was able to buy the best ones.

Hanging around with tramps was a valuable experience, but there were dangers as well. Many of my friends were kidnapped. I do not know

---

82  Makassarese: people from the southern part of Sulawesi; Madurese: people from Madura, an island off the north-eastern coast of Java.

exactly why, but some said that these children were killed and their organs sold. I nearly experienced the same thing. At that time I was about six years old, and was looking for bottles in the afternoon in front of gambling establishments in Gentengkali. Three men approached me. One of them pointed at me, and at that moment I knew that they wanted to capture me.

By reflex, I broke the bottle I was holding, to use as a weapon, before running away. They chased me. I decided to jump into a big river nearby and stayed under water for a long time. Eventually, they left – they probably thought that I would die in the river. I survived because I breathed through the broken bottle.

In fifth grade I started working with more focus. I bought broken rollerblades or bikes. After I fixed them, I sold them. If I did not sell them in a week, I brought them to a flea market. Later, in college, I played cards for money. I was so good at it that a Chinese man from Petemon took me with him to play as a professional gambler. But it did not last long as this card game was no longer trendy. Fewer and fewer people were interested in it, so I started gambling as a part of a crew. Several friends and I worked together, but acted as if we did not know each other. We went to villages to trap other gamblers, so they lost.

After graduating from high school, another job I did was selling the answers to state university exams. I usually sat in an exam with the applicants who paid me, and gave them the answers by sign language. One of the people who bought my services got into the medical faculty at Airlangga University in Surabaya and later became the head of a clinic and then co-founded a hospital in Sidoarjo. I sold answers to the examinees of various faculties at several well-known universities, such as medicine at Airlangga, mathematics at ITS [Institut Teknologi Sepuluh Nopember, a public engineering university in Surabaya] and computer science at ITB [Institut Teknologi Bandung, a university in Bandung]. I was able to answer the exam questions easily, because I was always in the top rank in school. I did this professionally from 1986 to 1990. For one exam, I could usually pass three people. I charged about Rp 5 to 10 million per person. [The price of a new motorcycle was approximately Rp 5 million at the time.]

## The Revenge against the Sasongko Family

The Sasongko family remained spiteful towards me. One time Sasongko's eldest son, Ton, who was a robber, was going to stab me. Fortunately, I escaped. But I started racking my brain for ways to challenge this nasty family. Because of my frequent visits to flea markets and my acquaintance with various gamblers, I could own and also design weapons, ranging from swords, air guns, little toxic knives, etc. I even got a revolver that I bought at a flea market in Pasuruan – of course, this was illegal. This made the Sasongko family rather afraid of me.

To revenge myself on Ton, I made a kind of role-play when I was in the second year of high school. I invited my friends from other towns. They pretended to be furious with me in front of my home, when Ton was around. Then, my friends slashed me with their swords, but I wore iron plates inside my jacket, so I did not get hurt. Then came another friend who intervened and stopped the fight. Ton saw this and thought I had some kind of supernatural power, so that I was resistant to knives. After that, every time he saw me, he seemed nervous. So I had more courage to annoy him by chasing him while waving a sword, because I was sure there would be no repercussion.

## The Return of *bapak*

In 1981 or 1982, *bapak* was released. My eldest sister picked him up. *Ibu* always spoke highly of our father during his imprisonment, so that we remained proud of him. My mother was a faithful wife and idealised her husband. When *bapak* came home, he was immediately surrounded by family and friends. My eldest sister kept hugging my father with tears flowing endlessly. My second eldest sister's eyes were also glazed with tears. My third eldest sister kept staring at him, while my elder sister seemed stunned, not knowing what to do. I kept observing their gestures and speeches.

When I approached *bapak*, I really wanted to get a hug from him, as I had heard so much about him from *ibu*. But he seemed rather indifferent and preferred to talk about the conditions in the prison. I thought that was not fair at all. He should have first asked how his family was while he had been gone. I decided to stay in my bedroom and began to realise that there had been a selfish person added to this household.

Not long after his release, *bapak* converted from Islam to Catholicism. And he also became somewhat anti-Islam and asked us not to get too close to Muslims. My other sisters converted to Catholicism, but my eldest sister remained a Muslim and father did not mind. I persisted with not having any religion, but when asked, I filled in my religious column with 'Islam'.

Not far from our house, Pak Sugianto was also released from Buru Island. However, his family was in a real mess. His eldest son became a robber. His second daughter became a prostitute. The third and fourth were gamblers. The youngest disappeared and no one knew where he was. Seeing the condition of his family, Pak Sugianto got a huge shock. Every day he just sat still and did not say a word, and shortly thereafter he fell ill and died.

## The Sex Business

Eventually, I tried my luck in the sex business. I mainly worked with women who needed money. No coercion, as they wanted to do this themselves. I was introduced to sex when I was in the fifth grade in elementary school. At that time, my neighbour who had just broken up with her boyfriend, asked me to follow her. She took me to an empty house not far from where we lived. Suddenly, she asked me to suck her nipples and vagina, then she sucked my penis. She also inserted my penis into her vagina. Then, she asked me to move forward and backward. I was surprised but also happy, because I actually had a crush on her.

We did it only three times, then she found another boyfriend: an adult man who had a job. She left me just like that. I was not heartbroken, but when I felt like doing it, I got really confused. Finally, I went to a red light district in Jarak. Because I did not have money, I waited patiently until it was quiet and there were no customers around. At that time, I could get a huge discount from the prostitutes there. These prostitutes were really nice to me, maybe because I was just a kid. Later, some of them even let me have sex with them for free when I had no money.

Around a year after, my aunt's friend raped me. He stayed at our home while visiting my aunt, and we slept in the same room, in one bed. He forced and threatened me. Because I was scared as well much smaller and weaker than him, I remained silent. However, my anus was really in pain for a few days, and it was bleeding when I defecated. When he came again, I did not want to sleep with him. I wanted to sleep with my sister instead. But my family was not sensitive at all. My mother even got angry and told me to sleep with him. Of course he raped me again. The man came back when I was in junior high school. At that time, I carried a knife everywhere, so he did not dare touch me. Anyway, when I was in my junior high, my courage grew and I was no longer afraid of anyone at all.

I had more knowledge about the ins and outs of the sex industry after I was married to a prostitute. In the presence of a religious leader, we had a *sirri* [unregistered] marriage. I was in high school, the sex worker was about ten years older, and we loved each other. The reason we decided to get married was just because we had been living together and did not want to get attacked by the people who lived near us.

From these various experiences, I finally set up my own sex business. The girls who wanted to become prostitutes did not dare to offer themselves to the customers, so they needed an agent. But I still did not want to take just any customer, willy-nilly. I was very selective. I met them first before I booked girls for them. Once, my customer refused to pay me after he got a girl. I was really angry and I managed to hold on to his driver's license. Despite this, my business went quite smoothly. However, eventually, my customers booked the girls directly, not via me. Many of these girls later even married their customers, although they had become the men's umpteenth wives.

## Other Jobs

I also tried to be a civil servant, although I knew there would be many obstacles because of my family background. I applied for a job at a BUMN [*badan usaha milik negara*, or a state-owned enterprise], and was accepted. But before my official appointment, I had to undergo a six-month trial and during this time, we were also required to fill out a 40-page questionnaire: we had to fill in the names, address and occupations of our parents, grandparents, aunties and uncles. Then, there were also questions about our knowledge of the state principles, Pancasila, and about citizenship. Of course, I failed this test. My friends who lied about their family histories also did not qualify, because apparently they checked our records with the local official and the district military.

Finally, I worked at whatever and wherever I could. I once worked at a steel mill. I had to make a steel structure for a factory warehouse in Cilegon, West Java. Afterwards, I moved to Sidoarjo-Surabaya, to be the head of a traditional medicine business. In 1998, I was hired by a company to make illegal detonators. This work taught me how to make bombs as well. After that, my willingness to kill Soeharto with a bomb grew. I bought bulletproof clothes, as I was serious about this idea. But Soeharto stepped down in May 1998, before I did it.

**Photo N   Rito Aji at his home in Surabaya**

# Now ...

The wound of the 1965 tragedy still lingers, especially for my eldest sister. She easily gets ill: breathing problems and headaches. She also often gets angry for no reason and she has nasal polyps. She is also very emotional: she can easily empathise with or be spiteful to people. Indeed, as a child, her life was pretty miserable. From the age of six, she had to be a maid for our mother's relative to help the family's income. Most of my mother's relatives hated the PKI. They did not even let us eat together with them. We had to wait until everyone had finished eating, then we could eat the remains on the table. One of our uncles, Pakde, even used to be a detainer of people accused as PKI and who were to be executed. Many people were afraid of Pakde. A few of our own relatives were murdered after being captured by Pakde.

Because we had been separated since childhood, my eldest sister hardly knew me. We rarely met. She knew about me only from *ibu* or from the news or stories of my family. Only now, I understand more about my sister, who used to say that I just wanted to have fun. Indeed, I want to enjoy life and do not want to burden myself with depressing things. Be happy, that is my principle. I am an atheist and want to live a full life as much as possible, and do not want to die old, weak and helpless in a nursing home.

What I do not understand is that my father is very religious. I believe that a good communist should be an atheist – they should challenge religion. Therefore, I once hid my father's statue of the Virgin Mary, for fun. But he was looking for it like crazy so I returned it.

I blame not only Soeharto but also Sukarno, for what happened in 1965. Sukarno did not take any action, even after finding out that there had been a mass murder of left-wing people.

*Towards the end of the interview, which took place mainly in mid-2014, I asked Rito for the names of his father and sisters. Then I realised that I had actually met Rito's father, Pudji Rahardjo, and eldest sister in Surabaya a few years ago, and that they had also told me a bit about Rito, and how proud they were of Rito's academic achievement. I told Rito about this meeting, and asked him to send my regards to them.*

*In June 2015, I met Rito several times in Surabaya at his home as well as mine. We often had dinner together, with several friends. I asked him whether his father ever put a letter in the sock or shoe of an international visitor on Buru Island. He answered: 'Several times. Any time he had the chance, he would try to do it.'*

# Soe Tjen Marching

The Secret of My Name

My name is Soe Tjen Marching.

Marching is not my husband's name or my family name, it is my name, given to me by my father. The name has often made me the butt of jeering laughter on the part of classmates. Even Soe Tjen was not a proper name in Indonesia back then. It was regarded as just a Chinese name, indicating that one was not quite 'right' there. With Marching, it was worse. And really, who else in the world is called Soe Tjen Marching?

What kind of a father anyway, would give his daughter such a strange name? Papa, when he died in September 1998, left me with the puzzle of who he really was and what really happened to him. I just knew him to be this tall dark man with a loud voice. When he was angry everyone would take fright. Even the dogs, the cats, the lizards on the wall. For he could hardly manage just to talk – he barked and yelled.

I was his favourite. At the same time, I was the one who was angry with him the most. I guess because I was aware that I was the favourite, I also had the opportunity and freedom to hate him more than my other siblings. This made our relationship difficult.

Just like the Chinese language that was not passed on to me, because the Chinese language was banned during Soeharto's rule, the story of my father remained a mystery for years. Out of fear for our safety, and to protect me, mama and my siblings did not want me to hear terrible things about papa, as I was the only one who had never seen him in prison.

My family told me all kinds of lies. Unfortunately none of them was a good liar. So, on one occasion when I overheard them saying that papa had been imprisoned, my sisters told me that the imprisonment was because his business partner tricked him. But sometimes they forgot the details, so the identity of the person doing the tricking changed from time to time. There were other stories, too. For instance: that my father was a journalist and he had written something that offended the government, but when I asked which newspaper he had worked for, they never replied. My mother, brother and sisters all had different 'tales' to tell about my father. Every time I asked about him, the possibilities seemed endless: it was like 'choose your own adventure' for me. Life was never boring! And all these possibilities have also made me into what I am and forced me to transform myself into several beings.

## I Became Chinese

When I was three, mama decided to buy a bigger house, as our house in Darmokali (a suburb of Surabaya) was getting too small for the six of us. We moved to Potroagung (also in Surabaya), with a big garden and banana trees behind our house, where I saw a *kutrik* [dragonfly] and a *kupu-kupu* [butterfly] with colourful wings like batik. It was not like in Darmokali, where I could chat all day with my friends over the fence and they often came to play with me after dinner. The street was narrower than that of Darmokali, and I did not see many kids around.

However, as I walked around the far end of the street, I saw several kids, which made me rather happy. This seemed to be a different area altogether. While on our part of the street, the houses were bigger and made of brick, the houses close by were much smaller and made of bamboo. I slowly approached the other children, but when one of them saw me, she stared at me for a while and jeered: 'Chinese!'

I did not even know what that meant, so I asked my mother, who told me that we were not Indonesian, that we were from a foreign country called China, and therefore I was different from those kids. But weren't all members of my family born in Indonesia? We had never been to China at all then! I was rather confused, but I accepted it. That day, I became Chinese.

## I Became Religious

In 1977, my mother sent me to the Christian school IMKA in Surabaya. It was a private school but considered a bad school at the time. It desperately needed students, so it was well known for attracting pupils from other schools who had failed to make the next grade. It was also very far away from my house. I often got jealous of kids who went to much more prestigious schools close to where I lived. Later, I found out that mama had sent me there because the headmaster had helped her when my father was in prison. So I had to travel a long way every day as a way of repaying this 'debt'.

At school, the teachers made me pray before we started and finished each lesson, before meals, and before going to bed. The teachers told me that God had created human beings, that He would punish everyone who did not believe in Him and that these unbelievers would suffer forever in hell.

At home, my father told me that praying was useless, and that there was no God. At school, the teachers told me about the murders committed by the communists in the 1965 coup, and that the communists were atheists and evil. At home, my father told me that atheists and communists were good (and don't you dare ask why).

At school, the teachers told me that Soeharto was a hero, and that he saved us by fighting against the depravity of left-wing people. At home, my father cursed whenever he saw Soeharto on TV.

At school, I was required to watch the film *Pengkhianatan G30S/PKI*: the communists slaughtering innocent people in a mosque, the Gerwani women dancing while plucking out the generals' eyes, the communists running amok destroying people's houses. I wondered whether my father had done something similar.

At school, one of the teachers found out that my father had been imprisoned as a communist. He said that my father was a sinner and that I was, too. Once, when we had to do some work, I had a short chat with the classmate who sat behind me. The teacher came to my table and slapped me really hard, calling me a troublemaker. Could it be partly my father's fault that this was happening to me?

At school, they condemned the children of PKI. At home, my father was domineering and bad tempered.

At school, I had to show to everyone that I was religious. At home I had to pray in secret when my father was around. I had to be constantly aware of the identity I represented vis-à-vis different people.

My self became elusive, shaped differently in different times and places. I had to be aware of where I was and who was around me, so that I could present myself safely. Just as former political prisoners had to be guarded about everything they did, I had to, too. And the most frightening authority then was my father, as he was the one who seemed the closest, the most constant and the most real.

Becoming religious was a way to rebel against him. So, I aspired to be a nun, and later this was not good enough. I wanted to be a saint or a martyr, for every now and then I imagined that I was being persecuted by communists like him. I was the saint who was about to be fed to the lions by the brutal Emperor Nero – someone like my father. But then, he was my father, not just a ruler who had no blood relation to me. And I did not want my own father to go to hell. So, I tried hard to convert him, for only those who believed would be saved. I sometimes wanted to be the saint who was able to convert him to the right path.

At other times I wanted him to just disappear, but then who would pay for our tuition fees, for our clothes and food? Wouldn't it be good if the money was there for us, but he wasn't? The hatred for my father often burned in me, and it must have been painful for papa, witnessing his children, especially me, being swallowed up by the authority that had imprisoned and humiliated him.

## There Were Times ...

There were times when I was relieved that he was not home. He tried to bribe me by buying things I really liked, so I would accept him more. But there were also times when we shared jokes and laughed at certain things that I dared not laugh at with other people: at my teachers, at some high officials on TV, or at Indonesia's first lady. Papa would defend me when mama told me off for dirtying my clothes, for playing with dogs too much, for climbing trees, and for not behaving like a lady.

There were times when he asked me to show him my hands, only so he could hold them for a while. There were times when he walked many miles, just to get the food I really wanted. There were times when he came to my room at night, when I was asleep, so he could look at me for a while – during the day, he had to work hard to make money.

There were times when he was not an atheist, a communist or an ex-convict. He was just a father. I often ignored these moments when I was young, but now these are the memories I remember when I see the word 'father'.

*And what made him evil?*

There were many questions that I was unable to ask or answer. I heard about what happened to him mainly from my mother – later, after Soeharto had stepped down, after my father had passed away.

## This is What She Told Me ...

Your father was born in 1933 in Malaysia and migrated to Indonesia on leaving school at the age of fourteen because his widowed mother could not cope with raising seven sons. Your grandfather died really young, when your grandma was just 30 years old. Your father never forgave his mother for sending him to Indonesia. He never returned to Malaysia after she sent him away.

In Indonesia, papa went to Jakarta and stayed with his aunt. She and her husband were quite well off, and owned a shop. They asked your father to help them with the shop. But every now and then, your father would steal a huge bag of rice from the shop to give it to the poor family who lived next door to them. Of course, this made his uncle and aunt really angry, so your father decided to leave them. He went with just the clothes on his back, a bicycle and not much money at all, to Surabaya, and there he got help from some people from a Chinese left-wing organisation.

He met me through a friend, and told me later that he fell in love with me because of my intelligence. I wrote poems and short stories, and this impressed him, because he was basically uneducated. He had just a school-leaving certificate, but he hardly felt inferior to me, who was better educated than he was. Well, he did lie to me at the beginning, saying that he had graduated from high school.

After we were married, I worked as a teacher at the Chinese high school Xin Chung [Central Star] in Surabaya, and your father owned a cooperative bank. We lived quite a comfortable life then. He could even buy me a car, at a time when many people still couldn't afford one. In the early 1960s, I heard rumours of an imminent anti-Chinese movement. My uncle had been murdered in a riot in 1947 in Blitar.[83] He and other Chinese were dragged from their houses one night by a group of men, and forced to dig a huge hole, only to be thrown in there and buried alive. Chinese people will often be blamed and attacked if anything goes wrong in this country. Even now.

At the end of 1965 (I have forgotten the exact date) when I had just started teaching, the headmistress came into my class. 'The school is to be shut down today', she said, 'Please teach as normal and show dignity.'[84]

That was what I did. I taught, until the very last minute, a short story by the French writer Alphonse Daudet, entitled 'The Last Lesson'. I had not finished discussing this story with my students when a group of young men entered the classroom and told the teachers that everyone had to go home. The students and teachers stood in rows, then went out. That was the end of their school day. Many of them were crying. One of the men who told the students to leave, said: 'This is amazing. They are so disciplined.' Well, that was all we had left: dignity to the end.

The next day, the school was guarded by the troops. Many students still came to school and gathered at the front, begging the troops to be let in: 'We want to study.' But the troops could not be bargained with. Obviously, I lost my job that day.

---

83  Blitar is a small town in East Java, where most of my mother's relatives were born and grew up.
84  All Chinese schools in Indonesia were actually shut down in April 1966. This shows that my mother's memory of the date is not precise, but that she still cannot forget the details of the incident.

The government shut down all Chinese schools and confiscated the buildings. Later, they turned the buildings into whatever they liked: hospitals, universities, state schools. I tried to make a living by opening a small shop, selling sweets and dishes that I cooked myself. I set up a big table, arranged all the goods, then opened the front window of our house, and that was it: people could see my goods and tell me what they wanted to buy from the window.

Your father was not involved in the Communist Party, but he helped several human rights organisations. I knew that he was one of the targets because many Chinese people had been accused of being communists. I asked him not to leave the house. But papa was so stubborn. He could never keep quiet and even took home one of his best friends, a PKI member, who was being chased by the military. Your father hid him in our bedroom. He did not want to tell anyone about this guy, even me. He stayed with us for a few months, had meals with us, and after meals he was back in the bedroom. Yet, after all this time, I did not know who he really was and what his real name was. Later, your father asked him to go to church and to become a church activist, to be protected and to hide his identity.

Because of his fear of being caught, this friend decided to move to another house, but your father still sent him food and clothes through my cousin. Then, one night, at the end of 1966, troops banged on the door of our house. The children were asleep, and after I locked the door of the kids' bedroom, I opened the door to the troops. They came in with their weapons and told your father to sit. Your father remained calm and asked me to get him a cigarette. He sat down and puffed his smoke while the troops started searching our home. I was pregnant with your elder sister, Yin, at that time. Maybe because in Java there was a belief that you must respect pregnant women, they were quite polite to me.

The troops took most of the books they could find in our living room. My schoolbooks and notes were taken. I also had books on Marx and Mao in our bedroom. I had signed my name in some of the books, because I was proud of having them, so they would have known that those were mine. I was certain then that the troops would come for me, too (*What would happen to the children?*), especially when one of them said to his commander that he would search in my bedroom.

After the officer came back from my bedroom, he said: 'All clear!' I realised then that he could have been a communist spy. I was saved, and so were my books, but soon after the troops left, I burnt them all.

The last word your father said to me before he left the house was 'Don't be afraid.' Then he was loaded onto a truck like a chicken. They accused him of being a communist, although he was never involved in any communist organisation at all. I did not have the chance to be sad or frightened, as I had to look after the children and try to make a living by selling whatever I could in a market, especially food like *kacang goreng* [fried peanuts].

I still remembered the name of the officer who searched my room, and I tried to get more information about him, only to find out that he had been murdered, too. Somehow I wondered whether he died for saving me.

I looked for your father in the military prison but could not find him there, so I went to the *koramil* [regional military office] in Wonokromo.[85] The commander said to me: 'I don't know, Bu. Don't look for him at the moment. It's useless. Just go home. Open your shop and look after your children. Actually, I don't even know whether I will survive this or not.'

I did as he suggested. A few days later, a large number of people came and bought from my shop. I am not sure where they came from. My customers were numerous, a lot more even than before your father was imprisoned. Of course, I was very pleased: I made a lot of money! I also received a big bag of sweets (with a message saying it was to be sold in my shop), but the person sending the sweets never asked for any payment. Once, a customer got something from my shop and instead of giving me money, he exchanged it for a lamp, and asked me to instal it in the shop: 'Your shop is too dark. With this lamp, more people will be able to see it.' It was a very special lamp, quite beautiful.

After I had lit the shop with the lamp, more customers came. They were very friendly as well, so I often had a chat with them, and knew their names. Several of them seemed like intellectuals. But slowly, these customers began to disappear. It was only later that I found out that my customers had been imprisoned or murdered. Many of them had also been accused of being communists.

The head of that *koramil* might have helped me. He might have asked those people to buy from my shop. He might have been one of us. And I never thanked him, as I was too confused by everything going on around me. Those customers might have been sent by him, and they might have told other sympathisers to buy from my shop. And the lamp?

The lamp may have been a signal of some sort. So other sympathisers knew that it was my shop that they had to come and buy from. Alas, all these theories are only speculation as we never knew what really happened. The man who gave me the lamp never returned to the shop, so he might also have been imprisoned or murdered. The commander of the *koramil*

---

85  Wonokromo: an area in Surabaya.

also disappeared later. Some people whispered that there were several communists in the *koramil*, and they had also been taken away.

It was only after two months and after bribing several officers for some basic information, that I found out that my husband was in Kalisosok prison in Surabaya. I went to Kalisosok straight away, but I was not allowed to see your father. At least it was confirmed that he was indeed there, and that he was alive. A few weeks later, I could send him food but was still not permitted to speak to him. I sent messages to your father in the form of codes on the paper I used to wrap the food. I wrote this code in such a way that my writing blended with the pictures on the paper, so the guards weren't suspicious. I did not know whether your father would be able to understand it, but I kept writing. I wrote to him that your elder sister had been born, that I could earn a living by selling food.

But I did not tell him that I had to send the two eldest children away, your brother to your grandmother's and your sister to your aunt's. I did not tell him that your elder sister could not drink any milk. Because I was under such stress, no milk came out of my breasts. Yin only drank rice water, for milk was too expensive for me. I couldn't afford it. I did not tell him how tiny and quiet my newborn baby was, for Yin may have felt the sorrow into which she was born.

I often tried to make something new, so people did not get bored with what I was selling. I learnt how to make *enting-enting* [peanut snap], and people really liked it. I sent a code to tell your father that I was earning a lot of money by making this new sweet, so that he did not have to worry about us. When I visited him again, I was given an *enting-enting* roller by your father. The guard passed it to me. It had been made by your father and his fellow inmates: a way of saying thank you, because papa often shared the food I sent with his fellow prisoners.

That was when I realised that he understood the codes I wrote. He was able to read what I told him about the children. He knew that Yin was born, he knew your eldest brother and sister had gone to school, he knew that we could survive while he was imprisoned. He knew.

And I had been telling the children about him as well, so they would not forget their own father.

Eventually, I was allowed to visit your father regularly. When I saw him for the first time after that Independence Day, he could hardly stand because his back had been ruined by the beatings and he had been electrocuted in several places.

I tried my best to send good food to him. But he told me that the guards took the nice food away, and left the rest for the prisoners. Money was hard for me so the children got barely enough to eat, and the guards still ate some of the food I sent to your father. So, I made rice with a bit of meat and vegetables, crushed them all together, mixed it well and dressed it up to look like dog shit. This trick worked. The guards let the 'dog shit' in.

## The Unexpected Visitor

It was late at night, in early 1969, and I was about to go to bed. There was a knock on the door. Quite loud. The troops banging on the door that night still haunted me, so the knocking at night always made me nervous.

I opened the door. And there he was: your father! Had he been released? No, he had not been released nor had he run away. He was about to be released in three weeks' time, but the new prison commander had let him visit me briefly to tell me the good news. Indeed, the new commander was one of my friend's relatives, so he did this as a favour. The commander asked your father to return to the prison on time, or else they would think that he had run away. I did not even have the opportunity to wake the children to meet their father, because he had to go back to the prison. So, he just saw his three kids sleeping in bed, then left. But he was due to return in a few weeks. For good.

On the day he was released, I was not allowed to pick him up. I waited at home and cooked fried noodles for him. At about 10 am, your father came with a prison mate, and they ate so much and for a long time. It was like they were making up for all the years they couldn't eat in prison.

Yin cried from shock. But your eldest sister and brother did not: they were just happy. Later, your two-year-old sister Yin brought him all kinds of things: shoes, clothes, toys. Anything she could find for him. She wanted to make him happy.

## The Story of When Your *Engkong* Was Imprisoned

Your *engkong*[86] had been imprisoned by the Japanese. He was a sailor and accused of being a spy. He was very close to your father and told me before your father proposed to me that even though he seemed rough and not very polite he was a kind and responsible person.

---

86  *Engkong*: grandfather (on the mother's side).

*Engkong* often talked to your father about his past, and said that if one day he was ever caught and questioned for any political reason, never to betray his friends: 'Because when you betray one friend, the guards will want more information from you. One name will lead to other names, and they will think that you know a lot. They will promise rewards, but they will not keep their promise. In fact, they may punish you worse, and after you are released from the prison, you will feel guilty for having done such a thing to your friends.' Your father had thought that your *engkong* was mad for saying this to him. But when he was imprisoned, your father followed the advice of your *engkong:* he never betrayed his friends.

When several prisoners in Surabaya had been sent to Buru Island, your father was not one of them. I heard the news that your father would be released soon instead. Later, your father told me that usually only people who were considered 'dangerous' were sent to Buru. The more the prisoners talked or betrayed their friends, the more the guards would think that they knew a lot and were 'dangerous'.

From that, I know that people who were sent to Buru Island must have either been important people in the party, or considered important or divulged their friends' names.

Your father worked really hard after his release, contacting his friends in the hope of being able to do any kind of business and offering to do accounting for them. On the weekend, he also sold the ice I made, on his bike. He did anything and was not ashamed of doing any kind of job, even the ones considered really low by his friends.

Your father did not enjoy his freedom for long. As he started being successful, as he started to rise up from his tragedy in prison, someone reported him and he was sent to prison again. This time, for half a year.

### Her Suspicions

Of course my mother's assumptions about the people sent to Buru were not completely wrong, but they were not right either: there were many people who were sent to Buru Island for no obvious reason. From the people I interviewed, I also found out that they might have revealed the names of their friends, not as an act of conscious betrayal but out of ignorance. They did not know why they were arrested, so they answered all questions as honestly as possible. They gave out information as much as possible, whatever the officers wanted, without knowing how this would affect the people around them.

Assumptions often produce suspicions and even fiction, especially when silence predominates. The relationships in my family have often been driven by this: we make assumptions which easily crystallise into suspicions. The assumptions of my eldest sister, who was only two years old when my father was taken, have led her to suspect that my mother did not really love her. My mother sent her away to my aunt and uncle, and my sister did not have a good experience with them. My mother couldn't really explain to her properly why she had to do it, as she believed silence was the solution for most questions and at times, for everything. Thus, even when we try to break the pattern, it feels like a sin. Even now we can't talk about my father without creating tension.

## I Was Born after His Release

I was swayed between extremes of love and hate towards my father, for he was psychologically damaged. He often went quiet for a long time and got angry for no reason. He liked keeping dogs, chaining them and beating them when he was annoyed. Another hobby of his was torturing rats. He enjoyed it when they screamed in pain.

He wanted us to be successful. He wanted us to eat well, I guess because he hardly ate well when he was young, and in prison he hardly ate at all. Food and education became very important for us. He bought us a piano. Even though it was a cheap one, that piano urged me to compose music. My father asked us not to get involved in politics at all, and to work hard, to make money. That was his definition of being 'successful'. Sometimes he called us 'stupid' because we did not know enough about politics, and at other times he said how heartless and narrow-minded business people were.

I sometimes lay down with my father on Sundays, when he was not working. I saw his body, especially his chest, full of holes. Some big. Some small. I had never seen holes like this on other people's bodies. So, I asked him: 'What are these?' He did not answer, shushed me and told me to go to sleep.

So, next time I lay down with him, I asked him again. But papa got suddenly furious and yelled: 'Never ever ask again!'

When I told my sisters and brother how my father got angry with me for nothing, they said how lucky I was for I had a much better life than they did. Their answer did not make sense. Even as a child, I was aware of it. And when I was annoyed with my father, sometimes my eldest sister would often shut me up and say that I had never seen my father suffer.

With that, I was burdened by guilt. I felt guilty when I hated him. I also felt guilty when I loved him, for I did not know whether I really loved him or whether I felt that way just because I could not, should not and must not hate him.

## What is in a Name?

My father has different surnames. In some documents, his surname is Oei. On others, his surname is Oei Go. When I was at elementary school, my teachers often asked me about the differences between my father's names in several documents. This problem continued when I was at junior high school. I was very frustrated because my parents never told me why.

I was really angry with my father about this: 'Why do you have different names and make my life difficult?' I was sure he would yell back at me, louder, as he had to be in power and in control of everything. But he did not. He kept quiet and went away. He seemed very hurt. Of course, I did not understand why then.

This confusion about my name followed me everywhere, and created further problems later, as in the early 1990s the Indonesian government required people to give their father's name on official documents, but my family insisted that I should never use my father's name. So, history repeats itself: I have documents with different names as well. Soe Tjen Marching and Soe Tjen Marching Go. With regard to immigration and border controls in Europe and Australia, this has caused me many problems.

The explanation only came much later, after a long period of confusion and anger:

While most political prisoners had the stamp ET after they were released, my father got the stamp G (meaning Gestapu). My parents knew that they had to get rid of this stamp at all cost.

So, my mother kept an eye on the *kecamatan* [sub-district administration] office. She knew one of the staff there often stayed later than the others. She approached him one day, and told him that there was a typo on my father's identity card: 'Look, my father's family name is Go not G.' Now my grandmother's family name is indeed Go, but my grandfather's family name is not Go. My mother said: 'Because my husband lost his father when he was really young, he had to take his mother's surname.'

The young and inexperienced official believed what my mother said. So he changed all my father's papers. The letter G became the name Go. But this meant that my father had two surnames on that document: Oei and

Go. And on his other documents, he only had one surname: Oei. The name 'Go' had saved us, but it caused us another kind of trouble as well.

## Threats Were Always Near

My father meanwhile refused to shut up. He sometimes said to his friends that Soeharto was an arsehole and corrupt. Many of them just smiled and shook their heads. My mother often got really angry with him because of this and she often said: 'Your father is crazy!'

He had a new friend now, an elderly man of about 60 years old, an uncle of my mother's best friend, Yati. Yati was a medical doctor and used to live in Solo, Central Java. My father could at least talk to Yati's uncle, his new friend, about many things. Yati's uncle was soft-spoken and had a much younger wife, and Yati told my parents that she was a daughter of a former Gerwani member. Every time I came to their house, his wife gave us a cup of sweet tea and let me play with their cats.

But all of a sudden my father stopped seeing Yati's uncle. 'He threatened to attack me with an axe', I heard my father say to my mother one night. Only recently, my mother told me that Yati's uncle used to be a mass murderer and when he found out about my father's past, he flew off the handle. Yati had to interfere to calm everyone down, so nothing worse happened. My mother later discovered that the young wife was willing to marry this old man to save her family.

Such threats came every now and then, as my father still could not shut his mouth, and this often caused arguments between my parents. Now, history has repeated itself here, too.

Because of my own activism, I receive many threats of beating, acid attack, death and rape. This causes my husband too a lot of stress. My mother and my husband have grown quite close because of this as they feel that they are in the same boat. At the beginning, their concern made me angry as I interpreted this as their effort to obstruct my wishes, my dreams and ambitions. And I felt that I was often torn between my duty to be a good daughter to my mother (who has suffered), and my duty to the 1965 victims.

## As He Got Older, His Temperament Got Worse ...

My father could always find fault with us. At times, he was impossible to deal with. He started regretting that we did not learn Mandarin, or that we were not 'Chinese' enough according to his standard. He felt he had been persecuted because he was Chinese and we had been discriminated against because we were Chinese, so he had to insist on being 'Chinese'. I never told him I had gone out with any men, because none of them could be classified as 'Chinese' by him. And somehow, he knew that I was hiding something.

In December 1997, when my application for a PhD scholarship at Monash University in Australia was successful, he was not happy. He was worried instead: he was afraid that I would be Westernised. He even asked me to refuse the scholarship. But my mother backed me and finally he let me go. Only a few days before I left for Australia, he said that he was proud of me. But then he made me promise: 'You will only marry a Chinese, won't you?' I nodded because I could not be bothered arguing with him, but later, in 2002, I married an Australian instead.

Soeharto stepped down in May 1998, and it was a big thing for my father to see this, for he despised Soeharto so much. That year I also won the national competition for contemporary composers held by the German Embassy in Indonesia. I was invited to receive the award in Erasmus Huis in Jakarta in September that year, but was not sure whether I would attend because this meant I had to travel from Australia.

In the end, I did fly to Indonesia – not to receive the award, but to see my father, for my sister rang and asked me to come home: 'Your father is critical. He may die any time.' His smoking habit had taken a terrible toll: incurable lung cancer.

He was still alive when I arrived. He had told me that he and my mother were planning to accompany me to get the award in Jakarta, but it was now impossible as he was too ill. I decided to stay and not leave for Jakarta but he insisted that I had to get my award. 'I will wait for you and I will not die before you get the award', he promised. So, I left for Jakarta. On the way to Surabaya, I was so worried that he would pass away, but he kept his promise. He held on until I came back. I showed the cheque I received as the prize but he read it upside down and said: 'Good. Really good.' I knew his time was near, but he still wanted to show us that he was OK. He did not want to make us worry. He passed away the day after.

## Years Later ...

It is really disappointing for me that the school textbooks still do not tell the truth about the tragedy of 1965-1966. I really wanted to write about my parents to reveal this dark history. A few years ago, a publisher in Indonesia said that they would be happy to publish my parents' story, but my mother said 'No!' She was still worried and this made me angry with her because I thought she was just a coward for not wanting to speak up.

After a long negotiation, she agreed that the story could be published in English, but not in Indonesian. But then she kept changing her mind, sometimes asking me not to publish it at all. She is still very worried. On another occasion, she said I could publish it only using pseudonyms. I had, however, made up my mind. The tracing back of my father's past began. I went back to Indonesia in 2013, to interview my sisters and my mother and also other people who were willing to open up to me about the tragedy in 1965. My eldest sister still did not want to talk about it when I asked her. However, every now and then, she mentioned fragments of things my father told her: 'Papa said that in prison, he ate live cockroaches, lizards, mice, anything.' Then another time, without my asking her, she said: 'Papa could survive in prison because he never ate much and he had a hard life when he was young. The others who used to eat a lot and had better life usually died first because of the torture or the starvation.'

## One Last Secret

A few days before I headed back to London at the end of 2013, my mother called me. She asked me to sit down, then said slowly: 'Your father was actually one of the committee members of the Indonesian Communist Party in Surabaya.'

So, all the stories I had heard had been lies? About my father who had never been involved in any communist group?

My mother thought it was too dangerous to be honest even to her children. I was the first person in my family who finally heard the truth from her. So many years of silence, of keeping secrets. How could she do this?

And how could he be alive if he was a committee member? 'He was just appointed when Gestok happened. Not many people knew about this. I burnt all of the papers immediately after I heard that there were many arrests. I also burnt the certificate of his appointment, a letter from the central PKI office, and other letters from important figures of the party. So, when the army got into our house, they found nothing.'

This explained why my mother often burnt books and letters, when she heard that there was any political turbulence or social riot. The old beautiful books she had are all gone, because burning papers saved her husband's life.

I wonder what other secrets there are, which I may never know. But this last revelation about my father was like a huge slap in the face. I really did not expect this. For I could completely understand if my mother hid bad things happening to my father, but concealing the fact that my father was one of the committee members of one of the largest communist parties in the world (after Russia and China)? For an elementary school graduate to be able to acquire such a position, isn't that an achievement? However, this turned into a big secret that my mother kept for years and years.

I did not know with whom I had to share this news. It was just too much for me to handle it by myself. But to whom should I talk? I decided to email Joshua Oppenheimer. He was the first person I told about this. His reply: 'What a moving story, Soe Tjen – but not surprising given the 'Marching' in your name! …'

Yes, that's why my name is Marching. From the Long March of Chairman Mao. My father may have never talked to me about his past or about the history of 1965, but he slipped a part of it into my name. Maybe he did want me to find about it one day, some day.

*I am no longer religious now, and when I remember how my father used to quote Marx that 'religion is the opium of the people', I agree with him more and more.*

*In October 2015, at the start of the commemoration of the semi-centennial of the genocide of the alleged communists in Indonesia, journalists from America, the United Kingdom and Indonesia interviewed me about what happened to my father during the political turmoil. But my father had buried his past, long before we buried his body. I can no longer ask him for that specific information. I cannot tell him that it is no longer taboo for us to talk about this and that he should be proud of his past. I cannot. It is simply too late.*

# Part 5

The Accounts of the Grandchildren

# Kusuma Wijaya

The Day I Found Out about My Grandpa

*Kusuma Wijaya was born on 22 March 1972 in Surabaya. We had been friends on Facebook for a few years before I started interviewing him. Kusuma is now a lecturer in English literature at Dr. Soetomo University in Surabaya. In September 2013, we met for the first time in Surabaya. I also knew Kusuma's best friend, Bagus Hariyono Kohar, who is a lecturer at the same university. Both Bagus Hariyono and Kusuma Wijaya are known as the 'red' lecturers of the university.*

*Bagus Hariyono told me that he only found out about Kusuma Wijaya's grandfather recently, after Kusuma had revealed his story to me. Bagus Haryono said that this explained why his best friend, Kusuma, was a leftist and why he knew a lot about Marxism and other Marxist theories, which is rare for Indonesians. Here is Kusuma's story.*

One evening in 1986, when I was still in the third year of junior high school, I came home, after watching the movie *Pengkhianatan G30S/PKI* [The treason of G30S/PKI] with my schoolmates. I told my father about it and asked him further about the cruelty of the Indonesian Communist Party [PKI] that was portrayed as evil and brutal in the film.

I did not expect that my question would trigger the revelation of my family's big secret: the identity of my grandfather. 'The man you've believed to be your grandfather is not actually your *kakek* [grandfather],' my dad said. 'Your grandpa is not Sumo Salikin but Kasmadi, and he died years ago. Sumo Salikin is just a good friend of your grandpa.'

Kasmadi, whose name I heard for the very first time then, was an elementary school principal in Gorang Gareng, a village on the border of Magetan and Madiun in East Java. As a teacher he joined PGRI [Persatuan Guru Republik Indonesia, or the Indonesia Teachers Association], as all teachers were required to participate in this organisation. In 1965, PGRI split into two groups, PGRI NV (Non Vaksentral), which was linked to the PKI, and PGRI V (Vaksentra), which was non-communist. PGRI NV was more vocal in seeking the improvement of conditions for teachers as a group, and they also expressed loyalty to Sukarno. My grandfather was a member of PGRI NV.

My *kakek* was also active in the folk art of his village, such as in *wayang* [a shadow puppet performance]. He was a gamelan player and was involved in Lekra [Lembaga Kebudayaan Rakyat, or the Institute for the People's Culture]. Lekra was generally associated with the communists. Although listed as a member of PGRI NV and Lekra, *kakek* was never active in politics. He was mainly concerned with teaching. He chose to be in PGRI NV simply because he was more at ease with the socialist motto of this organisation.

After the 30 September Movement and the mass killings, all activities of PGRI NV and Lekra were also halted, and all of the members were required to report to the military command once a week. My father, *bapak*, never told me about the treatment of the military command, as *kakek* never said anything as well, maybe because he didn't want his family to get stressed out. But during that period, the neighbours started distancing themselves from our family. Eventually, our family was rather ostracised. My grandmother Sukarti never again got together with the neighbours. During the Friday prayer, no one shook hands or greeted my uncle, after they found out that my grandpa had to report weekly. *Bapak* (who was only about seven years old then) no longer had friends of his age, because many parents forbade their children to play with my father.

Around the month of March 1966, as usual *kakek* and his friends had to report. But after dark, he still did not come home. My grandma Sukarti went around everywhere to find information about the whereabouts of my *kakek*. *Nenek* [grandmother] tried to contact the people who also had to report together with my *kakek*. But these people also had not come home yet. So from hints and whispers here and there, my grandmother found out that her husband was taken by soldiers and *santris* [Muslim students who go to Muslim boarding schools] to the village of Rejosari [near the location of the Rejosari sugar factory now]. He and his friends were killed there, and their corpses were chucked in the nearby pit.

We thought that *kakek*'s death might have been caused by the old anger originating from the communist rebellion in 1948 in Madiun [East Java], which victimised many people, especially amongst the Islamic religious leaders and their students. We believed that during 1965 these people took the opportunity to take revenge. They just blindly struck back, without thinking much about whether their victims were responsible for or related to what happened in 1948 or not.

The farmers who had joined the BTI [Barisan Tani Indonesia, or the Indonesian Peasants Front] also met a similar fate: many of them were murdered although they did not know much about politics and many knew nothing about communism. They just joined the organisation to meet other farmers.

After the murder of my *kakek*, the neighbours started to show more and more contempt. My *nenek*'s field was confiscated, and the people of the village worked on it as if it was theirs. They were getting worse and worse, and in the end, my grandmother's family was not allowed to own anything at all, because *kakek* was a communist. The murder of my grandpa was a proof for them that he was indeed guilty, and that my grandmother's family had been cursed.

A month after the murder, my grandma Sukarti with her nine children (my father, three uncles and four aunties) decided to leave Gorang Gareng. *Nenek* and her children left quietly in the middle of the night, for Surabaya, and came to one of my *kakek*'s best friends, who was also a member of Lekra in Surabaya. His name is Sumo Salikin. He lived in Wonorejo II, Pasar Kembang in Surabaya. With his help, *nenek* Sukarti started a new life, from zero. She sold vegetables in Ngagel market and my uncles and aunties got whatever work they could in this city.

At that time, almost all of the people in Wonorejo II were *abangan*.[87] Many of the people here were also communist sympathisers or members of the PNI,[88] so my *nenek* felt quite protected there.

Not long after they moved to Surabaya, my grandma called all of her children. This was what she said to them: 'From now on, you must not mention the name of your *bapak*. Never mention Kasmadi and his death. Kasmadi has to be totally forgotten, or else, your lives will be in danger.' So from that day, Kasmadi disappeared completely. He never existed. My grandmother said that, while her tears flowed like rain. The family had to kill Kasmadi and all of the memories about him.

Because of the fear and panic when she was about to run away from her village, my grandmother didn't bring the documents or any proof of identity. So my grandmother and the children had to create new ones. And my *kakek* was murdered for the second time. First by the soldiers and Muslim people, and the second time, by his own family. *Nenek* had to get rid of his name on every piece of paper – the name Kasmadi had to be removed from every

---

87  *Abangan* refers to Javanese Muslims who practice a more syncretic version of Islam than the more orthodox *santri*. They were more sympathetic to communism. The term was derived from the Javanese word for 'red' (*abang*).
88  PNI: in 1927, Sukarno established an organisation called the Indonesian Nationalist Association. In 1928, this group became the PNI (Partai Nasional Indonesia, or the Indonesian National Party). After Sukarno was imprisoned by the Dutch government for several years, the party was dissolved in 1931. In 1946, the party was revived but without Sukarno, who was the President then and was considered to be above politics.

document. Her children became the adopted kids of Sumo Salikin. That was how they introduced themselves to anyone from then on.

Although several officials of the *kampung* knew my grandfather's history, they kept this secret because many of them were members of Lekra and also because Sumo Salikin had a huge influence in that *kampung*. The younger brother of Sumo Salikin was a soldier of Siliwangi (the military division that fought during the Dutch colonial period). So the family of Sumo Salikin had power in the army and they could help many people in the *kampung*, including the officials and their families.

Since we came to live in Surabaya (in the beginning of 1966), no one ever knew that my cousins and I were the grandchildren of Kasmadi. It was a secret that our extended family protected tightly. However, I sensed something strange ever since I was young. Unlike other parents, my father asked the children to learn about communism and Marxism, although these teachings were considered evil in Indonesia, but he insisted that the children at least read about them.

Most of my aunties and uncles even kept the secret from their spouses. But my father did not. He could not keep a secret from my mother, because she was a daughter of Sumo Salikin. My father did tell her when they started going out, but my mother just said that she had known about it already. My mother was indeed brought up in a left-wing family. My grandmother on my mother's side [that is, the wife of Sumo Salikin] was once a member of Gerwani.

My uncles and aunties told their children that grandfather was a freedom fighter and was shot dead by the Dutch. His grave was not known. They did not seem to be troubled about this story, although if they wanted to think a bit: how could there be a war against the Dutch in 1965? Only a very few of my cousins knew the real story of my grandfather but they seemed to just want to forget about it and did not want to discuss it at all.

After what happened to my *kakek*, all of my uncles became Christian. My father did not: he remained Muslim. When I was at junior high school, I asked one of my uncles about this but he did not answer. Years later, when I nearly completed my bachelor degree, my uncle suddenly mentioned this again. Maybe because he found out that I already knew about my grandfather, so he could be more open with me as well. He said, that he did not think any religion was bad. He never thought that Islam was bad. But he was really angry with the Muslim people who had killed my *kakek*, and this had made him leave Islam.

**Photo O  Kusuma Wijaya in Surabaya**

*Nenek* actually knew who had murdered her husband, although she never revealed this to anyone. But in her sleep, she often mentioned particular names while cursing them: 'That – is an arsehole! Fuck that –!' No such words came out of her mouth when she was awake, even on her deathbed. Maybe she did it to prevent us from taking revenge, because the names she mentioned were those of our previous neighbours in the village.

After I graduated from high school, my anger suddenly exploded. I wanted to take revenge. I wanted to go to Gorang Gareng and finish off the murderers of *kakek*. I knew their names, so I could look for them. *Bapak* just said: 'Go ahead and bring a revolver if you want to go there. But if you want to kill them, that is stupid. Because they have also been victims of the mastermind of this tragedy and of his ideology. The person you have to kill is Soeharto!' With this, my anger towards the people of that village subsided.

After my father revealed this family secret, I asked *mbah* [grandfather] Sumo Salikin about my grandfather Kasmadi. He told me that Kasmadi was a great teacher and headmaster. He loved his work and paid much attention to his students. At that time, a headmaster had a high social status in Indonesia, but Kasmadi remained very humble. This story really inspired me. When I teach now, I want to be a good lecturer and pay attention to my students as well.

We have never gone back to Gorang Gareng. I also do not have any desire to see what it is like. The bitter memory of my *kakek* has prevented us from setting foot in that place again. But at least *bapak* revealed his big family secret to me – all because of the very film that tried to further smear the victims of the mass murder.

*Kusuma Wijaya helped me hold a public screening of* The Act of Killing *at the end of August 2013 at Ontel Hotel in Surabaya. Since then, he has given several talks about the 1965 tragedy and also the story of his grandfather. In 2014, he became the coordinator of the NGO Bhinneka in Surabaya, an organisation I established to fight against the increase of religious fundamentalism in Indonesia. Now, he still helps me with the publication of* Majalah Bhinneka [Bhinneka magazine] *to commemorate the 1965 genocide after half a century. I am really impressed with his calmness and intelligence. Apparently, Kusuma really looks up to Njoto (Irina's father), who remained calm, even when facing his tragic end.*

# Haidir Svj

Born and Raised on Buru

*At the beginning of August 2013, Haidir requested me to become a friend on Facebook, and soon after I received his email: 'Thank you for accepting me as your friend. Please allow me to introduce myself: I am from the ex-political prisoner family of Savanajaya.'*

I call my grandfather *mbah* or *embah*. His name is Usup. He comes from the small town of Tenjo, in West Java. One time, he told me his life story, which led him to the cruel jungle created by the New Order government, the island of Buru. It began in 1970, when two men grabbed him at gunpoint. Then he was dragged into a car. My grandfather was not interrogated for a long time. They just asked him where he worked, and *embah* answered: 'P.T. Unilever'. He was imprisoned from then on; first he was sent to Bandung then to Nusakambangan Island, before ending up on Buru. After that, his life started in the world of prisoners, unbeknown to his wife and son. He was imprisoned in the barracks of unit 4 [Savanajaya].

But there remains a question which has no answer even now: 'Why was he arrested?'

## The Time of Release

In 1976, *embah* was 'rehabilitated'. He decided to stay on Buru, rather than move back to Java. After the political prisoners were released, and the migrants from Java arrived in Buru, the government gave the people there a plot of land to build a house and to raise livestock. Thus, the ex-political prisoners usually started a new life with farming and animal husbandry. My grandfather chose to be a farmer. The indigenous people of Buru treated prisoners quite well. In fact, many were grateful to the former political prisoners, as they developed a pretty efficient farming system so that the locals too could harvest their own crops.

When the families – wives and children – of the ex-prisoners were sent from Java to live on Buru, my grandfather's wife and son never arrived from Tenjo. So *embah* married a widow, an ex-wife of his cellmate. Her name was Sriyanah and she was originally from Lamongan in East Java. But my grandfather still could not forget his family in West Java, especially his son. He kept looking at an old photo of his little boy, which he tucked in his service cap. He never stopped looking at that picture. Then came a hope for him, when several builders arrived from Java, to work in Savanajaya, and one of them was from Tenjo! He asked this builder to give a letter to his son. I wrote the letter on his behalf. My grandfather still remembered the address vividly, although tens of years had gone by. But he got no news at all afterwards. Maybe that builder could not find the address or maybe his wife and son had moved somewhere else. No one knows.

## Growing up on Buru

I was born on Buru Island on 27 September 1993. Even though this was the dawn of the twenty-first century, the facilities around me were very poor. There was no proper hospital nearby, so I had to be born with the help of a shaman. My mother was also born on this island, and married a man from Malacca. I cannot tell much about my mother, because I lived with *embah* since I was little. My mother followed my father on duty to Ambon (the capital of Malacca). When there was a conflict between Muslims and Christians in Ambon (many of them murdered each other), my parents moved back to Savanajaya. I was still at elementary school and we lived in a hut given to *embah* when he was just released from prison.

*Ibu* told me that when she was still at school, everything was much worse here on Buru. For many reasons, the schools did not want to accept the kids of ex-political prisoners, even though these children were often quite smart. My mother had to get special permission from the commander of the local military in Buru, just to be able to go to school. After they finished school, many of the ex-political prisoners' children have been quite successful, and they could build up Savanajaya. Nonetheless, after my mother graduated from high school, she could not find a job; and because of our economic situation, she could not study in Java either. So she tried to survive on Buru Island, looking after cows and ducks – the work she had done as a child.

Even now, the kids of the ex-political prisoners are still discriminated against at school. Many indigenous kids were nicer to us and they often asked us to teach them. After that, they usually gave us vegetables, durian, sago or fish from their *kampung*. However, other kids often called us 'the unit kids', referring to the prison system which used unit divisions. Especially when we were punished by the teachers, the jeering of 'the unit kids' often came up. We had to duck-walk, stand for hours under the blazing sun, or crawl like a dog – those were some of the punishments we had to endure in elementary school. If we were late, we would be punished; if we forgot to do our homework, we would be punished. They would look for any small mistake, especially from 'the unit kids'. If we forgot to greet the teacher or our hair was considered too long, we would be punished.

Our school was very simple and in fact, quite poor. The distance from our home was very great. To go to high school, I had to travel 21 km. So it was 42 km per day. We often had to go to school by getting a lift on a truck that delivered sand or other stuff to Savanajaya. But if we could not find any trucks, then we had to walk. Especially when we went home from school, usually there was no car at all to take us home. But we had such a big desire to learn, and to survive.

We, 'the unit kids', often got together and discussed things, especially politics. Most of us had been aware of Soeharto's propaganda since we were young, we had more awareness than other schoolchildren here. Because most of us had been taught by our parents or grandparents to express our opinions, we had better general knowledge about many things, such as the economy, socialism and capitalism. Our knowledge was just alien to the other kids.

**Photo P    Haidir Svj in Yogya**

## The Argument

It was the history class. The teacher told us about Soeharto, the PKI's betrayal of the government, and the 'sins' of the political prisoners on Buru Island. I could not stand keeping quiet, although I knew the risks: anyone who challenged a teacher would be punished. 'Our grandfathers were on Buru Island and they did not betray this country', I said. 'They were not involved in the murder of the generals in Jakarta. They were just the scapegoats of Soeharto, who was craving power and wealth.'

In front of the class, I showed our teacher the book *Diburu di Pulau Buru* [Hunted on Buru Island], written by Hersri Setiawan, which tells the story of the suffering of the political prisoners on Buru. I also gave him my notes on discussions with Solihin [an ex-political prisoner in Savanajaya] about his life story and experience before and after he was transported to Buru.

I left that school to study in Yogya, but my younger brother, Mukram, is now studying at the same school and he is taught by the same history teacher. He continues the debate between me and that history teacher, and on 30 September 2013 he read his essay at school about the tragedy of 1965, in front of everyone.

This is what he told me over the phone: 'Kak [elder sibling], I have delivered a piece of *embah*'s aspiration. On Monday, in the middle of the flag ceremony, the students flew the flag at half-mast to commemorate the death of the generals. I took the flag down. I was quite nervous actually, but I did it anyway. The teachers were really angry and one of them waived a rattan stick, threatening to beat me up. But I just ignored him and started my oration: 'This is a very sad day for Indonesia, because millions of people had to meet their tragic ends or suffered from injustice. This tragedy has affected the children and grandchildren of the victims. My *embah*, their fathers and grandparents have been the victims of the New Order. Our parents and grandparents have worked the land on Buru, so that all of you [I pointed at everyone there] can live here …' The phone got cut off.

## Savanajaya

Savanajaya is a pleasant place for me. We are all very close to each other, like one big family. If you want to visit us, you will not find any problem staying with people here. The grandchildren of the ex-political prisoners have also formed a solidarity group, to promote the pride of being the kids of Savanajaya. So we decided to use the abbreviation Svj as part of our names and recently, we also created Savanajaya T-shirts, stickers, etc. Maybe because of this, many people love this place as well, including an intelligence agent who was ordered to spy on us. He moved to Savanajaya in 2008 and told us that he came from Java. He rented a house besides us. He made a living by making and selling tempeh. After a few months in Savanajaya, he started questioning us. But by then he felt at ease with the people and the environment here. He decided to leave his job and stay in Savanajaya. Later on, he told us that his supervisor sent him to find out whether anyone in Savanajaya was planning some kind of revenge or rebellion, but he fell in love with the people and never wanted to go back to Java.

It is just such a shame that the education on Buru is still very poor. Therefore, I had to go to Yogya to study. So did my cousin. Before we left, many people told us that studying at university in Yogya was very hard, because the school on Buru was so backwards. But this made me work harder, and I am doing well now. Recently, I have also challenged my lecturer in Yogya, because he said that Islam could solve everything and that the communists were the real problem for Indonesia, while criticising the ex-political prisoners. I did not keep quiet. I explained about the real history of the New Order. I do not know what he will do to me after this. But I have made up my mind not to keep quiet. My *embah* is not well now, as he is getting older, all he can do is lie in his bed, but he remains my motivator and inspiration.

*I met Haidir in Yogya in September 2013. He came with his cousin, whose last name is also Svj. He has the same kind of spirit as Haidir – that of opposing manipulation by the government regarding 1965. In July 2015, I met Haidir again at Bu Mamiek's home. It turned out that Haidir and Bu Mamiek lived quite close to each other. Leo's daughter, Pipiet, and her husband (whose father was also an ex-political prisoner) joined us later. If was another touching meeting of members of the 1965 family. Now, every time I see the name Svj, I know that most probably they are from Savanajaya.*

*On 27 August 2015, Haidir contacted me: 'Mbak, I just want to let you know that embah Usup has passed away today, at 4 pm. He was still unable to trace his son in Java, who he kept missing dearly to the day he died.'*

# Diah Wahyuningsih Rahayu

My Grandfather's Earlobes

*On Friday, 21 September 2014, Adi Rukun (the main character in Oppenheimer's movie* The Look of Silence), *wrote to me via Facebook: 'How are you, Mbak? I would like to introduce you to a granddaughter of a 1965 victim. She is from the same district as I am in Sumatra. Her Facebook name is Diah Wahyuningsih Naat. She really wants to share her experience with people in the same boat.' That was how I came to know Dian Wahyuningsih Rahayu, who teaches history at a high school in Batam.*

When I was around thirteen or fourteen years old, I asked *ibu* regarding the strange ceremony they had been performing in *mbah*'s room. Before Eid, *ibu* and her extended family often visited *mbah wedok* [grandmother] in her village in Kotasan – Deli Serdang. This is where *ibu* was born, before she moved to Tanjung Morawa in North Sumatra. There, *ibu,* her brothers and sisters, and *mbah wedok* gathered in one of the rooms, carried out a ceremony and read *surah yasin* from the Quran. My cousins and I were not allowed in. But *ibu* did not explain much about it. When I asked how *mbah* died, she just answered that he got sick, of old age.

Only when I was about to go to college in 1993, did *ibu* talk to me about *mbah* for the first time. But this was only because she wanted me to study to be a teacher and to major in history, although I was not interested in it. She told me that she really wanted me to do it to continue the aspirations of *mbah*, who was also a teacher. That was all she said. I obeyed her and went to a teacher-training college.

When I was in my second year at college, *ibu* told me a little bit about her father. Then, she told me some more a few years later. From my mother's fragmentary stories of my *embah*, I am able to tell you about him now.

### My *embah*

The name of my grandfather is Djayus Darmosoewirjo. Remembering him is not easy because I never met him at all. I only know about him from scattered stories and conversations amongst our family and relatives. He was a highly respected teacher in his village. He was the first person who took the initiative to build a residential area in a woodland in Deli Serdang.

Then he established a school and paved the way for access to the population. The school and the street were named Budi Utomo. He did not want the residents there to live far away from others, as this made it more difficult for them to survive.

Because of his efforts, many village children eventually were educated at least to an elementary level, and my grandfather was known as *mbah* Guru.[89] Now, the school he established has turned into a state school, managed by the local government. But the achievements of my grandfather, *mbah*, that I should have been proud of, were kept hidden from me for years.

In 1965, *ibu* and *bapak* were working at a state-owned bank, Bank Dagang Negara. The people of Deli Serdang heard about the murder of the generals in Jakarta about a few weeks after and many noticed that tension began to increase. At that time, *bapak* was sent to the branch at Lubuk Pakam on a Saturday, because the situation in North Sumatra was starting to become chaotic. *Ibu* decided to stay with her father and mother. When *ibu* stayed with her parents at the end of October 1965, my grandfather was ill so he did not teach at his school.

Early in the morning, my mother was woken by the loud cry of my eldest brother, who was then only four months old. He did not stop crying – maybe this was a premonition. Not long after, people in camouflage uniforms surrounded their home. They were really rude and ordered *mbah* to get out of his room. *Ibu* tried to defend *mbah* by arguing against these men, but guns were quickly pointed at her. They asked *mbah* to admit that he was a communist. *Mbah* was never active in politics at all, but they still took him away.

Of course, I was shocked to hear this story from my mother. I was taught in school to hate communism and the PKI. And because my mother and I did not talk about *mbah* or the events of 1965 again, when I became a teacher, my understanding of the PKI was still the same: the PKI were traitors to the country and the nation, and they deserved to be despised.

Only in 1999, during the era of reformation in Indonesia, did I ask *ibu* again about *mbah*. I insisted that she tell me as much as possible about him. My mother started the story by asking me to be careful, as even the walls in our home had ears. I could sense her intense fear, as one of our neighbours was a civil servant who did not like my father. *Ibu* told me that the neighbour once reported to the local officials that *bapak* was the son-in-law of a PKI member. Fortunately, nothing came of the report then. Now, *ibu* was at last willing to tell me why they had been performing the secret ceremony in that

---

89 *Mbah* or *embah* means grandparent. *Mbah guru* means a great guru.

room: because that was the grave of *mbah*. Previously, she kept telling me that *mbah* was buried in Kebumen, the village in which he was born. But how could his body be buried in that room? *Ibu* said that only his earlobes were there.

*Ibu* continued that when the attackers pushed my *mbah* to admit that he was a member of the PKI, *mbah* did not say anything at all. This made them furious, so they cut both of *mbah*'s ears, and hung these ears on the bedroom door. *Mbah* did not scream at all when they did this. He remained silent. This made my mother really angry and she tried to challenge them again. However, it was in vain as they kept threatening her with their guns.

Before *mbah* was taken away, one of those people gave him an opportunity to write a last message to his wife on a piece of paper. '*Mbok, aku arep muleh*' [I am going home] – that was all he wrote. He knew that that was his last day so that was his goodbye. They immediately dragged *mbah* into a truck. *Ibu* got out and tried to chase the truck while screaming for help from the people around. However, nobody helped her. The *kampung* residents only watched and did nothing, for it would have been too risky for them to help.

*Ibu* and *mbah wedok* then buried the earlobes of my grandfather in his bedroom. They deliberately buried them there, so as not to make the villagers suspicious. In order to save his children, *embah wedok* decided to move away from the village. Initially, they moved to the Lubukpakam and finally, they settled in Tanjung Morawa.

According to *ibu*, *mbah* was arrested for two possible reasons: he was active as a cadre of PNI, the party considered as pro-Sukarno. Another reason was the slander of his neighbour. One day, a group of young men from Lekra, a leftist art organisation, visited *mbah*. They told him that they wanted to perform *ketoprak* in the village and asked for donations. My grandfather had no money then, but he happened to have just harvested rice. So *mbah* decided to donate some bags of rice for them to sell to get the money for their project. One of the neighbours saw this, so *mbah* was accused of being a communist. That was the last story I heard from my mother, who passed away in 2003.

## The History Lesson

'Bu,[90] the PKI is a group of rebels, right? The PKI is the Indonesian enemy, right? The PKI were atheists, right? Communism is a malicious ideology, right?' These were the questions of my high school students when we discussed the events of 1965 in class. Now that I know the story of *mbah*, I have experienced a barrage of feelings as a history teacher. It is really hard for me to discuss the issue with my students. On the one hand, I want to reveal to them what really happened then, but I also know, on the other hand, that these students have been indoctrinated for a long time, and changing their views will not be easy.

At one time, a student came to me with a book entitled *Saksi dan Pelaku Gestapu* [The witnesses and perpetrators of Gestapu], published by Media Presindo in 2005. This was her question: 'Bu, it turns out that, according to the book I read, the 1965 incident is not like what the textbooks describe. Which one is the correct version?' I felt honoured to answer this question that had never before been asked by other students.

Because of her, I had a burning passion to find the right moment to talk about this history in front of my other students. I tried to start with my personal story as a granddaughter of one of the victims who had been slandered and then slaughtered without trial. When I opened up this family secret, I felt something warm on my cheek: my tears. I was very emotional then. Soon after I ended the story, one of my pupils said. 'Bu, these school textbooks are full of lies then.' Yes, Soeharto was a great brainwasher, and was very successful in manipulating history so that people like me keep being stigmatised even now.

After I attended the premiere of the film *The Look of Silence* in Jakarta in November 2014, I talked with all four of my brothers and tried to convince them that it is time for us to open up and reveal the true history about *mbah*. Two of my brothers agreed, but a huge debate took place between me and my other two brothers. They were frightened that one day my honesty would backfire on them and our extended family. They also did not want me to take part in your project, Soe Tjen. Likewise my uncles and aunties intend to never mention or talk about this, although I believe that one of my uncles knows a lot about *mbah* and what happened to him in 1965.

I do not want to keep quiet, no matter what. I am happy that my mother required me to major in history, so I could follow in the steps of *mbah* as a teacher and have the opportunity to debunk these manipulations in

---

90   *Ibu* or *bu* means mother. It is also a form of address for elder women in Indonesia.

the history of Indonesia. I am proud to have a grandfather like mine and consider him as the source of my inspiration and a hero of the family.

*A few months after I interviewed her, Diah contacted me and told me about the screening of* The Look of Silence *she held at the high school in which she teaches. While the public screening of this film had been banned in several places, Diah was persistent and she successfully showed it at her school. She has opened up about her family history in front of her students, and she told me that now she has been determined more then ever to reveal the truth about 1965.*

*However, many of Diah's family members disagree with her activism. We often talk about this, as I also have to face much opposition from my family. In April 2016, Diah tried to apply for a scholarship in the United States to continue her studies, however her headmaster refused to support her application because she disapproved of Diah's activism in relation to the events of 1965.*

# Kiky

The Eternal Fear

*Kiky (pseudonym) contacted me after reading one of my writings about a victim of the 1965 genocide on Facebook. She introduced herself as a victim's granddaughter, and would like to share her story as long as I write it using pseudonyms. 'Please ask me any question, and I will try to answer or ask my mother if I don't know', she wrote.*

*As I set up the '1965 Family' group for the survivors of 1965 as well as the relatives of the victims to share their experiences, I invited Kiky to join. But Kiky said that she was not yet ready to open up to other people. As an Indonesian of Chinese descent, Kiky felt the pressure and threats were greater. She also felt in awe of my project and that people were willing to reveal their stories using their real names and identities. For her and her family, this was unimaginable.*

My grandfather, *kung-kung*, was gone long before I was born. I just heard that *kung-kung* died around the mid-1960s. Only when I was in high school, mama told me a little bit about him. She said it in a whisper, although we were at home then, but she was still afraid that someone would hear us. She also made me promise not to tell anyone else, as she was about to reveal the biggest secret of the family.

Mama decided to uncover this secret only because of her fear that my *koko*,[91] who had started to become interested in various organisations, would meet the same fate as *kung-kung* did. My grandfather and my grandmother, *pho-pho*, lived on Bangka, a small island to the east of Sumatra. They had eight children, seven daughters and the eldest child was the only son. My mother was the fourth.

*Kung-kung* was active in both the PKI and a labour union. Mama said that *kung-kung* had quite important positions in both the PKI as well as the union. Organisational meetings were usually run at the home of *kung-kung* and *pho-pho*. When the G30S took place in Jakarta, there was no unusual activity whatsoever in the family house on Bangka. Everyone stayed at home, except for mama's eldest brother, who was in Jakarta because he was studying there. Most people on Bangka Island heard about the G30S from the radio. Approximately two to three weeks later, the army stormed mama's house and dragged *kung-kung* out, witnessed by his wife and children. Only

---

91  *Koko* = elder brother in Mandarin.

after several weeks they found out that *kung-kung* had been taken to a jail in Belinyu, Bangka.

Mama was only seventeen years old then, and had dropped out of high school. According to my mother, before the G30S, intimidation of her family had already taken place, mainly because they were of Chinese descent. A few years earlier, people of Chinese descent were required to choose to become either Indonesian or foreign citizens; my mother chose to be an Indonesian citizen. The schools for foreign and Indonesian citizens were separated on Bangka at that time. After mama became an Indonesian citizen, she went to school with non-Chinese people. As a member of a minority, mama was often bullied and called names. Unable to stand this treatment, mama decided to quit school and looked for a job. Subsequently, she taught elementary school children in first or second grade.

Soon after *kung-kung* was arrested, the police regularly interrogated mama and her elder sister. Often, the police summoned them several times a week. One of the questions the police always asked was: 'Where are the weapons from China hidden?'[92] One day, when mama and her sister were being interrogated at the police station, *kung-kung* appeared at home with the army. *Pho-pho* was really surprised to see him. Has he been repatriated? It turned out that they took *kung-kung* home only to find out where he had hidden the weapons from China. But *kung-kung* had never received any weapons. The army also searched the house and because they could not find anything they were very angry. They dragged *kung-kung* back to prison and destroyed almost all the sweet potato crops planted by my grandmother, which was the food the family relied on. But there was a kind officer who asked *pho-pho*'s family to be vigilant, because there might be people who wanted to slander us and plant weapons secretly in our house.

When *pho-pho* and the family were allowed to visit my grandfather in prison, they saw that he was carrying a lot of deep scars. *Kung-kung* never talked about these injuries. When the family asked him, he never answered. According to several people, they tortured the political prisoners by lashing them with iron chains. A few months after being imprisoned in Belinyu, one afternoon the prisoners were taken to Palembang.

The night before the army dispatched the prisoners, their families were allowed to pay a visit to them in Belinyu prison. *Pho-pho* and the children came to see *kung-kung*. Most of the detainees were sure that it was the last day of their lives. Not far from them, a Gerwani member sobbed horribly and

---

92   Press reports between the end of 1965 until 1966 stated that the PKI members received and stockpiled weapons from China (Roosa, 'The September 30th Movement', pp. 32-33).

asked her mother to pray for her: 'Mak,[93] please pray after three and seven days from my departure to Palembang, *ya*. I will definitely be killed there.' *kung-kung* remained calm and asked *pho-pho* not to worry. He said that the prisoners would be taken to Palembang for a trial. And because *kung-kung* was innocent, he was sure that everything would be fine. *Kung-kung* only requested *pho-pho* to give him some soya sauce for his journey.

The next day at about 11 am, only *pho-pho* witnessed the departure of *kung-kung* in a truck covered with a tarpaulin. My mother was teaching so that she could not come. Eventually, mama decided to leave her teaching career because she could not stand the intimidation she was subjected to and she became a tailor instead. Indeed, after *kung-kung* was arrested, she was required to get a *surat kelakuan baik* [good-conduct certificate] if she wanted to continue teaching. She had to get this letter every three months, and she had to face intimidation from the officers every time she tried to get one. At least tailors did not need a good-conduct certificate. *Pho-pho* tried to support her family by selling cakes. Her youngest child was only five years old then, and my mother's *koko* could continue his studies in Jakarta only with the help of a relative.

After *kung-kung* was taken to Palembang, the police continued interrogating mama, and especially her elder sister, about the weapons from China. The interrogations made mama's sister severely stressed out. Eventually she decided to leave Bangka, by getting on a truck and then a boat to Palembang to avoid being terrorised by the police and army, although at that time she was seriously ill. Perhaps it was fortunate that she left, because shortly after that Udayana soldiers came to Bangka to receive training. They loved to knock on the door at any time of the day and harass and even molest women, including my mother.

Unexpectedly, a stranger turned up from Palembang. He brought a letter from *kung-kung*. *Pho-pho* and the family recognised the handwriting and signature of my grandfather, so they believed that it was indeed a letter from him. In the letter, my grandfather asked them to send him green beans and garlic, and give them to their relative in Palembang (*Pho-pho* had relatives in Palembang), so that this relative could send them to *kung-kung*.

But *pho-pho* was very much frightened that the letter was some kind of a trap. She did not want anyone else to know where her relatives lived, so she just gave money to that stranger, to buy what *kung-kung* wanted plus delivery fees to send the stuff to my grandfather in Palembang. *Pho-pho* suspected that *kung-kung* suffered from beriberi, because many people

---

93  *Mak* is short for *emak*, meaning mother.

in Bangka at that time believed that green beans and garlic were the best cure for beriberi.

After the letter, there was no more news from *kung-kung*. None at all. A few years later, *pho-pho* met the Gerwani member who asked her own mother to pray for her. It turned out that she was one of the fortunate few who was able to return alive to Bangka Island. She told *pho-pho* about the sadistic tortures in Palembang. She saw *kung-kung* in Palembang prison, but only very briefly. After that, they were separated. *Pho-pho* and the family tried to figure out what had happened to *kung-kung*. But to no avail. Even now, it remains a mystery. They just heard that most of the detainees taken to Palembang were killed by tying their bodies with a rope made from banana stems and dumping them into the Batang River. From various stories, mama concluded that possibly *kung-kung* died around January or Febuary 1967.

Before papa married mama, he had heard about *kung-kung,* and it was not a problem for him at all. In fact, he respected *kung-kung,* for what *kung-kung* had done for the people. Our family decided to move to Jakarta in December 1982, to improve our finances. Many of our extended family members also moved to Jakarta, possibly because they were traumatised by what had happened to *kung-kung*. Moreover, many people on that small island knew that we were descendants of a member of the PKI. But *pho-pho* stayed in Bangka until she got really sick in 1986. Then she went to Jakarta to get medical treatment but died in the same year, of uterine cancer, when I was still in the fourth grade in elementary school. I did not understand about the PKI and did not have any opportunity to ask *pho-pho* about it at all.

In Jakarta, no one knows about our backgrounds, so there is no problem with regard to the history of *kung-kung*, but we encounter problems because we are of Chinese descent. The *kampung*[94] fees, for example, are higher for us because we are Chinese. The local officials often asked us to contribute for this and that activity. We never know whether the activities are real. When they ask for a donation, they often say that other people have given 'this much' – pointing to large numbers only – so we are pressured to give a similar amount. My younger sister once saw one of them changing the numbers on their paper by adding a zero, making Rp 10,000 into Rp 100,000.

In 2004, I went to Bangka for the first time after we moved to Jakarta. The neighbours there were kind to us. Several of them must have known about

---

94  *Kampung*: a small community of houses. In Indonesia, every *kampung* has a head who can ask residents to donate money for *kampung* activities.

*kung-kung*. But they never mentioned the incident at all, maybe because many of them there are also of Chinese descent.

Even now, my extended family never talk about this. Mama's elder sister recently warned mama never to tell her children about *kung-kung*. But because of your project, Soe Tjen, mama was willing to reveal more to me. She did not object to your writing our story, as long as you use pseudonyms. We are still afraid that a similar incident may befall us again one day.

*Although at first Kiky did not want me to introduce her to anyone related to this tragedy, near the end of the interview, she asked: 'Soe Tjen, have you ever met with victims from Bangka Island or those around Palembang? If so, I'd love to ask them about kung-kung. I'm still curious about what actually happened to him. I want to know how he died.' The conflict between haunting curiosity and fear is often apparent amongst the families of the victims. Even finding out more about their own family often makes these people feel guilt ridden, for this means entering a forbidden ground, the place they had been protected from by their family.*

# Epilogue

## The Corollary of Memory

As I was finishing this book, a scene from Joshua Oppenheimer's film was haunting me: an elderly man of over a century, whose skin was sticking to his bones, creeping over a cracked floor. Towards the end of *The Look of Silence,* Adi's father, Rukun, is lost in his own home and thinks that someone is about to beat him up. However, no one was about to beat him up. He was in a room with his own son, Adi, who was filming him.

Rukun has forgotten about the gruesome events of half a century ago. He cannot even remember the name of his son, who was brutally murdered in 1965. Yet the memory of the murder has not been deleted. Rukun has buried his memories so deeply that he no longer remembers what he has buried. Still, his unconscious remembers. And his sense of powerlessness has not simply vanished, especially because his son's murder remains unresolved and involves severe injustice. These submerged memories seem to return in a transformed state: the pain and terror do not disappear.

Rukun is certainly not the only one. The survivors and families of the 1965 victims are not allowed to express what gruesome incidents they had witnessed and have been forced to accept the manipulated version of the atrocities. This has caused many of them to repress their memories and also their identities, in the same way that Rukun has done. I have seen many victims enter into old age while being haunted by their pasts. They tend to forget more recent events, but those that are in the more distant past can suddenly resurface. Memory might have dispersed the details of the incidents, but the sediments of painful episodes can become even more powerful and harrowing with time.

The inability to express 'real' anguish has trapped many victims in a kind of hallucinatory fear. But doesn't fear have to be hallucinatory for it to work efficiently, so that the victims remain subdued, regardless of whether any danger is nearby? The fear implanted by Soeharto's government has been potent in maintaining the hatred directed against the communists, as well as sustaining the sense of powerlessness experienced by the victims and their families.

The terror created by the New Order was able to endure for decades and across different generations. Although incredible strength and bravery have been demonstrated by the victims, fear still persists long after the New Order has ended. This seems to have been the strategy of Soeharto and his cronies: be as brutal as possible, so that fear can become like a ghost and scares anyone, everyone, even the generations to come. The brutality remains alive in the people's memories, even in those who were born long after the atrocities happened.

Soeharto's troops often insulted and degraded the victims in such a way that the victims would feel ashamed of revealing what happened to them. This is the latent danger of the New Order. Hence, denial is common amongst the victims and their families: many of them simply claim that the atrocities never happened. For many of the victims, self-enclosure and withdrawal are ways of protecting themselves and their families.

What ostracises the victims even more is that as a way to shield themselves from the continuous prejudice and the reaction against their powerlessness, they tend to detach themselves from certain groups. Accordingly, many of the victims have created 'irrational' prohibitions for the children: never be friends with or date soldiers' and police officers' families; never marry Muslims; never join any organisation; never study politics. Prohibitions emerging from fear and anger linger on, if victims are still not recognised as victims, if they still have to remain silent. This repression will contribute to widespread animosity amongst different groups in Indonesia, as well as discrimination and conflicts: the side effects will keep spreading if this incident is not addressed humanely and justly.

My original intention behind writing this book was actually very simple: to reveal how the 1965 atrocities were perceived by the victims and the victims' families, and how these had affected them. Nevertheless, my simple intention has often raised eyebrows and been met with many challenges as well as disagreeable questions: 'Why do you want to keep digging into the past, to disturb the peace? Why do you want to create trouble?' Many in Indonesia are still reluctant to hear the truth about what happened half a century ago, especially because the cost is too high: it will bother and even anger the people in power. Fear often instigates society to appease the people in power, and keep repressing the victims, because this way is easier – this is a common calculative strategy to avoid risks. When the victims are too frightened to speak up, that is the time when the crime becomes perfect. By sustaining fear, the remaining representatives of the New Order can even turn their victims and the victims' families into their agents: victims even silence others who are desperate to tell the truth. However, because many of the victims are used to living in fear, they embrace it and in this situation, pleasing the authorities is a must, and the oppression and brutality of the authorities are perceived as a just punishment for them.

It is not surprising that the main hindrance of the 1965 activists and survivors who strive for their rights has often been their own families. And these particular 'agents' are difficult to ignore or challenge. It is easier for 1965 activists to challenge people who are not related to them: they can ignore other people's warnings or even threats, but challenging their own mothers, fathers, grandparents or other family members who have suffered from the 1965 atrocities? How could they do that, especially because these family members are part of the history they were about to reveal. Thus, most people had to face the dilemma of either being selfish (for ignoring the feelings of their family members) or being cowards (for not speaking the truth).

The children and grandchildren of the victims who are willing to share their family histories with me heard them orally and they have to guard these histories with caution. The two main reasons behind the revelation of these family histories are to counter the formal history told by the state (Kusuma Wijaya, Adi Rukun and Haidir Svj) and to reveal it only after it is considered safe (Dyah Wahyuningsih Naat, Irina Dayasih, Kiky and me). For others, such as the family of Kristianto Budi, the family history related to these atrocities remains a taboo, and they had to find out about it from other sources. The fear internalised within the family is often unobserved, as it is kept behind closed doors and is manifested only as silence.

From these oral narratives, however, more and more internalised fear has been detected. The process of writing these narratives has also become a means of fighting this internalised fear for some of my respondents. Because of this, my project has undoubtedly created tensions within the victims' families as well as in my own family, because they believe that those involved in my project are putting their families in danger. Nevertheless, this collection of testimonies has also linked the people affected by this tragedy together. They, who have been separated, silenced and isolated by the government, can identify others in the same boat.

The memoirs gathered in this book function as testimonies of how the atrocities that happened over fifty years ago have influenced people from different generations, personally, socially as well as politically. Various and even paradoxical reactions can be found, especially because there is still confusion about what actually happened, even amongst the survivors and their families. For instance, while most of the people affected by the 1965 atrocities despise Soeharto, the people in the village of Wayan Windra in Beringkit (Bali), do not. A village considered to be 'red', where most of the men were slaughtered, Beringkit used to be dominated by the supporters of Golkar (Soeharto's party) during the New Order period, because the right-wing section of the PNI (which used to be Sukarno's party) was involved in the mass murder there. So, most of them sided with Soeharto for they believed that Sukarno was one of the culprits of the 1965 genocide.

Undoubtedly, the 1965 genocide still has a tremendous impact on contemporary Indonesian society. The perpetrators and their cronies are still in power, and their ambition to be considered as heroes is shaken as the victims start speaking up. To maintain their image as 'heroes', the perpetrators' identity actually relies on that of their victims: as long as the victims keep quiet about the stigma, this supports the belief of the perpetrators and their cronies that they are heroes. This book has given the space for the survivors and their families to challenge the chronic stigma maintained by the perpetrators and their cronies: it is time to end the silence.

# Bibliography

Anderson, Ben. 'How Did the Generals Die?' *Indonesia* 43, April 1987, pp. 109-134. http://cip.cornell.edu/DPubS?service=UI&version=1.0&verb=Display&handle=seap.indo/1107009317.

Anderson, Benedict R. O'G., and Ruth T. McVey. *A Preliminary Analysis of the October 1, 1965 Coup in Indonesia*. Ithaca: Modern Indonesia Project, Cornell University, 1971.

Arendt, Hannah. *Eichmann in Jerusalem: A Report on the Banality of Evil*. New York: Penguin, 1994.

Bjerregaard, Mette. 'What Indonesians Really Think about *The Act of Killing*'. *The Guardian*, 5 March 2014.

Brewster, Todd. 'Remembrance (More or Less) of Things Past'. *Civilization* 6.4, 1999: 71-84.

Central Intelligence Agency. *Research Study: Indonesia – The Coup That Backfired*, December 1968. https://www.cia.gov/library/readingroom/docs/esau-40.pdf.

Chomsky, Noam. *Year 501: The Conquest Continues*. Boston: South End, 2015.

Crouch, Harold. *The Army and Politics in Indonesia*. Jacarta: Equinox Publishing, 1978.

Curtis, Mark. *Web of Deceit: Britain's Real Role in the World*. London: Vintage, 2003.

Drakeley, Steven. 'Lubang Buaya: Myth, Misogyny and Massacre'. *Nebula* 4,4, 2007: pp. 11-35.

Farid, Hilmar. 'Indonesia's Original Sin: Mass Killings and Capitalist Expansion, 1965-66'. *Inter-Asia Cultural Studies* 6.1, 2005: 3-16.

Hearman, Vannessa. 'Uses of Memoirs and Oral History Works in Researching the 1965-1966 Political Violence in Indonesia.' *International Journal of Asia Pacific Studies* 5.2, 2009: 21-42.

Hughes, John. *Indonesian Upheaval*. New York: McKay, 1967.

Kolko, Gabriel. *Confronting the Third World: United States Foreign Policy, 1945-1980*. New York: Pantheon Books, 1988.

Öhman, Arne, and Susan Mineka. 'Fears, Phobias, and Preparedness: Toward an Evolved Module of Fear and Fear Learning'. *Psychological Review* 103.3, 2001: 483-522.

Pauker, Guy J. 'The Role of the Military in Indonesia.' In John J. Johnson, ed., *The Role of the Military in Underdeveloped Countries*, ed. John J. Johnson. Princeton: Princeton University Press, 1962, pp. 185-230.

PRO DEFE 25/170. Tel. 1863 FO to Singapore, 8 October 1965.

Raymont, Henry. 'Holt Says US Actions Protect All Non-Red Asia.' *New York Times*, 6 July 1966.

Robinson, Geoffrey. *The Dark Side of Paradise: Political Views in Bali*. Ithaca: Cornell University Press, 1995.

Roosa, John. *Pretext for Mass Murder: The September 30th Movement and Suharto's Coup d'État in Indonesia*. Madison: University of Wisconsin Press, 2006.

Roosa, John. 'The September 30th Movement: The Aporias of the Official Narratives'. In Douglas Kammen and Katherine McGregor, eds, *The Contours of Mass Violence in Indonesia, 1965-68* (Honolulu: Asian Studies Association of Australia in association with University of Hawai'i Press, 2012), pp. 25-49.

Scott, Peter Dale. 'Still Uninvestigated After 50 Years: Did the U.S. Help Incite the 1965 Indonesian Massacre?' *The Asia-Pacific Journal* 13 Issue 31, 2015: 1-15.

Thompson, Paul. *The Voice of the Past: Oral History*. 3rd ed. Oxford: Oxford University Press, 2000.

Vickers, Adrian. *A History of Modern Indonesia*. Cambridge: Cambridge University Press, 2005.

Wertheim, W.F. 'Suharto and the Untung Coup – The Missing Link.' *Journal of Contemporary Asia* 1.2, 1970: 50-57.

Whitington, Paul. 'Chilling and Effective Murder Poses', *The Independent*, 28 June 2013.

Wieringa, Saskia. *Sexual Politics in Indonesia*. New York: Palgrave and Macmillan, 2002.

# Index

Aidit, D.N. 42, 53, 134
Aji, Rito 163-170
Ambarawa (prison) 47-48, 51, 88-89, 92, 110
American government 22-23
Amnesty International 63, 101
Anderson, Ben 19, 26, 29
Antara 128-129, 132
anti-communism, anti-communist 19, 24, 30-31, 26, 42, 139
Arendt, Hannah 31
army, Indonesian 29-31, 44, 47, 56, 69-71, 74, 80, 98, 100-101, 108, 116, 124, 129, 148-150, 152, 154-159, 163, 185, 192, 205-207
artist 107
atheist 27, 101, 117, 126, 152, 161-162, 170, 174
Australia 81, 182, 184
Australian 24, 184

BAT (British American Tobacco) 68-69, 71
Baperki 56-57, 67
Batam 52, 200
Beijing 129-130, 132
brainwashing 48
British government 24
BTI (*Barisan Tani Indonesia* or Peasants Front of Indonesia) 56, 57, 95, 113, 140, 190
Buddhist, Buddhism 62, 145
Budi, Kristianto 30-31, 148-151, 213
Buru island 25, 33-34, 41, 45, 49-50, 53-54, 58-64, 66, 72-74, 78-79, 81-82, 102, 123, 126, 136, 146-147, 163, 167, 170, 180, 195-199

Cakrabirawa 152
campaign 19, 21, 27
cancer 35, 184, 208
capitalism 197
Carter, Jimmy 63
Catholic 89, 91-92, 96, 103, 145, 151, 162
Catholicism 81, 91, 167
CGMI (*Consentrasi Gerakan Mahasiswa Indonesia,* or the Unified Movement of Indonesian Students) 42, 46, 85, 135
China 53n, 128-132, 172, 186, 206-207
Chinese 175-176, 184, 205
Christian 58, 172, 192
Christianity 62
CIA 18, 22-23, 29
colonial 87, 100, 110, 192
communism 20, 22, 24, 27, 29-30, 111, 117, 119, 126, 130, 132, 138, 140, 145, 190-192, 201, 203
communist 15, 17, 19, 22-25, 27-28, 30-31, 36, 42-43, 53, 56-57, 59, 69, 93, 95, 101, 119, 123-125, 128, 134, 139-140, 149-150, 152, 157-158, 161, 170, 173-174, 176-177, 185-186, 189-191, 201-202

Communist Party 15, 17, 22-23, 53, 59, 69, 95, 152, 157, 176, 185, 189
community 33, 57, 62, 90, 93, 118, 142, 208n
Council of Generals 18, 42, 69, 148, 152
coup 15, 26, 29, 69, 148, 152-153, 172
culture 33, 131-132

Darul Islam 129, 148, 148n
Dayasih, Irina 134-141, 213
Dutch 55-56, 63, 80, 87-88, 91, 100, 110, 140, 142, 191-192

economic 25, 119, 139, 196
economy 197
Edhie, Sarwo 20-22, 149
education 62, 101, 113, 136-137, 145, 151, 161, 181, 199
English (language) 50, 77, 103, 185, 189
ET (*Eks Tapol*) 28, 51, 65, 80, 125, 150-151, 182

FAKI (Front Anti-Communist Indonesia) 30, 139-140
fear 13, 17-30, 33-36, 58, 93, 115-116, 120, 126, 142, 145, 147, 171, 176, 191, 201, 205, 209, 211-213
freedom 21, 33, 41, 72, 78, 80, 86, 143, 145, 171, 180, 192

G30S 19, 28, 97, 103, 148, 150, 173, 189, 205-206
generals 15, 17-20, 25-29, 42, 55, 69, 87, 96, 103, 117, 130, 148, 152-153, 173, 198, 201
*genjer-genjer* (song and dance) 51
genocide 13, 20, 22-24, 30, 32, 34, 36, 92, 94, 104, 149, 186, 194, 205, 214
Gerwani 15, 17, 19-20, 25-28, 42, 85, 87, 96, 103, 107-108, 115, 123, 173, 183, 192, 206, 208
Gestapo 27
Gestapu 27, 182, 203
Gestok 55, 68, 134, 161, 185
Golkar 145, 213
Guided Democracy 25

Habibie 52
Hearman, Vanessa 36
Hindu 21, 62, 145
history 18, 24, 26-28, 30-34, 36-38, 51, 81-82, 107, 111-112, 119-120, 123, 128, 137, 149, 161-163, 182-184, 186, 192, 198-200, 203-204, 208, 213
Hitler 31, 45, 49
Holt, Harold 24
human rights 32, 92, 176

identity card 140, 150, 182
ideology 18, 27-28, 30, 35, 93, 117, 125-126, 130, 132, 144-145, 193, 203

imprisonment 67, 78, 135, 137, 166, 171
International People's Tribunal (IPT) 32
IPPI (*Ikatan Pemuda Pelajar Indonesia*) 94-96, 100, 107-108
Islam 62, 68, 81, 92, 129, 133, 148, 162, 167, 191-192, 199

Jakarta 15, 18-19, 44, 51, 53, 55, 57, 62, 65, 68-69, 77, 117, 124-126, 128-132, 134-136, 141, 145, 148, 152, 154-155, 174, 184, 198, 201, 203, 205, 207-208
Japanese 74, 85, 87, 179
Java 21, 27, 42-43, 47-48, 51, 55-56, 61-64, 68, 75, 80, 88, 93, 107, 110, 123, 129, 135-136, 140-141, 148-150, 152, 154-156, 164, 168, 175-176, 183, 189-190, 195, 199
journalist 70, 107, 131, 171

Kalisosok 56-58, 71-72, 140, 178
Kalla, Jusuf 33
Kamah, Iwan 128-133
Kiky 205-209, 213
Koaksi (*Komando Aksi*) 114-115, 117
Koblen 50, 70-72
Kopkamtib 60, 78
Koramil 159, 177-178

left-wing 15, 18, 21, 23, 54, 95, 134, 150, 157, 170, 173, 175, 192
Lekra 25, 42, 107, 109, 136, 190-192, 202
Lenin 161
Lubang Buaya 15, 18-19, 27, 96

Madiun (East Java) 68, 149, 189-190
Malang (East Java) 55-56, 65, 67, 150
Malaysia 149, 174
Mandarin (language) 36, 183
Mao (Zedong) 176, 186
Marching, Soe Tjen 34, 104, 111, 127, 140, 146, 171-186
Marhaenism 126
Marlina, Sari 152-162
Marx, Karl 108, 161, 176, 186
Marxism 126, 145, 189, 192
mass grave 92-93, 124, 160
mass murder 15, 20-22, 26, 28-30, 81, 107, 123, 146, 157, 170, 194, 214
massacre 20-22, 24, 29, 81, 87, 149, 151
Muhayati, Sri 85-93
Mulyono, Leo 41-54, 88
murder 15, 17-22, 26, 28-31, 55, 71, 81, 107, 117-118, 123, 129, 146, 148-149, 157, 170, 191, 194, 198, 201, 211, 214
muslim 62, 65, 89, 92-93, 126, 148, 162, 167, 190-192
mutation 18, 35
mutilate, mutilation 15, 19-20, 26, 29, 96
Muzakkar, Kahar 129

Namlea 60, 73, 75, 79
nationalism 41, 46
Nazi 27
New Order 20, 28, 30, 33, 35-37, 41, 60, 80n, 92, 111, 118, 145, 151, 161, 195, 198, 199, 211-213
Njoto 134, 137, 140, 194
Nusakambangan 45-46, 49, 57-58, 73, 195

Oei Hay Djoen 64, 136-137
Oei Hiem Hwie 25, 34, 41, 55-67, 136n
Oppenheimer, Joshua 13, 31-32, 34, 113, 118, 120

Pancasila 27, 30, 51, 64, 80, 101, 168
Partai Komunis Indonesia (PKI) 15, 17, 19-20, 22, 24-25, 27-29, 34, 42-43, 51, 53, 56-57, 64, 70n, 80, 85-86, 90, 92-93, 95, 98, 103, 107, 110-111, 116-117, 124-126, 128, 130-131, 134, 136-137, 142, 144-145, 149, 153, 157, 161, 163-164, 169, 173, 176, 185, 189, 201-203, 205-206, 208
Partai Nasional Indonesia (PNI) 146, 191, 202, 214
Pemuda Pancasila 30
Pemuda Rakyat 69, 86, 96, 98, 142
*Pengkhianatan G30S/PKI* 28, 103, 173, 189
Permesta 128-129, 148
Plantungan 51, 100, 102, 104
Pram (Pramoedya Ananta Toer) 25, 51, 53, 59-61, 63-64, 66, 74, 78, 131
propaganda 15, 19-20, 22, 24-26, 29-30, 103, 197

Rahardjo, Pudji 41, 68-82, 163, 170
Rahayu, Diah Wahyuningsih 200-204
rape 94, 183
religion 21, 48, 58, 62, 81, 92, 126, 133, 163, 167, 170, 186, 192
Res Publica University 43, 46, 57n
Revolutionary Council 15, 19, 42, 69
Roosa, John 29, 29n, 206n
RPKAD (*Resimen Pasukan Komando Angkatan Darat* or the Indonesian Special Forces) 69, 108, 149, 153-154
Rukun, Adi 32, 113-120, 141, 200, 211, 213
ruler 26, 173
Russia 53, 132, 186

Santiaji 51-52
Savanajaya 49, 59, 62, 74, 78-79, 195-199
Semarang 47, 64, 75, 89-90, 100, 101, 154-155
silence 13, 117, 181, 185, 212-214
silent 35, 78, 87, 98, 100, 117, 126, 137, 167, 202, 212
socialism 111, 123, 126, 197
Soeharto 15, 15n, 16-20, 22, 24, 26-30, 34-37, 42, 50-53, 55, 60, 63-64, 67, 94, 100-101, 103-104, 116, 124-125, 129, 132, 138, 145-146, 153, 161, 169-170, 173-174, 183-184, 193, 198, 203, 211, 213-214
Solo 107, 110, 135, 149, 153-154, 183
starvation 45, 72, 185

INDEX

stigma 28, 33-34, 36, 100, 117, 145, 150, 214
Sukardi, Usmantri 123-127
Sukarno 15-16, 18-19, 22, 24, 27, 29-31, 53, 55-58, 68, 94, 126n, 129, 138, 146n, 148-149, 152-153, 170, 189, 191n, 202, 214
Sumarmiyati, Christina 94-104
Sumatra 30, 32, 113, 135-136, 154-156, 200-201, 205
Sumitro 60, 78
Supersemar 15, 15n, 16, 30
Surabaya 55-57, 61, 64-65, 67-71, 80, 140, 148, 151, 163, 165, 168-170, 172, 175, 177-178, 180, 184-185, 189, 191-194
Svj, Haidir 195-199, 213

taboo 137, 148, 186, 213
*Terompet Masyarakat* 55, 70
terror 13, 17, 20, 27-28, 36, 111, 144, 149, 207, 211
testimony 33, 36-37, 213
Toer *see* Pram

torture 19-20, 25-26, 33, 54, 56-57, 71-72, 74, 79, 85, 94, 99-102, 126, 135, 185, 206, 208
trial 78, 125n, 131, 134, 168, 203, 207

Untung, Lieutenant Colonel 18-19, 28, 69, 152

Wieringa, Saskia 13, 19-20, 22n, 25, 29
Wijaya, Kusuma 28, 189-194, 213
Windra, Wayan 22, 142-147, 213
Wirogunan prison 44, 85, 90, 98-99, 110
Wiwoho, Sriyono 107-112
women's emancipation 94
women's movement 15, 17, 19, 87, 107
women's theatre project 134

Yani, Ahmad 18-19
Yogya, Yogyakarta 19, 27, 42, 44, 46-47, 51-54, 85-86, 88, 90-91, 94-95, 97-98, 110, 123-127, 138-140, 150, 197-199

For Product Safety Concerns and Information please contact our EU
representative  GPSR@taylorandfrancis.com
Taylor & Francis Verlag GmbH, Kaufingerstraße 24, 80331 München, Germany